DAVID NOUR

NOURGROUP.COM

Best from NFPA!

Nour

THINKERS
5O
RADAR
2021

Best Business
Strategy Books
of All Time
W I N N E R

GLOBAL
GURUS
TOP 30 2019
LEADERSHIP

CURVE BENDERS

Praise for Curve Benders

"If you're looking for a roadmap to remain relevant in the future of work, *Curve Benders* is your compass."

– Harry M. Jansen Kraemer, Jr., Clinical Professor of Leadership, Northwestern University Kellogg School of Management; former Chairman & CEO, Baxter International

"I really enjoyed Nour's lens on the personal S-curve in *Curve Benders*; what a brilliant way to think about your reinvention to remain relevant in the future of work."

– Garry Ridge, Chairman & CEO – WD-40 Company

"David Nour is among this century's greatest business minds. He keenly sees a world through a lens identifying game-changing trends and emerging new business models. He is a critical thinker, and *Curve Benders* incorporates both a strategic thought process along with practical solutions for organizations seeking excellence. A must read for leaders in their lifelong learning journey."

– Bob Weidner, President & CEO – Metal Service Center Institute (MSCI)

"The year 2020 was the year of non-linear growth. In *Curve Benders*, Nour has captured what it takes to learn from the global pandemic and dramatically elevate your relevance in the next two decades."

– Ray Harris, Chief Information Officer – Adtran

"The pace of change is now accelerating even more rapidly. Adapting and transforming is becoming a way of life, not a way point. *Curve Benders* is a must-read for anyone leading businesses into the future."

– Joseph Schroedel, Brigadier General, USA (Ret), Executive Director – Society of American Military Engineers

"In *Curve Benders,* Nour offers readers a practical and inspiring handbook to remain relevant in the future of work. Let yourselves be seduced by this refreshing manifesto for strategic relationships."

– Yves Pigneur, co-author, Business Model Generation

"*Curve Benders* is a dynamic roadmap for doing business now and in the future. It pieces together key principles that will allow me to better align my priorities, ways of working, and my relationships with employees and customers. This refreshing direction will make a real difference in my professional and personal life."

– Shaun Roedel, Senior Vice President, Manufactured Products – Oceaneering

"*Curve Benders* brings fresh insight to unleashing higher orders of leading and guiding a dynamic company in a dynamic environment. Boards need to pay attention. Nour hits multiple homeruns with his section on the Chief Entrepreneur role and the exciting new frontiers that can be birthed alongside core areas of focus. Get this book, soak up the wisdom, and make things happen for your personal growth, your board, and your company."

– R. Eric Mccarthey, Board Director/CEO/Venture Capital Partner; former Senior Global Customer, Operations, and Strategic Planning Officer – The Coca-Cola Company

"For two decades, my work has been about engineering S-curve leaps for organizations and teams in the face of complexity. Nour's lens on the personal S-curve in *Curve Benders* is a brilliant way to think about your reinvention to remain relevant in the future of work."

– *David Komlos, CEO – Syntegrity; co-author of* Cracking Complexity: The Breakthrough Formula for Solving Just About Anything Fast

"In this incredibly timely piece of work, Nour challenges us to think about our post-pandemic realities, both professionally and personally. As a higher-ed administrator constantly thinking about how to educate students for future relevance and impact, *Curve Benders* is my new favorite resource."

– *Diane M. Ryan, Ph.D. Associate Dean, Tisch College – Tufts University; former Deputy Department Head, Behavioral Sciences and Leadership – United States Military Academy, West Point*

"In his newest book, *Curve Benders,* Nour provides fresh new insights and tools for leaders to successfully deal with crisis leadership, build resilience, and develop agile transformation projects to excel in the new world driven by extreme change."

– *Antonio Nieto-Rodriguez, author, Thinkers50, Past Project Management Institute (PMI) Global Chair*

"Nour has given us *Curve Benders* as the recipe for crisis leadership and resilience, that will prepare us for the next global disruption that we all know is coming! Practical advice that will serve you well at work and in life. Two thumbs up!"

– *Chester Elton, bestselling author of* The Carrot Principle, Leading with Gratitude, *and* Anxiety at Work

"Nour's insights on the Organization of the Future and what it really takes to innovate is well captured in *Curve Benders*. For every CEO and board that aims to be more intentional and strategic in their innovation investments, here is your guide."

— Damon Griggs, CEO — Dovel Technologies

"Nour's fast-moving prose defines curve benders as relationships that power our growth. But *Curve Benders* is bigger than that, tying together different concepts in a persuasive whole about our blended personal and professional lives and how we might do everything better."

— Erik Pritchard, CEO — Motorcycle Industry Council

"Nour sets himself apart from his contemporaries with *Curve Benders. Relationship Economics* gave me insights into my most valuable relationships. *Co-Create* was the recipe book for real innovation with those relationships. *Curve Benders* completes the trilogy with its guide to the future of work and the impact of certain relationships on my life."

— Kevin Brogan, EVP — The Wine Group

"After my Sales Community podcast interview with Nour, I was impressed by his breadth, depth, and natural comfort in engaging senior execs. Subsequently, he provided a unique lens and an independent perspective on my personal and professional growth journey. As I learned more about his books and global keynotes, I invited him to deliver a keynote at our SKO. It was a resounding success as our global sales team ranked Nour's Co-Create session as one of the best they've experienced - even virtually. We've since engaged Nour to coach me, and my revenue leadership team, and we're exploring opportunities to expand the scope of his work and impact. I can't recommend Nour enough. If you're looking for a fresh, intelligent, thought-provoking speaker, coach, and advisor, Nour is a pro."

– Bill Hogan, Chief Revenue Officer - SecurityScorecard

"David Nour brings that rare combination of executive polish, with incredible insights, due diligence, and a necessary level of candor to push you to think and lead differently . . . a thought-leader in strategic relationships, co-creation, and creating a culture of innovation. Having worked with Nour across three global corporations (HP, Dell, and Samsung) over the past decade, I can personally endorse the value he brings to every engagement."

– KC Choi, Corporate EVP, Head of Global B2B Mobile –
Samsung Electronics

"David Nour is intelligent, engaging, can quickly frame an organization's challenges and opportunities, and his Strategy Visualization service has been of great value to my team and me. I would highly recommend his process, diligence, candid guidance, and utmost professionalism."

– Chad Johnson, Chief Procurement Officer – Humana

"David Nour is world-class when it comes to an understanding of the real needs of his global clients and bringing just the right mix of candor and actionable insights. At Sun Microsystems and HP, I engaged him multiple times to support our organization, and he never disappointed. From speaking engagements to thousands, to a strategic advisory with senior leaders, to executive coaching, you can't go wrong in working with Nour."

– Randy Seidl, Board Member, CEO, CRO,
Sales Community Leader

CURVEBENDERS

CURVE BENDERS

How Strategic Relationships Can Power Your Non-linear Growth in the Future of Work

DAVID NOUR

WILEY

Published by John Wiley & Sons, Inc., Hoboken, New Jersey.
Published simultaneously in Canada.

Curve Benders, Growth Grid, Personal Market Value, Refraction Points in Your Personal
S-Curve, Nour Strategy Visualization (NSV), and Nour Innovation Sprint (NIS) are trademarks
of The Nour Group, Inc.

Illustrations by Lin Wilson.

For general information on our other products and services or for technical support, please
contact our Customer Care Department within the United States at (800) 762-2974, outside
the United States at (317) 572-3993 or fax (317) 572-4002.

Wiley publishes in a variety of print and electronic formats and by print-on-demand. Some
material included with standard print versions of this book may not be included in e-books or in
print-on-demand. If this book refers to media such as a CD or DVD that is not included in the
version you purchased, you may download this material at http://booksupport.wiley.com. For
more information about Wiley products, visit www.wiley.com.

Library of Congress Cataloging-in-Publication Data:

Names: Nour, David, 1968- author. | John Wiley & Sons, publisher.
Title: Curve benders : how strategic relationships can power your
  non-linear growth in the future of work / David Nour.
Description: Hoboken, New Jersey : Wiley, [2021] | Includes index.
Identifiers: LCCN 2021008532 (print) | LCCN 2021008533 (ebook) | ISBN
  9781119764212 (cloth) | ISBN 9781119764236 (adobe pdf) | ISBN
  9781119764229 (epub)
Subjects: LCSH: Social networks—Economic aspects. | Social capital
  (Sociology)—Economic aspects. | Interpersonal relations. | Business
  networks.
Classification: LCC HM741 .N677 2021 (print) | LCC HM741 (ebook) | DDC
  302.3—dc23
LC record available at https://lccn.loc.gov/2021008532
LC ebook record available at https://lccn.loc.gov/2021008533

Cover image: Lin Wilson
Cover design: Lin Wilson

SKY10025692_031721

To Wendy for your extraordinary strength, unparalleled support, and unconditional love;

To Grayson for your boundless grit, brilliant mind, and Nour tenacity – Go Jackets!

To Justus for your shreddedness, kind heart, and intelligent street smarts.

I'm in awe of the three of you every day. Thank you for your love.

CONTENTS

INTRODUCTION: DON'T DOUBT WAZE!

The most difficult thing is the decision to act. The rest is merely tenacity. The fears are paper tigers. You can do anything you decide to do. You can act to change and control your life; and the procedure, the process is its own reward.

– Amelia Earhart, American aviation pioneer

The COVID-19 pandemic illustrated how woefully underprepared we are. Attempting to predict the future is often futile. The future of work is a different game, predominately, because many variables can dramatically impact our world. If I had told you back in January 2020 that a wet market in Wuhan, China, would shut down a roaring global economy and cause major industry sectors to fall into an economic crater, cause over a million deaths worldwide, and leave tens of millions unemployed, all in a matter of few months, you'd be highly suspicious.

No matter where you are in your personal or professional journey, you must be growing. *This is your journey from now to next*. It must become a journey of inquiry, exploration, and experimentation. If you're privileged to manage a team or lead an organization, inspiring others on their personal growth journey will pay significant dividends on your human capital investments.

It is critical to understand that growth is made up of significant moments. Like relationships, the most memorable growth moments are fostered strongest and fastest between individuals. On this journey, collaborative relationships are an essential part of gaining new knowledge. The best version of you will often come from fundamental changes in how you engage and influence others. These are the most difficult behaviors to internalize and master.

And make no mistake about it, there is a Grand Canyon–sized gap between intent and action. For example, if you want to get in shape, unfortunately, you must do more than just read about it. Your fitness goal is a tightly integrated ecosystem of the right education, a healthy diet, and appropriate exercises, performed consistently for months. Losing weight is seldom an event. It's a lifestyle change that incentivizes you to not only get to your optimal weight but also to keep the pounds off. It's a commitment to real and lasting change. It doesn't happen overnight, and there are no shortcuts. The same goes for staying relevant in your work.

You have to get off your ass and own your personal and professional growth journey: no one is going to pull you up off the couch. Only your legs can push you up. You must become the chief architect of a blueprint for your future.

If you think about any journey, you need a roadmap to get to your destination. For a physical journey, GPS has supplanted the roadmap. Career and personal journeys have no such guidance system. It's good to have a copilot to help you stick to the time frame, avoid hitting squirrels, and remember why you are going in the first place. You'll need resources (time, effort, and capital) and perhaps even a new skill or two to enhance the experience, if not create greater efficiency.

I've lived in Atlanta since I immigrated from Iran back in 1981. I've grown up and worked in various parts of town. Uncle Ken, with whom I lived as a teenager, had a business designing and deploying air pumps at gas stations all around town. We'd drive out to hundreds of locations each week to service these machines, occasionally getting lost and relying on the fold-up, keep-in-the-glovebox maps to get around. After living in the same city for almost 40 years, I began using Waze.

Waze's network effect differentiates it from Google Maps. Over 100 million active monthly users provide critical insights, ranging from potholes and other road hazards to police locations. With this pool of information, it is up to the minute on information about traffic congestions, accidents, construction, and roadblocks. With this abundance of input, many algorithms instantaneously recalculate my path and keep me on the fastest track. So, although I know Atlanta intimately, Waze has made my commutes less time-consuming. Even if it takes me through an odd neighborhood (which it does), Waze knows the most efficient route. My family has committed to *not doubting Waze*! Waze has been transformational. And, as we'll learn later, transformational encounters always beat transactional ones.

Your personal and professional growth journey will be a similar experience. You know your core competencies today, and you are inclined toward your future aspirations. You can't possibly know all the structural, political, and behavioral obstacles in your path. Beyond your professional background, your single biggest asset in that growth journey is the insights from your portfolio of authentic relationships.

That's what this book is about. *Curve Benders are strategic relationships that will power your non-linear personal and professional growth in the future of work.* Great bosses, mentors, or coaches can and do incrementally improve your performance. But Curve Benders do so much more. They profoundly impact both your direction and destination in life. Not everyone will have the same Curve Bender. Yours will be unique to your growth needs. Most business relationships offer incremental improvements in our careers, not exponential changes in our lives. Curve Benders are profound relationships. They create the greatest change in you in the shortest time. They are scarce. People have impacted my career, but I can say confidentially that only a handful have provided more value than I could have anticipated for my personal and professional growth.

For profit and loss (P&L) leaders, Curve Benders dramatically accelerate your path to outcomes. If you're concise in your strategic vision, and prioritized pursuits, surround yourself with exceptional talent that's aligned with your value agenda, Curve Benders become that X factor that will set you apart from your peers. Regardless of how you're measured, they create more than a spark; they harvest hope, amplify aspirations, and deliver multiples in your efforts to create enterprise value.

Curve Benders are rare. They could be a coach or a mentor, or perhaps someone unexpected. Marilyn Monroe was a Curve Bender. In the 1950s, Ella Fitzgerald was a rising star, but racial prejudice kept her out of the biggest clubs. By happenstance, Marilyn Monroe wanted to improve her singing, and a music coach gave her one of Ella's records. Lying on her floor, Marilyn would spend hours listening to

Ella's records. Marilyn went to see Ella perform in Los Angeles and reached out to her. The two quickly bonded over being orphans and their career limitations of their appearance and gender. Ella complained about being barred from bigger stages. So, Marilyn used her status. She called the managers of the Mocambo, the most prominent jazz club of the time, and told them she would be front row if and when Ella played there. Marilyn did come and brought other celebrities every night Ella performed. Ella never played at a small jazz club again.

Ella was a seeker, looking for someone to help transform her path, and Marilyn was her solver. Curve Benders help you achieve far greater heights than you ever imagined possible because they see the best version of you. They inspire you to push yourself beyond your perceived limitations. They encourage you to become the leader, spouse, or parent you want to become. With Curve Bender relationships, you can create the impact you want in all facets of your life and leave the legacy you want for your team and your loved ones.

This example doesn't show all this. Marilyn didn't inspire Ella to push – and her limitations were *real*, not perceived. MM pushed for EF. I doubt that MM made EF a better leader, spouse, or parent. She "made" her a more successful singer.

Don Peppers, the founding partner of Peppers & Rogers Group, exemplifies a Curve Bender relationship with his long-time collaborator and coauthor, Martha Rogers, PhD. "I was out giving speeches when I met Martha back in 1992," he shared in our interview. "She came up to me and asked if I was planning to write a book about the topic of my speech. If I wasn't already doing so, she said, then she wanted to write it with me," he added. They agreed, spending three years writing what became *The One to One Future: Building Relationships One Customer at a Time* (Currency Doubleday, 1993).

The book came out and, for six months, did well but not spectacular. Then two things happened:

1. Tom Peters called it the "Book of the Year," and George Gendron of *Inc.* magazine wrote, "Peters was wrong. This is not the book of the year. It's not even the book of the decade. It's one of the two or three most important business books ever written."

2. The web became more prevalent, and with it, conferences that attracted innovators and entrepreneurs. *The One to One Future* became a must-read among this group, and Don and Martha became in-demand speakers. They founded Peppers & Rogers Group to offer consulting and training services, growing the company from 10 to 150 employees in the first three years. It partnered with VC-backed tech companies and served as a *Who's Who* of leading firms around the world, all of which wanted to get closer to their customers and serve them better.

Since 1993, Don and Martha have coauthored 10 books and three editions of a graduate school textbook on customer-centric competition. These books have sold over a million copies in 18 languages. Many believe Don and Martha to be the parents of the modern CRM sector. Martha elevated Don's gravitas, and Don helped Martha reach an executive audience beyond her academic realm. Together, they've become synonymous as the global authority on one-to-one marketing, if not customer-centric business models.

Curve Benders have the power to reroute our growth journey. So, who and where are these Curve Benders? How do we find these magical, mystical creatures? Do they serendipitously appear in our lives, or can we become more deliberate in meeting and engaging them? A more profound question to ponder is: How do we become someone else's Curve Bender? By the way, certain relationships can also take you in the complete opposite direction – I call those Fender Benders! In the coming chapters, I'll challenge some of your assumptions and give you a personal roadmap to explore critical questions in your future, with blended ways to work, live, play, and serve others.

TRANSACTIONS VERSUS TRANSFORMATIONS

Jim Coulter is the co-CEO and founding partner of the private equity firm TPG Capital, which has $84 billion in assets under management. Jim was mentioned in a recent CNBC interview on growth opportunities in periods of change.[1] The report shared that for most of Jim's career, business change had consisted of long evolutionary changes iteratively with continuous improvements. These slow-and-steady changes were assumed to be Darwinian. The global markets today represent a new type of change where industries are forced to reinvent themselves radically. COVID-19 has reinforced that assertion. Think about how we consume music. For several decades, we played music with a physical recording. Then, after a period of pure chaos, our music consumption began to be reimagined by old and new enterprises that experimented with digital technology. These competitors created a new market, pricing models, and strategic partnerships. After the carnage of Napster, Milk Music (by Samsung), and Rdio (acquired by Pandora), we ended up on the other side, with Spotify as the musical juggernaut of the twenty-first century. Coulter refers to this phenomenon as a *punctuated equilibrium* moving across industries. Punctuated equilibrium is a hypothesis in evolutionary biology that highlights isolated episodes of rapid speciation between long periods of little or no change.[2]

The global pandemic brought a new kind of turmoil into the business world. To grow stronger from inevitable chaos, we need a new approach. We must approach our business relationships with an eye for transformations rather than transactions. Transactions are commonplace. Two people make a simple exchange but have no emotional investment past the trade. Transactions reinforce linear growth. However, they don't foster faster and more robust growth that you can attain with transformational relationships.

If you are motivated only by transactions, you will sooner or later find yourself in a personal or professional slump. Transactions give you set plays, timeouts, unlimited substitutions, and room to coast on the field of play in many lethargic organizations and outdated industries. Transactions are omnipresent in cultures of mediocrity where good enough will suffice. Transactions are often the decay brought on by complacency and a sense of entitlement to employees, customers, and partners. Transactions are an event, focused on short-term goals, objectives, and incremental improvements as they defend the status quo. Transactions masquerade as innovation theater. Real relationships are continual. They can accelerate non-linear growth because learning is intertwined with feelings of connection and a higher purpose. When we have transactional relationships, we just check off boxes and stay in our routines. But, when we encourage transformational relationships, evolution begins.

Take soccer. If you have ever watched a game, you might notice that most players rarely have the ball. The best teams have players who are constantly scanning the field; multiple perspectives allow them to see numerous opportunities. Team-minded players can see the opposition's play developing. They are consistently motivating their teammates and putting their team in the best possible position when they get the ball. Success in these games is often predicated on extreme team cooperation, commitment to a winning culture, and severe time pressures. Passing the ball may seem transactional, but the crux of playing is teamwork. When players unite their skills and perspectives, they have a better chance of winning.

Transformation is what you'll need in your journey from now to next: the commitment and a clear vision that can act as your roadmap to reach a dramatically better version of yourself. In your journey, you'll need to plant aspirational seeds for a more significant impact, influence, and reach. Transformations are a journey to play for the longer-tail horizon, driven to problem-solve through creativity, collaboration, and co-creation. Transformations thrive on meritocracy. Transformations happen when we unite ideology with real-world practicality. Like polished, professional sales leaders with analytical insights to dramatically improve their client's conditions. Or clinical professors who balance theoretical constructs with real-world application and implementation practices. Transformational relationships accept and celebrate prudent risk-taking, turn failures into creative explorations, and tear into our egos. *To truly transform, you must challenge the status quo.*

Many business leaders have aimed for transactions to transform their significance or industry presence. Yet, transformation seldom happens. Cultural norms guide transactions. They're constructed with rules we know and are comfortable applying in traditional business metrics. Our perfect execution box will keep us stagnant. Traditional businesses are confined to organizational structures, job descriptions, pay grades, corporate ladders, performance reviews, committees, and nonstop attempts to prove just how smart we are. A transformation cannot succeed if it is derived in a transactional ecosystem, with a transactional mindset.

With all due respect to friends in these positions, I've long thought of many chief compliance, chief legal, chief risk, and chief financial officers as oncologists! Their role in a perfect execution box is to eradicate glimmers of creativity, risk, and potential failures. Far too many cannot accept anomalies in how they design, develop, and deliver their perfect execution boxes. New approaches toward the market are seen as cancers to accepted norms. This mentality sprouts vastly in the U.S. education system. My kids' private high school curriculum makes me cringe every time I read it. It is derived from the Georgia Department of Education's Curriculum and Instruction guidelines, originally by the "Committee of Ten" established by the National Education Association, back in 1892! They unanimously recommended that "every subject which is taught at all in a secondary school should be taught in the same way and to the same extent to every pupil so long as he pursues it, no matter what the probable destination of the pupil may be, or at what point his education is to cease."[3] The global education ecosystem has evolved dramatically since 1892, and we now understand that epistemology is multifaceted and that not everyone learns the same way.

Now, if you're designing the SpaceX *Falcon 9 Heavy* rocket system, by all means, compliance and that perfect execution box are expected. Take a closer look at the team members and you'll uncover fascinating, highly diverse, and divergent career paths, comprised of transformational learning and growth journeys.

No one thought SpaceX would beat Boeing and Lockheed Martin until Elon Musk and the team at SpaceX designed rockets that not only propelled their payloads to orbit but also landed back on Earth to be reused. That transformation took 12 years, propelling SpaceX to rarefied air in NASA's "commercial crew program," relying on a private contractor to design and build spacecraft to send humans to orbit. Ultimately, the SpaceX vision is to fly people to the Moon and Mars, an ambitious feat that will require the next generation of spacecraft, known as *Starship*.

What strategic relationships will support your version of a SpaceX 12-year transformational journey? How will you muster the courage to be really bad at something first, while you challenge existing business models and explore new tools and processes previously deemed unimaginable? How can you gain the stamina to explore, test, fail, and keep coming back for more? I believe your most authentic and value-based relationships can motivate you to reach previously unimaginable heights.

How Will You Get There?

The best possible times to discover Curve Benders in your personal and professional growth journey are a handful of points along your S-curve. I call this your *refraction point* (Figure I.1). Back in high school physics experiments, you may recall attempting to shine light through water. The change in velocity of the light changes the light wavelengths, creating several possible boundary behaviors. Similarly, you're focused on continuous improvements toward your outcomes in your personal and professional growth journey. That's the light shining

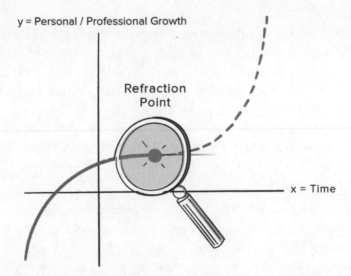

Figure I.1   Your Refraction Point

directly at something, and, although essential to focus, there is no bend or flex at entry or exit. When light travels along the normal to the boundary, it changes its speed but not its direction.

Only when you change your approach will your path reveal alternative possibilities. Curve Benders change our lens and, in the process, often change our angle to solve challenges and address opportunities right in front of our eyes. Curve Benders are the compass of our lives that help us explore different directions. They elevate us and show us what a transformation looks like, personally and professionally.

The journey toward a better you will rely on your roadmap and hitting critical points along the way. At times you feel stuck in a rut and without any forward momentum. Sometimes the barrier may be an organizational structure. It's easy to blame external factors for problems of our own making. One of the earliest obstacles in your roadmap will be accepting a new path toward growth.

Growth for many people is a linear proposition. However, the expectations around real growth will continue to increase in widely diverse ways. You'll need to connect the dots between *what* skills, knowledge, and behaviors you must gain and *how* to acquire them quickly and efficiently.

As I'll discuss in subsequent chapters, the most competitive and valuable firms have mastered the challenges of dynamic market environments. New business models, maneuverability, and applied technologies will flex the organization's labor. Labor flex refers to the willingness and ability of the organization's talent to adapt to new skills and ever-changing market demands. As such, the ability to learn and relearn becomes critical in redeploying talent in every organization.

The S-curve framework – used in a broad array of disciplines to represent the start, accelerated growth, and maturity of something via an S-shaped curve – can help you understand the *what* and the *how* in your growth journey. S-curves are a form of linear growth in your career ladder. I believe that what will get you to the top of the S fastest is climbing a career *lattice*. By crisscrossing over a chain-link path, you will ensure that you are picking up a variety of skills along the way that will enhance your overall market value. For example, Children's Healthcare of Atlanta hired the former head of Supply Chain at Home

CURVE BENDERS

relationship economics®
the art & science of relationships

CO-CREATE

Strategy
Visualization

NOURGROUP®

**Thank you for an
Amazon Review
if you like the book.**

stay in touch

NEED Strategic Growth	**MEET** David Nour, CEO
WRITE dnour@nourgroup.com	
TALK +1 (404) 419-2115	**LEARN** NourGroup.com

Depot. Last I checked, CHOA doesn't sell drills, and Home Depot is not in the healthcare business. This is how you can leverage your transferable skills to jump across industries and add new value and perspectives to an organization. These new capabilities will keep you relevant and increase your personal and professional value, and other organizations will want you. It bolsters a new pull for your personal brand.

The refraction points on our personal S-curves are a direct result of a sharpened self-awareness. Research suggests that having a clear lens on who and where we really are in life helps us become more confident and creative. We make more data-driven, sound judgments, build dramatically stronger relationships, and influence others in our communication and collaboration efforts with far greater effectiveness. We are less likely to fabricate, mislead, misjudge, and blame others when we are self-aware. Beyond better leaders, we become better teammates, often leading to higher performance, execution, and results for our organizations.[4] Other refraction opportunities can be driven by a desire to find greater purpose and meaning in one's work and life.

THIS BOOK'S PROMISE

For P&L leaders to remain relevant in the uncertain future, they must identify and leverage their strategic relationships to create non-linear growth opportunities. This book is your roadmap in *your journey from now to next*. My goal is to convey the subject-matter expertise you'll need to identify, assess, and build strategic relationships in your personal S-curve. Over time and through the exponential network effect, these relationships can introduce you to potential Curve Benders to accelerate the trajectory of your life's path.

Throughout this book, key parts of the Curve Benders Roadmap will define insights you'll need on your growth journey. From understanding 15 forces that will dramatically impact your future and what to do about them now to paving your path to curve-bending relationships, the Curve Benders Roadmap is your GPS. It will guide you to own your personal brand, accelerate your relevancy, identify Curve Benders as risk mitigators, and drive your continued reinvention. Although written with a prioritized context of your professional role within organizational challenges and opportunities, the uncertainties of the future extend beyond any geography, your collar's color, and your life beyond your career. The Curve Benders Roadmap will challenge you to amplify the servant leader in you, to become profound in the lives of others, and to create a life of significance.

And if you're looking for a motivation to keep reading, here is food for thought: the most important person in the next 10 years of your life, you haven't met yet!

So, let's get started.

– Nour

CHAPTER 1

Work–Life Blending

Education is the most powerful weapon which you can use to change the world. The power of education extends beyond the development of the skills we need for economic success. It can contribute to nation-building and reconciliation.

– Nelson Mandela, South African anti-apartheid revolutionary, political leader, and president of South Africa, 1994–1999

Curve Benders need multiple on-ramps to enter our lives. These on-ramps could be leaders in other industries exploring similar growth opportunities, scientists analyzing the impact of our lives on a sustainable climate, and like minded parents across the globe struggling to help their kids understand racial inequalities. You could undoubtedly explore your future of work, with a plethora of resources. The opportunity is to expand your purview to other aspects of your life as well. When you intentionally invest in how you live, you create opportunities to meet and grow through Curve Benders. It is essential to surround yourself with those who don't think like you do. Cognitive diversity in your network keeps you fresh. From generational to geographical differences, cognitively diverse relationships help us understand that the rest of the world doesn't believe or behave as we do.

The holistic nature of Curve Benders makes them fascinating people. Although a strong work ethic often creates their professional success, their broader lifestyle provides a glimpse into their significance. As you design your Curve Benders Roadmap, you must create space for serendipitous and intentional relationships to influence your reflections, planning, and priorities. Diverse perspectives around you will create a dramatically more vibrant and fulfilling future. These intersections forge new branches in your life to explore not just what you can accomplish, but also who you can become as a leader, a partner, a parent, and a global citizen.

Alan Weiss, PhD, is one of my Curve Benders. I met Alan in 2007 when I was asked to pick him up at the airport. He was there to speak to the National Speakers' Association (NSA), Georgia chapter. I never imagined that this chance encounter would dramatically change my business direction and my life over the next two decades. During dinner and his speech, I became increasingly impressed by Alan's intellectual horsepower. He is well-read, well-traveled, and has great depth as an advisor. Like most Curve Benders, Alan has strong opinions on a broad spectrum of topics and can quickly frame challenges and opportunities. He is jovial with a zest for the finer things in life. But he also has an edge. If you're wasting his time, he quickly becomes impatient. He has no problem asking, "What's your question of me?" if you call him for help and give him background info he doesn't need. You don't have to like Alan, but you'll be hard-pressed not to respect his insights. Invest time and effort in his content and he will transform a solo practitioner's business and life. Although he's a solo practitioner, he has amassed wealth from corporate advisory, training, and speaking engagements since the 1980s. More recently, he has developed a thriving community made up of thousands. Speakers, consultants, and trainers all want to learn from him, if not become him.

Alan showed me the transformative power of a Curve Bender. With his advice, I recalibrated my focus. He helped me think differently about the value that I bring to my clients and taught me his unique approach to value-based fees. I enhanced my command of the English language and committed to reading broader-based books. I often share Alan's insights, modified to fit our specific conditions, with my community. Following Alan's teachings, I doubled my revenues in less than one year.

But Alan does more than just make me want to become a better advisor. He does more than push me to think, to consider multiple sources of intelligent perspectives, and to make better decisions. He sees the best version of me. Once, in passing, he said, "you are one of the best-kept secrets in America." Talk about a personal slogan! I felt a deep extrinsic motivation that fueled me to never disappoint him.

Alan has also given me a front-row seat into his notion of *ONE life*. He says that none of us separate personal and professional lives. *We all have one life*. Although many professionals struggle with *work–life balance*, Alan lives by what I call *work–life blending*. For the past 30 years, he has run his practice from his home office in Rhode Island. Around 2 p.m. every warm day, you can find him by the pool. He combines professional programs with cities and activities he wants to experience. From weekends in London and Sydney, Alan integrates his work into that which brings him enormous joy. Mastering that balance is priceless. He has traveled globally to conduct educational programs and woven family time into the trips. He has served on the boards of nonprofits, academic advisory committees, and even coached a Ms. America contestant. I met Alan after a decade of consulting by the hour – a fundamentally flawed model, due to its capacity constraints. Nonlinear growth through Alan's content, experiences, community, and work–life blending has dramatically improved my professional skills, as well as quality of life. He is the epitome of accelerating one's relevance.

Many Americans derive their last names from ancestors in England. As the country's populations grew after the Norman conquest in 1066, people found the specificity particularly relevant.[1] Most of the estimated 45,000 different English last names have origins in one of seven types: occupation, personal characteristic, English location, estate name, geographical feature, ancestry, or patronage.[2] For almost a thousand years, our jobs have defined us to the extent that they are embedded into how we are identified. So, your friend Thomas Baker's great-great-great-grandfather probably made a mean sourdough.

As someone with strict parents, I learned a strong work ethic early in life. It was normal to be up early each morning, active on weekends, striving to do my best. Late hours were the norm. I remember how hard my parents worked multiple jobs to make ends meet when my sister and I were young in Iran. When I moved to the States, my Uncle Ken, with whom I lived as a teenager, held a full-time job and was a part-time entrepreneur, so Saturdays and Sundays were just two more days in the workweek. Working multiple jobs, I paid cash for both my undergraduate and graduate degrees. I was doing side hustles that I found in newspaper ads before the gig economy got to be a thing. In the early days of my career, 6 a.m.–8 p.m., Monday through Friday, was the mandatory workweek. As a fledgling entrepreneur, I'd work every weekend, missing out on family time. I would stay at the office late to get more done. What an awful example of work–life imbalance, as I saw my kids grow up way too fast. You could say that work has always defined me, as it does most men with whom I associate.

Through a thoughtful observation of how other leaders lived, I saw that one could be successful by societal measures. *Pursuing a more fulfilling and well-rounded life opens fascinating new paths to Curve Benders you would never encounter otherwise.* Here is one example: I used to have a strong interest in Scouting. For a decade, I was involved in my son's Scouting experiences, where I proudly supported him to earn his Eagle Scout rank. Through Scouting I met Clint Hunter, who led me to discover a new passion for riding motorcycles. I now regularly take weeks off for long-distance global motorcycle rides with amazing people I would have never met otherwise.

This approach to work–life blending has allowed me to prioritize service to others. My son and I have spent weekends on a construction site, helping to rebuild homes for the less fortunate. We make meals and put together toiletry kits for the homeless community in Atlanta and meet incredible men and women of deep faith. Both kids lead summer mission trips to Ecuador where they witness firsthand the toll of poverty. We sponsor less fortunate families throughout the year, demonstrating the love of God when we give, serve, and love others.[3] Through our family's volunteer work, I've grown closer to other dads at my kids' school.

A commitment to a fuller, more vibrant living creates an impetus for more meaningful relationships, beyond the transactional contacts. Work–life blending allows you to develop deeper relationships. These relationships extend and expand your horizons far beyond what you do for a living. They create a life well-lived.

Life in the future will require more authentic relationships. Giving others a chance to get to know the whole you will encourage them to like and trust you. They'll see more than just your professional progress; they may get a glimpse into your personal aspirations, how you learn, grow, have fun, challenge your assumptions, and give to others.

INFRASTRUCTURE OF OUR LIVES

Acela Express, the American high-speed train, is capable of 186 mph, but can travel up to 150 mph in only three sections of the track, which totals 460 miles from Boston to Washington, DC. Why? Because the track can't sustain higher speeds.[4] Our cars, high-speed boats, and passenger aircrafts struggle from similar limitations. The vehicles we travel in are reliant on the conditions in which they operate.

The same applies to your growth in the future. You'll always rely on your environment, resources, and relationships. In addition to developing your talents and modifying your behaviors, you will need to invest in life's infrastructure.

A good way to think about your life's infrastructure is to consider how city leaders consider investments. In our cities, infrastructure improvements enhance the efficiency in production of value, ease transportation, and dramatically boost communication. Infrastructure improvements provide incentives for public- and private-sector participants. Infrastructure enhances our productivity, making us more capable and competitive, and improves our quality of life.

Infrastructure investments are expensive. The good news is that creativity, resourcefulness, and co-creation can lower the costs. Your Curve Benders Roadmap is best served with a candid assessment of your life's infrastructure. What upgrades does your environment need to allow you to reach your full potential? Astute infrastructure investments include lifelong education, fresh and unusual experiences, tools, and technologies to keep your infrastructure efficient and upgraded. An essential investment will be to diversify your portfolio of relationships with those who can shed a new light on unforeseen learning and growth opportunities.

Ken Ashely is one of those relationships in my life. Ken, an Atlanta commercial real estate professional, builds strategic relationship in all facets of his life. He sits on the local Boy Scout Council board and is very active in the Atlanta community, adding value in every interaction. During a recent lunch visit, he mentioned that he was membership chair for Leadership Atlanta, one of the nation's oldest community leadership programs. The expansive network of distinguished alumni is made up of Atlanta's community, civic, academic, and industry leaders.

He encouraged me to apply. I am elated to participate in the nine months of retreats, day-long seminars, service projects, discussion groups, and community tours, where leaders explore critical community issues, examine their leadership competencies, and build lasting relationships of trust and mutual understanding.[5] But the crucial thing is that if I had not invested in a portfolio of diverse relationship like Ken, I would have never realized an opportunity like Leadership Atlanta.

In the future of living, your smart personal infrastructure will have three layers (Figure 1.1). First will be a technology base, which includes devices and physical networks — at home, at work, and on the move. You must go beyond having access to the internet and a computer to being digitally competent and collaborative. The second layer consists of a tech stack of applications, like Miro, an online whiteboard app. When holding an online meeting, I use Miro to clarify, communicate, and cascade visual ideas. The third layer will be digital acumen in how you adopt and adapt to different behaviors with this infrastructure.

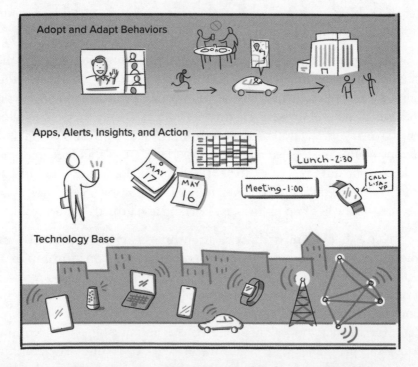

Figure 1.1   Three Layers of Your Personal Infrastructure

In the post-pandemic world, like many, I have become as effective online as I am in person. As we discuss in the next chapter, technology will have a profound impact on our lives. Smart infrastructure will add digital intelligence to our urban interactions to solve problems and achieve a higher quality of life.

ALIGNING CORPORATE STRATEGY

I've long believed that business relationships go bad with misaligned expectations. You can't completely eliminate misalignments, so to minimize their potential damage, it's critical to align and recalibrate mutual expectations early and often. In my executive coaching, misalignment is the single biggest source of the chip on an executive's proverbial shoulder. They're frustrated because their personal aspirations are not in sync with their organization's vision and priorities. Your Curve Benders Roadmap will be heavily influenced by your organization's strategy and prioritized pursuits. So, it's ideal if your current efforts and future aspirations are on the same page with both your leader's and organization's priorities.

We use Strategy Visualization to help clients clarify and cascade their strategic path forward. We walk alongside leaders to examine the current state of their strategies and relationships. Through a new lens, we create a visual story to help articulate a direction that's simple to understand, easy to internalize, and fast to implement (Figure 1.2).

Most organizations don't lack innovative ideas. They struggle with barriers that prevent great ideas from being implemented. The top six barriers our team consistently uncovers in our clients is shown in Figure 1.3:

1. **Confusing Vision and Direction** – Your vision is brilliant but a failure if nobody can understand it.

2. **Culture Inhibits Innovation** – If your culture won't encourage real innovation, what can?

3. **Resistance to Change** – If people are to change, they need to understand why they should and why they should do it now.

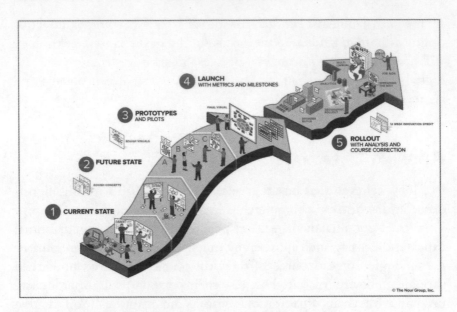

Figure 1.2   Nour Strategy Visualization (NSV)

Figure 1.3   Top Six Barriers to Strategy Execution

4. **Misaligned Initiatives** – Projects go sideways when nobody understands why they exist.

5. **Audiences Can't Understand** – What's the best way to lose your people's focus? Confuse them.

6. **Unclear on Our Why** – People work for more than financial rewards. Communicate with clarity why your organization exists.

Strategy Visualization is particularly helpful in clarifying a leader's vision and the path forward. It drives concise communication of prioritized pursuits and can keep the team from getting distracted. It cascades the vision with consistency and clarity of intent. It often transforms how an organization communicates to various stakeholders. In several opportunities, it has conveyed a more compelling fundraising event or a merger/acquisition story on why the path forward is the best competitive option among a set of fierce competitors. Figure 1.4 is one example, illustrating the clarity of a strategic path forward for TK Elevator Americas.

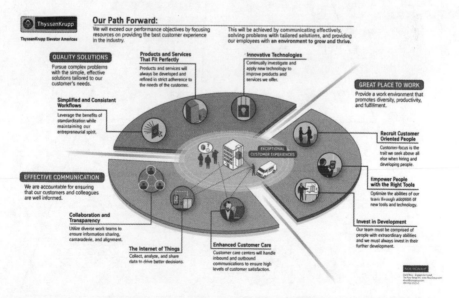

Figure 1.4 TK Elevator Americas "Our Path Forward" Strategy Visualization

Similarly, your Curve Benders Roadmap should be the path toward future you. Curve Bender relationships will help widen the scope of what your future can become.

You can think about and begin to place your aspirations into a two-by-two matrix that I call your *Growth Grid* (Figure 1.5). Across the x-axis are the two fundamental phases of any significant challenge or opportunity: pain points and resolutions. Along the y-axis are general approaches in mindset and skillset development necessary to begin addressing them: concrete direction and abstract concept.

At a high level, the Growth Grid has four stages:

1. *Inquisition* – Identifying key pain points with a concrete direction

2. *Formulation* – Turning concrete direction into a viable plan

3. *Exploration* – Gathering feedback on the plan's viability

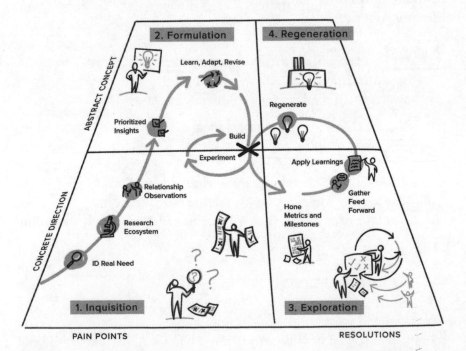

Figure 1.5   Growth Grid
Source: Inspired by the Nordstrom Innovation Lab.

4. *Regeneration* – Incorporating learnings into the next version of the plan

In the bottom-left quadrant 1, your focus should be deep *Inquisition*. Get beyond the historical negative connotations and focus on exploring the challenges you face or upside growth you seek with empathy for a target audience you're trying to serve. Here you'll want to:

1. Identify your real needs,

2. Research your environment, and

3. Gauge insights your relationships may have observed in the market.

Let's say, for example, that your pain point is to identify, engage, and influence new prospective clients.

In the top-left quadrant 2, your focus should shift to conceptual *Formulation*. The information gathered through your inquiry around ideal client profiles, their key challenges, and opportunities for you to serve them in a unique manner should help you refine your path to the right prospect profiles. You will have to use brainstorming skills, knowledge, and synthesize patterns to make forward progress when you begin to form your hypothesis on how to attract them.

As you progress on your aspirational journey, in the bottom-right quadrant 3, you embark on iterative *Exploration*. Here you are implementing solutions and iterating with agile, applied learnings. You're testing different ways to attract clients and taking note of what works and what doesn't. You're gathering feed-forward from trusted sources, ideally honing your metrics and milestones, and refining with leading indicators.

The final quadrant 4 in the top right is for investments in *Regeneration*. You should be able to regenerate ideas and initiatives from your learnings. When you sufficiently apply your solution, have a consistent and robust feed-forward network, and lead indicators, you should have solved how to attract more clients. That journey should lead you back to the first quadrant to inquire about incremental, if not exponential, improvements. Too many leaders bypass the regeneration efforts, as they mistakenly believe that a step back to inquiry and reassessing their progress before taking two steps forward will slow them down.

This agile execution of your aspirations will instill a disciplined approach to gaining the right skills at the right time. When you apply said skills, you'll gain the knowledge you need to devise new and pertinent ideas and solutions. Ultimately, you'll improve your performance, execution, results, and behaviors to create lasting change.

ORGANIZATION'S VALUE AGENDA

Curve Benders have this path highly interwoven into our lives. In 2015, Marshall Goldsmith, the number-one executive coach in the world, attended a program, Design the Life You Love, by one of the top designers in the world, Ayse Birsel. Asked to name his heroes, he listed Frances Hesselbein (former CEO of the Girl Scouts and recipient of the Presidential Medal of Freedom), Alan Mulally (former CEO of Ford and CEO of the year in the United States), Dr. Jim Kim (former president of the World Bank), Peter Drucker (founder of modern management), Paul Hersey (noted author, teacher, and his personal mentor), and Warren Bennis (one of the world's greatest leadership thinkers). Then Ayse asked Marshall to tell what made them his heroes, to which Marshall responded, "great teachers" and "very generous." She then challenged Marshall to "be more like them" in designing the life he loves.

From this, Marshall proposed to teach 15 people everything he knew at no charge. In return, he'd ask these 15 to pay it forward by doing the same for 15 others, for free. It was his way of recognizing the incredible contributions many great teachers and leaders had made in his life. Marshall made a 30-second video, which became one of the most widely viewed videos on LinkedIn, that inspired more than 18,000 global applicants to become part of 100 Coaches.

Having met Marshall in 2008, I eagerly threw my hat into the ring. To my surprise, Marshall called me in September 2017 and invited me to join this fantastic group of individuals, many of whom are leaders in their respective fields. Since then, MG100 has become an incredible source of inspiration, friendships, collaboration, and growth for me. MG100 has served as the genesis for this book, evolved my personal growth, and elevated the value that I bring to my clients.

In December 2017, at the MG100 gathering at The World Bank, I met Sandy Ogg, founder of CEO.Works. Sandy has spent over three decades working with and learning from successful global CEOs. Sandy had been an operating partner in the private equity group at Blackstone and the chief human resources officer for Unilever. From his front-row seat to successful CEOs, he developed Connecting Talent to Value™. This methodology helps organizations bend the value curve by getting the right people into the right jobs.

Most CEOs lack the ability to see the importance of each individual role in their organization. Sandy feels that no organization can afford to be ignorant about what's driving value in times of significant disruption.

Inspired by his model (Figure 1.6), Sandy made a compelling argument. Many CEOs think their job is to set direction, execute strategy, and manage performance. Talent is often relegated to HR while the value is driven by finance. He observed how rarely CEOs, CFOs, and CHROs come together to flag specific roles in the organization

Figure 1.6 Seeing the Importance of Individual Roles in an Organization
Source: Inspired by Sandy Ogg, Connecting Talent to Value™.

that drive enterprise value. Even more rare is the monitoring of individuals in those roles for their contributions to value, level of engagement, and capacity. Yet those very contributions are what the organization relies on to secure current performance and future growth possibilities.[6]

Instead of treating roles, contributions, and capacity as separate activities under the overarching umbrellas of organizational design, performance reviews, and talent pipeline, it's time to connect talent to value.

The value agenda must come first. With input from the board and the leadership team, the CEO should make a set of strategic choices to focus on how the organization's talent will increase in value over time. This value agenda has two critical components (Figure 1.7):

1. **Momentum**, which defines the value expected from the business-as-usual path. This is today's source of value, and it may grow or contract based on market conditions, industry disruptions, or geographic market challenges and opportunities.

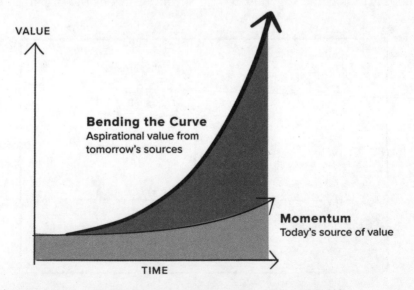

Figure 1.7   Two Critical Components of the Value Agenda
Source: Inspired by Sandy Ogg, Connecting Talent to Value™.

2. **Bending the Curve**, which defines the possible value the company may realize if it accurately anticipates future market needs and flawlessly executes a few strategic initiatives to deliver. This is the aspirational value from tomorrow's sources through implementing innovative business models and co-creation possibilities.

The next essential step is to understand precisely what roles have the most potential to deliver to the organization's ambitious value. This is where your aspirations would align. If your current role isn't one of these, you have to make it so or change roles. Many of these roles don't sit nicely in a traditional organizational hierarchy. The question in identifying the critical roles is to make a list of 25 to 50 of the most important roles in the company that create or enable substantial value.

Roles that deliver exponential value can be broken into two types:

1. **Value Creators** generate revenue, lower cost, or increase efficiency.

2. **Value Enablers** help lower risks associated with value creation, overcoming organizational hurdles such as talent shortages, cybersecurity issues, regulatory compliance, and legal matters.

In traditional organizational structure, the C-suite is a proxy for value creation. In reality, value creators are often much deeper in the enterprise, several layers below the CEO. If you rough out the value creation roles in the company and quantify the specific contributions expected of each of these roles, you can identify value "hot spots" (Figure 1.8). Clarification of those jobs highlights the risk and upside they influence. The quantifiable insights into each role will illustrate not only the less-than-optimal person in any of these roles but also how much value the organization has at risk.

You need to use an evidence-based approach to match talent to roles. Have your team look through multiple perspectives to get as clear a picture as possible of each candidate's capacity to fulfill the role's requirements. The evidence gathered should confirm how well

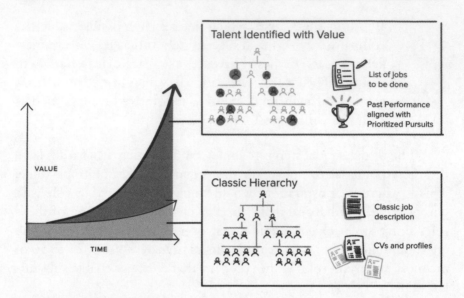

Figure 1.8 Traditional Organizational Structure versus Hot Spots in Value Creation

Source: Inspired by Sandy Ogg, Connecting Talent to Value™.

each candidate's knowledge, experiences, and behaviors match the role and deliver assigned performance results to it. Only when the preliminary match warrants, conduct interviews and review psychometric test results to assess a candidate's commitment.[7] This approach is unique from the traditional talent selection process in two distinct manners:

1. Instead of starting with a classic job description, create a list of jobs to be done to deliver the expected value.

2. Instead of looking at CVs and profiles to match the person with the job description, review the relevant jobs in which the candidates have done well and match their past performance with a set of priorities in the jobs to be done.

For example, instead of writing a job description for someone who needs to build a good relationship with suppliers in China, recruiters should look for an individual who has already done that job. By assessing the capabilities of the person to do a specific job, you eliminate the need to evaluate people as A, B, or (praying they aren't) C players. You simply look at the jobs to be done and the number assigned to each role and conduct a straightforward exercise to determine which candidate will give you the best match with the sets of jobs to be done, most likely to deliver the expected value.

In your own growth journey, quantifying your own value creation will lead to a better match with the critical roles every organization needs to link its talent to the value agenda. Then ask if you are in the momentum category of business-as-usual performance. Or are you consistently contributing to bending the value curve in your organization through net-new growth opportunities that quantifiably improve the business?

FOUR NON-LINEAR GROWTH STRATEGIES

The evolution of your organizational structures, strategies, and priorities will dramatically impact your Curve Benders Roadmap. Understanding these dynamics and adapting your contributions to value creation will increase your currency in the marketplace. As a leader, you also need to consider how these variables will influence how you lead and develop your team in *their* personal and professional growth journeys. Remember, in the future, the only job security we can expect is the value we bring! The only loyalty organizations should expect is the continuous learning and growth they create for their talent.

During a two-week online strategy sprint, Scott Galloway, NYU Stern professor of brand strategy and digital marketing, brought his T-Algorithm from his book, *The Four: The Hidden DNA of Amazon, Apple, Facebook, and Google* (Portfolio, 2018), to life with his signature over-the-top style. *T* refers to the trillion-dollar valuation of emerging business models.

Over the past 20 years, the four tech giants have generated unprecedented market value, in excess of $3 trillion, often "wreaking havoc on their competitive peers, performing infanticide on small companies, and prematurely euthanizing larger firms," as Scott puts it. Eight strategies are essential to reinventing parts of your organization, as well as your growth journey ahead. All eight are interesting and relevant to enterprise value creation. Four strategies are particularly relevant to your journey as they drive non-linear growth: *Career Accelerant*, *Benjamin Button*, *Likeability*, and *Visionary Storytelling* (Figure 1.9).

1. **Career Accelerant.** What do Pete Buttigieg, Sheryl Sandberg, Sundar Pichai, and James P. Gorman all have in common? They all worked at McKinsey. The firm is the rocket fuel that can set the trajectory for the rest of one's career. Attracting the best talent is a prerequisite to being an accelerant firm. These firms heavily invest in the top-tier recruiters who become ambassadors for a culture of excellence and internal growth probabilities. Accelerant firms also promote rising stars quickly. They aren't afraid of allowing the top of the pyramid to become crowded. By maintaining an up-or-out culture, McKinsey has created an environment where leaving the firm after a few years is considered a rite of passage. They not only make it easy for people to move on but help them into better positions. The firm's alumni website features successful alums, job postings, and upcoming networking events.

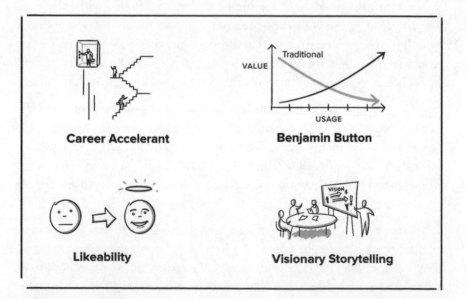

Figure 1.9   Four Non-Linear Growth Strategies from Scott Galloway's T-Algorithm

In your Curve Benders Roadmap, you must prioritize the recruiting process. As a leader, overinvest in your organization's recruiting talent. As a candidate, look for top-notch recruiters, armed with compelling assets to attract star players. Second, look for cultures of excellence with an up-or-out policy that creates room for young stars to shine and advance. Any firm reluctant to push senior management out often won't generate enough leadership growth opportunities. At firms like McKinsey or Goldman Sachs, short stints are the norm because they overinvest in supporting former employees in creating influential evangelists of the firm in the market. Attracting and promoting top-tier talent guarantees that high achievers will thrive at other top firms in a vast array of roles and across a multitude of industries. You should aim to become a part of a firm's no-lose proposition, where it pays to have worked in an accelerant firm. You'll also be well served by building strong relationships with partners at the big three management consulting firms – Bain, BCG, and McKinsey – due to their knowledge resources and strategic market relationships.

2. **Benjamin Button.** Benjamin Button strategies are ones whose services age in reverse, like the protagonist of F. Scott Fitzgerald's short story. Most products or services depreciate over time. Today's most valuable organizations leverage a digital network effect, which, with increased use, expands the organization's value. Every new user into the ecosystem makes the product or the service more valuable.

This increased value occurs in two ways:

1. The product's or service's core offering is interaction with other users. Think of LinkedIn. If all your colleagues, customers, and partners are on LinkedIn, it's much more valuable to you than if just one contact is on the platform. So, LinkedIn becomes more valuable with each new user added.

2. New users can make a product more valuable when the product learns from each user's behavior and

then improves based on that behavior. These companies increase in value with each additional use, not just each new user. Google, Wikipedia, and Waze are the classic examples here.

Today's best tech startups are attempting to use both strategies. They need to add more users and embed learning opportunities from each new use. Spotify sees your friends' playlists and then creates granular insights on your recommendations.

Organizations that can defy traditional biology of depreciation and grow more valuable with increased use enjoy clear economic benefits. So can you in your Curve Benders Roadmap. The greater quality, diversity, and relevance of each additional relationship in your ecosystem, the stronger your network's potential impact and market value. You should learn from every relationship behavior pattern – sociologists refer to this as being *Ambient Aware*. The more knowledgeable you become about what moves key members of your ecosystem, the more proactively you can nurture, engage, and influence your network.

3. **Likeability.** The basis of brand strategy is to attach intangible associations to an inanimate product or concepts. If you personify an organization with a positive animate characteristic, you make the brand more likable. Who doesn't love Tony the Tiger, Flo, Mayhem, or "Just do it"? But that likeability extends beyond just brand attributes. Iconic CEOs or founders become brand ambassadors. Almost anything Virgin does is likeable because of its maverick founder, Richard Branson. Being the first openly gay CEO of a Fortune 500 company is an admirable leadership position, and it makes Tim Cook more likable.

Likeability may sound too obvious. Nevertheless, likeability also offers protection, as likable organizations are less likely to have terrible things happen to them from government or external factors. Generally speaking, they're less prone to antitrust charges, unfair regulations, or district attorneys looking to make a populist argument against them. Sheryl Sandberg writing books and speaking gracefully on gender equality in the workplace and her personal loss makes her much more likable. Pairing the mature, poised, and accomplished Sandberg with the boy wonder Mark Zuckerberg helped keep the wolves of scrutiny at bay for an additional one to two years, despite multiple scandals rocking Facebook.

A word of caution regarding likeability: just as likable leaders can only improve a company's image for so long, you have only so long to clear the runway. Most people have a BS radar, and if they feel they've been lied to, they can be particularly scornful. It's critical that you walk the walk. Likeability will be an essential characteristic of your future success. It often means more internal and external support; it means funding for your key initiatives and attracting more competent and capable talent. In my executive coaching, I've observed people who have an easier time establishing relationships, those seen as leaders inside the organization and outside of it, advance further.

4. **Visionary Storytelling.** The ability to articulate a bold vision for your organization is more than a soft skill. In working with dozens of companies, I've observed that articulating a compelling vision will get everyone rowing in the same direction with the same vigor. No matter whom you're trying to attract, a bold vision and execution plan with key milestones definitively sets such leaders and their organizations apart from their peers.

Google wants to organize the earth's information. The benefits of this massive, difficult, and expensive vision are clear. And they're getting better at it every day. Facebook wants to connect the world – it's simple, easy to understand, and aligned with the different facets of their business model. They have an estimated 2.5 billion people globally, directly or indirectly connected. And they're getting better at it every day. Brands must also keep a sense of realism in their vision or risk their credibility. WeWork's mission was to "enable or elevate our consciousness." Really? From a co-working space? Peloton wants to deliver happiness. Again, really? Are they delivering happiness or selling expensive exercise equipment?

The key to success in your Curve Benders Roadmap is to balance a compelling vision with consistent performance. You must invest in consistently communicating what you're doing, what you are exploring, and the results you are creating. Jeff Bezos's 1997 letter to the Amazon shareholders said that they were going to focus on three things: value, convenience, and selection. Every year you can see how they've been delivering against those three commitments and the staggering investments they're willing to make to reinforce that core vision.

I believe immense power and insight come from using winning firms as a roadmap for your business and your personal growth. The foundation to your Curve Benders Roadmap will be your personal market value. Let's look at how to enhance it next.

YOUR PERSONAL MARKET VALUE

A critical step in your growth journey will be your personal market value. Just as an organization can increase its market value, you, too, have the potential to increase your personal market value dramatically. Like anything else you want to last, it's important to start with a stable foundation (Figure 1.10).

Your personal market value, at the center, requires a strong foundation across three critical areas:

1. **Core** – This singular topic impacts our headspace, emotional well-being, and focus on forward progress in a lifetime journey.

2. **Personal** – We're living and working longer, with a need for deeper roots than our institutional constructs as well as guardrails in a set of personal values.

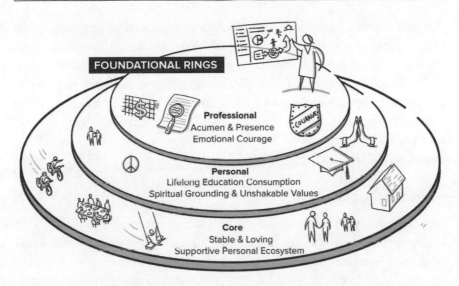

Figure 1.10 Personal Market Value: Stable Foundation

3. **Professional** – From acumen to presence and emotional courage, impactful and effective leaders engage and influence others, bolster the success of their teams, and demonstrate resolve with emotional courage.

Foundational Ring One: Core – Stable, Loving, Supportive Personal Ecosystem. A reliable ecosystem of family and personal friends nurtures our resilience. Ask successful executives to identify their bedrocks and most will credit their spouses, friends, and family members. "When we think about improving our lives, we focus our development inward," says Tom Rath, a Gallup Organization researcher and author of *Vital Friends: The People You Can't Afford to Live Without* (Gallup Press, 2006). "But the real energy occurs in each connection between two people, which can bring about exponential returns." Spouses shape how we feel about our employers, ultimately influencing workplace performance. Authentic friendships nurture our mental health and personal well-being. When we feel loved, we're eager to learn, grow, and demonstrate appreciation toward those who've bolstered our reach toward greater heights.

Foundational Ring Two: Personal – Lifelong Education Consumption, Spiritual Grounding, Unshakable Values. Organizations will face a massive human development revolution in the next two decades. Evolutionary tech will accelerate the speed of business, making lifelong learning no longer an aspiration but a necessity to remain relevant. According to the IBM Institute for Business Value study, 120 million workers in the world's 12 largest economies will need to be retrained or reskilled as a result of AI and intelligent automation.[8] The United Nations and the Office of National Statistics project that the average life expectancy in the United States will reach 95 years for females and 90 years for males by 2050, and an estimated 35% of babies born in 2012 will live to 100.[9] These figures all point to retirement pushed out to our 80s, extending our working years dramatically.

Personal and professional growth will eventually cross paths with business ethics. As people lose confidence in institutions and their leaders, a spiritual foundation is necessary to restore a sustainable future. With the reshaping of our global economies, political landscapes, and religious institutions, we need deeper roots than our institutional constructs. We need shared meanings and purpose. Unshakable values are the nonnegotiable principles by which you live your life. They will serve as guardrails in your future direction and destinations.

Foundational Ring Three: Professional – Acumen, Presence, and Emotional Courage. Acumen is the blending of knowledge and skill guided by experience. If you understand a P&L, you can apply different levers to improve your performance metrics and defend your actions because they're informed by your past experiences. You must see more than the bigger picture. You must learn to quickly frame why something is happening, evaluate available options, and make a logical decision confidently. Your ability to influence others to support you in achieving key priorities will demonstrate your resolve. Increasingly valuable deep generalists are asked to lead amid crisis or uncertain times if they have demonstrated:

- Financial literacy,
- Organizational knowledge,
- Ability to deal with ambiguity,
- Framing of cause and effect,
- Unparalleled self- and stakeholder awareness, and
- Contextual relevancy.

When you connect with others authentically, you demonstrate presence. The most important leaders bolster others in their success and demonstrate gravitas. These leaders improve their emotional intelligence, collaborate with equality of insights, proactively serve others, and embrace one version of the organization's truth. Lastly, in this foundational ring is what my friend Peter Bregman wrote in his book *Leading with Emotional Courage* (Wiley, 2018) and shared in our Curve Benders podcast. Emotional intelligence requires emotional courage and a willingness to experience discomfort, risk, and uncertainty in doing difficult things.

Beyond the foundational rings of core, personal, and professional, the next tier of that personal market value encompasses three fundamental assets of *Value Accelerants* (Figure 1.11).

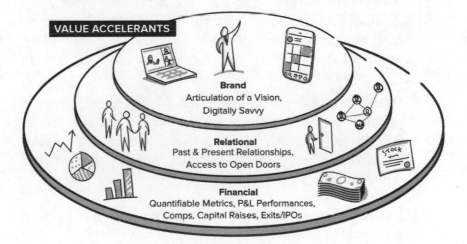

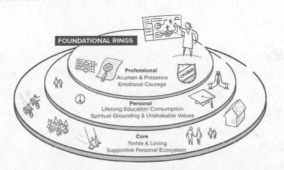

Figure 1.11 Personal Market Value: Value Accelerants

Similar to a business owner or management team monitoring the value of their business, you too should regularly assess real value creation in your personal brand. Most assume that this process is purely quantitative assessment. In reality, it's the foresight of future expectations. To reflect those expectations, you should understand what enhances and dilutes your value. Here are three key areas:

- **Financial** – This refers to the metrics, including your past and present compensation models, your P&L performances over the years for that remuneration, your ability to raise capital for a startup, or the financial scale of that venture to an exit or an IPO, and experience in M&A transactions.

- **Relational** – This is about the breadth and depth of your past and present relationships, access to open doors, and gaining net-new opportunities through your relationships. Your ability to connect the dots between the relationships you have and the ones you need will set you apart from your peers.

- **Brand** – From the talent you've led to the astuteness of your personal brand, the vision of the future you can articulate and how digitally savvy you are make you highly relevant to a broad set of organizational challenges and opportunities.

The next tier of that personal market value encompasses three fundamental *growth enablers* (Figure 1.12).

As we'll cover in upcoming chapters, these attributes dramatically propel you forward:

- **Resilience** – Think of this as your personal elasticity – to prepare for difficulties ahead, meet them with toughness and resolve, and to quickly recover from setbacks. In the next chapter, I'll cover 15 forces of possible disruptions. When they are proactively and consistently considered and planned for, the shift to a digital, knowledge-based economy translates to a vibrant workforce with incredible value.

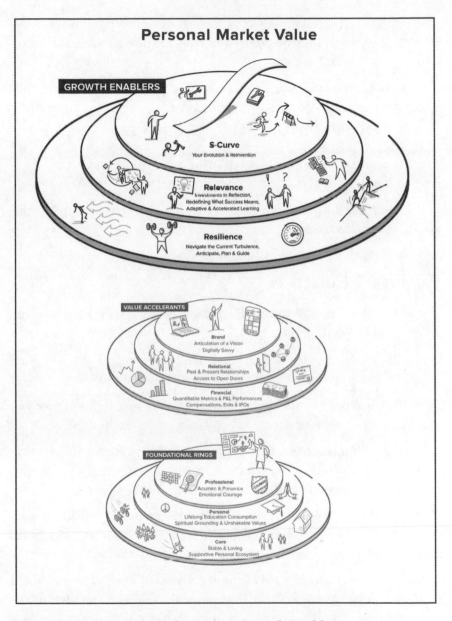

Figure 1.12 Personal Market Value: Growth Enablers

- **Relevance.** In later chapters, I'll focus on enablers of this attribute such as accelerating your relevance, focusing on your non-linear growth mindset, making consistent investments in reflection, redefining what success means to you, and leveraging your refraction points and relationships to adapt and accelerate your learning.

- **S-Curve.** This attribute is all about your willingness and ability to learn, grow, evolve, and constantly reinvent yourself via a personal S-curve.

As you continue to read, keep value accelerants and growth enablers in mind, as they become rocket boosters in your non-linear growth.

Next, let's look at 15 specific forces that will directly impact your ability to remain relevant.

CHAPTER 1 SUMMARY

1. The future of work will be based on what we are working on, not what we do.

2. Curve Benders are rare and need to be sought out. They can accelerate your personal and professional growth.

3. You need to assess your life's infrastructure to make sure you have the foundation to reach the growth you need.

4. Organizations must change the way they attract and develop talent to be more effective in aligning talent and roles with creating and enabling value.

5. There are four relevant strategies for your non-linear personal and professional growth: Career Accelerant, Benjamin Button, Likeability, and Visionary Storytelling.

6. Your personal market value consists of a set of foundational rings (core, personal, professional), value accelerants (financial, relational, brand), and growth enablers (resilience, relevance, S-curve). Invest in each proactively.

CHAPTER 2

15 Forces Impacting Your Future

The San Antonio Spurs have won five NBA championships. They have this quote hanging in their locker room that says something to the effect of "Whenever I feel like giving up, I think about the stone cutter who takes his hammer and bangs on the rock 100 times without showing a crack. And then at the 101st blow it splits in two. And I know that it wasn't the 101st that did it, but all the 100 that came before."

– James Clear, *Atomic Habits*

Uncertainties make our lives more complicated. The world is more connected now than ever before. This global interconnection will force us to focus on its dynamic growth. We will need to be deliberate and proactive with how we're going to evolve within it. In this chapter, I'll simplify *15 forces I believe will dramatically impact the ways we work, live, play, and give in the next two decades* (Figure 2.1). Think of these as faint signals and harbingers of change.

For each force, you need to evaluate yourself in terms of your comprehension and the degree to which the force will affect your particular situation. At the end of this chapter is a table that will help you determine the forces most relevant to your growth journey. More importantly, I'll challenge you to explore Curve Bender–centric actions you can take. Your existing relationships may be able to raise your thinking and perspective in each of these topics, as well as potentially introduce you to other subject-matter experts in their ecosystems.

Understanding headwind forces lets you be more proactive in maneuvering around them. You'll want to take advantage of any forces that may provide a *tailwind* to your journey. Being proactive will make you more attractive in the market. Other forces won't have a single

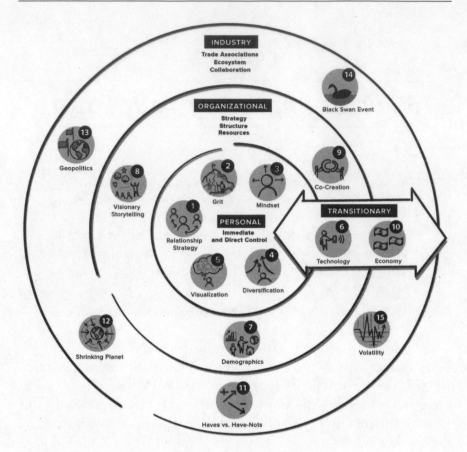

Figure 2.1 Fifteen Forces Impacting Your Future

vector. Alone, or in combination, they will create *turbulence*, to which you'll need to adapt.

Think about each force and ask, "How do I see this force directly affecting my business, organization, industry?" More importantly, "What will I do about it? How can I start synthesizing key observations into my future planning efforts?" As you read through each force, a good exercise would be to grade yourself on how well you understand the force and its potential impact on you, your team, and your organization today:

- *A* – I have an excellent understanding of this force and its potential impact.

- **B** – I have a good understanding of this force and am comfortable with my perception of its impact.

- **C** – I am not as comfortable in my understanding of this force or its potential impact.

- **F** – I don't understand much about this force or its potential impact.

Your grades in the table at the end of this chapter should prioritize your investment of additional resources (time, effort, or capital) to better understand that force and explore its implications on your future-focused skillset.

The best leadership teams I've worked with proactively explore the uncertainty in these faint signals. They continually challenge themselves to ask better questions on the meaning and consequences of each force. Intentional leaders must constantly question whether the faint signals demonstrate emerging patterns.

Some leaders have a lens that's too narrow. Regardless, their organizations face an onslaught of competitive threats. These threats come from known competitors as well as agile and nimble unknown competitors. Whoever thought that Amazon would be in the grocery or healthcare industries? Organizations that do not have a formal process to scan for environmental changes relentlessly are at a greater risk of finding themselves disrupted by these forces. Media conglomerates face several of these forces: a plethora of streaming services, bandwidth-hungry online gaming platforms, and increased regulatory scrutiny. These environmental changes will disrupt an organization's business model and create an existential crisis. Survival requires the courage to act and the insight to see how to act while there's still time to implement those actions.

Two threats to your organization's response to these forces:

1. **Organizational lethargy.** The global pandemic demonstrated that our standard operations should require fewer meetings, presentation decks, and explanations of concrete

deliverables. If we fail to adapt, we certainly miss a massive opportunity for our organizations to learn faster.

2. **Comfort threats.** Organizations often focus on threats they understand, particularly since they already possess systems to monitor existing risks. After months of researching competitive peers, building financial models, and diving deeper into the potential conflicts with other parts of the business, the changes most organizations attempt are seldom relevant. The mindset to defend the status quo is worthless. Although it may contribute to iterative changes, it won't produce opportunities to innovate.

EXTENT OF YOUR CONTROL

I've broken the 15 forces into three primary rings based on the extent of your control – as the rings expand, you have less control:

- **Personal** – These are within your immediate and direct control.

- **Organizational** – These are within the control of your organization, based on its strategy, prioritized pursuits, organizational structure, and dedicated resources.

- **Industry** – These are influenced or, ideally, addressed by your industry, trade association, or collaboration among powerful allies within an industry ecosystem.

- Some forces apply to more than one category, hence they're **transitionary** forces between two.

FIVE PERSONAL FORCES

With these five personal forces, you have the long term, direct control of your skills, knowledge, and behaviors. They are your **Relationship Strategy**, **Grit**, **Mindset**, **Diversification**, and **Visualization** (Figure 2.2). Let's take a closer look at each.

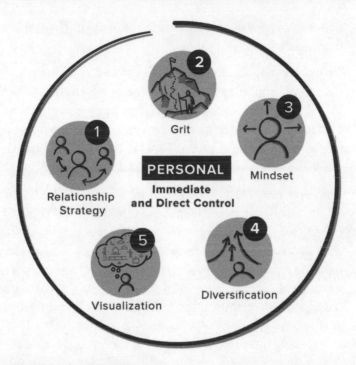

Figure 2.2   Five Personal Forces

Force 1: Relationship Strategy. Most of us, when we face a challenge or an opportunity, think, "What should I do, and how should I do it?" We seldom ask *Whom do I already know and need?* How can I connect the dots between the current relationships I respect to accelerate getting things done? Three key steps to consider in your relationship strategy:

- *Invest in Your Existing Relationships.* I call these your Relationship Bank. The depth, relevance, and diversity of your existing network will determine your influence footprint. The quality relationships you choose to invest in will accelerate your ability to reach key milestones more efficiency. You'll be well served to focus on a few authentic relationships with those you enjoy collaborating with, learning from, and growing through.

Ensure you're valuable by giving them as much as, if not more than, what you ask of them.

- *Prioritize the Relationships You Need.* I call these Pivotal Contacts. You may not have sustained these relationships. Who's that one executive whose email can move multiple obstacles out of your way? Who can sponsor your key initiative and prioritize it in the C-suite or with the board? These are the answers to your "Whom do I need?" questions.

- *Connect the Dots with Unique Value-Add.* I call these Relationship Currency Deposits. The third, and probably most crucial step, is to connect the dots between relationships you already have with the ones you need. Only when you have sufficiently invested in an existing relationship should you ask for a return on that invested time. Asking for a favor before real trust has been established puts the long-term relationship at risk.

Your Relationship Strategy should be integrated into all that you do. Ask yourself often, "What relationships will I need to address this challenge or opportunity? What relationships do I have that are authentic and mutually value-based? How will I connect the dots between the relationships I have and the ones I need to accelerate my path forward?"

After reading about Relationship Strategy, grade (A, B, C, or F) both your current understanding of this force and its impact on your future success. Be candid – that's where your growth will come from. _____

Grit

Force 2: Grit. Angela Duckworth's seminal work defines grit as *passion, purpose, practice, and pursuit*. Grit is a personality trait. It is the combination of passion for something unified with the perseverance to see it through over disappointingly long periods. Three key ideas about Grit will be most relevant to the direction and destination in your future:

1. *Grit is not related to IQ; it's highly correlated with conscientiousness.* Being thorough, careful, reliable, organized,

industrious, and self-controlled will help you get further than being highly intelligent without those qualities. What you need to excel is to demonstrate a sustained focus of your talents over time.[1] Grit is also resilience in coming back with an arsenal of learning *after you've failed*.

2. ***Both dimensions of Grit are required for performance:*** perseverance of effort and consistency of interest.[2] You must create opportunities to remain interested in your project, beyond an initial spark of inspiration. Eric Kandel, the 2000 Nobel Prize recipient in physiology, discovered *synaptic plasticity*. As we discover new ideas and learn more about them, we trigger neurotransmitters in our nerve cells. With each effort, the synapses expand and create stronger connections. When the same neurons fire together, it strengthens neural pathways. When consistently fired together, these neurons wire together, creating faster pathways, which leads to improved performance.[3]

3. ***Grittier people develop higher-level and purpose-driven long-term goals.*** Grittier people are more confident and effective in pursuing and reaching their goals because they understand they are in it for the long haul.[4] Jim Thorpe was a Native American from Oklahoma and won Olympic gold medals for the pentathlon and decathlon. In the picture shown in Figure 2.3 from the 1912 Olympics, you'll notice that Thorpe is wearing two different-colored socks. Before his race that morning, his shoes were stolen. Instead of giving up and going home, Thorpe rummaged through the garbage and found two pairs of shoes. One was too big, so he wore a second pair of socks so the shoes would fit. He won two gold medals that day. Exceptional P&L leaders don't make excuses; they find ways to overcome the most insurmountable obstacles.

After reading about Grit, grade (A, B, C, or F) both your current understanding of this force and its impact on your future success. Remember, Grit is equal parts *passion and perseverance*. _____

Figure 2.3　Jim Thorpe, 1912 Olympian Gold Medalist

Mindset

Force 3: Mindset. In the future there will be fundamental changes in our work. Our professions are being rewritten with the rise of the gig economy, the convenience of work-from-anywhere, and the limited connection between traditional education and our work. In the future, "What do you do?" increasingly becomes "What do you work on?" So, how should we think about navigating our future in a way that enables us to have the freedom to do the things that matter most to us? Digital, entrepreneurial, and collaborative mindsets will help fuel your curiosity, creativity, and connections.

Three ideas will be most relevant to you as you shift your mindset from how you work to your purposeful work:

1. ***Think career lattice and not ladder.*** A ladder is highly transactional and single directional. A lattice is

Linear Career Progression   Lattice Career Pathways

Figure 2.4   Career Ladder versus Lattice

transformational, as it opens up a plethora of opportunities to experiment and explore (Figure 2.4). Many people still operate under the assumption that there is a single path to a career goal. Those whose work energizes them often end up there through the myriad opportunities they chose to pursue. Too often, stale job descriptions, hierarchical pay rates, and outdated organizational structures discourage individuals and stifle motivation, numbing them into stagnation and helplessness. Trying different types of work allows you to embrace planned happenstance, open-mindedness, and flexibility rather than the specialization of a career ladder.

2. *Abundance, intrinsic motivators, and the pursuit of mastery.* An abundance mindset is fundamentally different from one of poverty. Many people believe, "If I don't get this job, client engagement, or promotion, I'll never eat again!" Instead, a mindset of abundance knows, "my success is directly related to the quality of the jobs, clients, or projects *I choose* to take on!" Only when you continuously reflect on what motivates you intrinsically will you be able to prioritize mastering your craft. When we are autonomous, we have the freedom to fulfill new paths. We do work that aligns with

our core values and redefine success based on our purpose. When we climb the career lattice, we can master the arena, not just one track.

3. ***Throw away your stopwatch and get a compass.*** How fast you reach your destination matters less than how deliberate and focused you are. This advice, which a mentor gave me almost 20 years ago, has guided me since. Guiding your personal and professional growth cannot be abdicated to anyone else, including the HR department. Here is just one example: an estimated 40% of topline revenue of many professional firms – think accounting, consulting, or law – is going away in the next five years because of AI/machine learning.[5] How will you remain relevant in this scenario? As my friend Ayşe Birsel advocates, you must *design the life you love* and integrate work that fits into it.

After reading about Mindset, grade (A, B,C, or F) your current understanding of this force and its impact on your future success. Remember, your clarity of intent enables you to resist distraction in your path forward. _____

Diversification

Force 4: Diversification. In investments, diversification protects the investor from potential losses in a single asset class. Apply the same strategy to your personal and professional growth journey by diversifying your knowledge and revenue streams. For example, I am coaching a client who was recently promoted to be the company's first chief digital officer because he previously ran a highly successful business unit. His company's decision, based upon his past performance, to have him run a technology organization allows him to use outside knowledge on a new problem.

As you explore diversification to expand the breadth of your interests and pursuits, three ideas will be most relevant:

1. ***With disruptive forces, you need expanded career options.*** Changing economic environments, regulatory compliance, company disasters can all impact your relevance. Expanding

your career choices increases your options, as job security becomes increasingly rare. According to a 2019 Gartner organizational design survey, 32% of organizations are replacing full-time employees with contingent workers as a cost-saving measure.[6] Another ongoing challenge is the accelerated global mergers and acquisition (M&A) activities. As more industries consolidate, the likelihood of job redundancies dramatically increases.

2. ***Organizational leadership pipelines will be designed for resilience versus efficiency.*** In the past decade, the leadership pipeline was focused on efficiency by streamlining roles, supply chains, and workflows. The pandemic highlighted fragilities, lack of flexibility to respond to disruption, and leadership export deficits. Conversely, our Crisis Resilience research showed that organizations with a leadership pipeline with highly diverse skills were able to respond, course correct, and move quickly and agilely. One client relocated leaders from Brazil to lead supply chain disruptions in Asia.

3. ***Growth paths in the future will be portfolios of work.*** A portfolio approach to work allows, even encourages, odd work styles. A friend is a Peloton instructor, an Airbnb host of her several properties in town, and a thriving startup entrepreneur. The future of how we work needs to be disciplined, adaptable, diversified, and highly personal. Our business models are at the intersection of what the world needs and the skills we are passionate about. The diverse skills, experiences, roles, and realm of responsibilities distribute risk. This in turn allows for greater experimentation.

Beyond diversifying your career options and your organization diversifying its leadership pipeline, one of your greatest diversification strategies will be to apply the same rigor to your *relationships*. Most P&L leaders tend to surround themselves with people who share their virtues. We often talk about and aim for ethnic and gender diversity, but I'd submit cognitive diversity in these relationships will serve you well.

After reading about Diversification, grade (A, B, C, or F) both your current understanding of this force and its impact on your future success. Remember, only when you diversify your knowledge, capabilities, and relationships will you also expand your opportunities for a diversified revenue stream. _____

Force 5: Visualization. In Chapter 1, I highlighted visionary storytelling as a fundamental leadership competency. Similarly, visualizing your future position, and a path to get there, creates clarity of intent and helps you attract specific relationships to bolster your success. By visualizing a desired outcome, you begin to see the possible steps, hurdles, and potential roadblocks, and, more importantly, opportunities to anticipate your next move. As such, visualization will have two unique meanings in your future:

Visualization

1. *A personal lens on your journey from now to next.* Michael Phelps is one of the most decorated Olympians of all time. Visualization greatly contributed to his success. Part of his training regimen was envisioning every aspect of his race.[7] His mental preparation took him beyond other world-class swimmers. He planned for positive and negative events – a great start from the block or broken goggles mid-race. By going through scenarios, he created a mental repertoire of responses, which programmed his nervous system to perform under pressure. His visualizations of different scenarios built his confidence. He didn't have to worry about adapting on the fly to competitive conditions because he had a plan for everything. Instead, he focused on being the best athlete he could in that moment. Bob Bowman, Men's Olympic Head Coach at USA Swimming, believed that Phelps's mental preparation was his biggest strength.[8]

   Successful executives often use visualization to hit key career milestones, pitch a high-profile client with confidence, or grow and scale their business. They are able to tackle large, complex projects without feeling overwhelmed. Here, visualization acts as a bridge between where they are today and where they want to be – by allowing them to see and feel success before it happens. This is a mindset tool to prepare you for the journey.

2. *The organization's vision and path forward.* This is the strategy visualization effort mentioned back in Chapter 1. It helps clarify, communicate, and cascade a succinct vision and a set of priorities the organization will choose to pursue. Similarly, visualization here creates a focused path for the leadership and the team to make the best possible choices for the best possible outcomes.

After reading about Visualization, grade (A, B, C, or F) your current understanding of this force and its impact on your future success. Remember, if you confuse, you'll lose. How can you distill the essence of your vision or path forward that sticks in your audience's minds? _____

Transitionary Force: Technology

Beyond the first five personal forces lies a transitionary force, Technology (Figure 2.5). It overlaps both your personal sphere of influence and much of your organization. Let's take a closer look at how.

Technology

Force 6: Technology. Future enterprise systems will accelerate value creation in our organizations by scaling innovation systematically. This fosters the agility they need to thrive. Today's P&L leaders are investing in available technologies, but they aren't necessarily unlocking their full value for their organizations. Visionary leaders who invest in future enterprise systems will do more than accelerate their profitability. They will learn to adapt to innovation faster and build boundless ecosystems. Here's how:

- *P&L leaders are under pressure to generate continued growth.* Enterprise tech can enable new competencies and accelerate

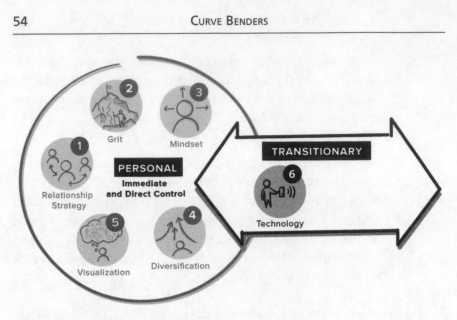

Figure 2.5   Transitionary Force of Technology

operational efficiency. Beyond iteration, uncovering innovation and scaling it organization-wide will continue to be a struggle. That's why Ray Harris, CIO at Adtran, Inc. (NASDAQ: ADTN) is spearheading a multi-year global implementation of the Adtran Enterprise System (AES), capable of continuous system-wide updates every 90 days. The system touches every facet of the enterprise value creation and delivery (Figure 2.6). Harris believes that "AES will enable increased speed of innovation, operational efficiency, and productivity while continuously improving our ability to deliver an exceptional customer experience."

- ***The gap between current organizational thinkers and future builders will widen.*** The current IT infrastructure of software apps, hardware stacks, telecom, and data centers isn't built for many future demands. We will prioritize deep analytics, sensors, mobile computing, AI apps, and IoT connections of a billion organization devices. Leaders with a clear intent to adapt to new tech will craft a clear vision of their organization's future system capabilities and make consistent progress.

- ***Optimal sequence implementations will fuel process innovation.*** Future enterprise systems will allow organizations to

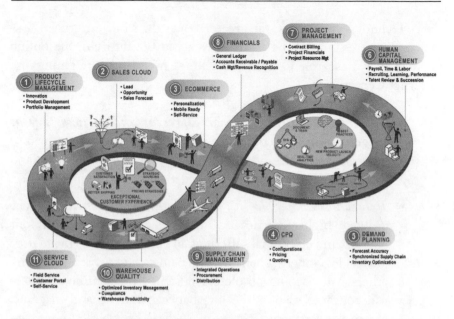

Figure 2.6   Enterprise Tech as an Enabler of Value Creation at Adtran

adopt complex, interdependent processes. These processes will fuel an interconnected, living system of apps and people capable of creating new spaces where ideas and partnerships will thrive. For example, leaders' expanding usage of the cloud would create a uniform approach to data, security, governance. This ubiquitous technology allows unlimited exploration of unconventional business and technology co-creation.

- *Adaptable future systems will learn and improve by themselves.* Advancements in data and intelligence tech will eliminate the friction that hinders organizational growth. It will help humans make better decisions much faster. Automation and AI in the data supply chain will power a stable, modular, extremely flexible, and constantly evolving architecture.

- *Future enterprise systems will be enablers of human creativity.* Systems will be able to talk, listen, and understand similar to human interactions today. Natural-language-processing and machine learning will bring simple elegance to tech as an enabler of human creativity. Over time, systems will become less artificial and more intelligent, making interaction with them easier.

Technology will have far greater reach than our enterprise systems. Here are some of the top themes about the future of life online from a Pew Research Center and Elon University's Imagining the Internet Center:[9]

- **_The internet will become omnipresent and as necessary as oxygen._** Seamless connectivity will be the norm, with apps integrated seamlessly within our homes, transportation, and wearables. AI will become embedded and ambient intelligence.

- **_Tech will help people live longer and healthier lives._** Tech-enabled, highly empathetic machines will address both our physical and emotional sufferings and be designed to make people feel less lonely. Thankless and painstaking work like serving others will become obsolete. Additionally, scientific advances will continue to blur the line between human and machine. Massive investments into areas such as prosthetics, neuroscience, and implants will continue to translate brain activity into physical form. Technology will further aid our mobility, memory, intelligence, and other physical and neurological functions.

- **_AI tools will take over repetitive, unsafe, and arduous labor._** This will help create more time for meaningful work, for which people have an intrinsic need. Advances in AI and robotics will help humans create purposeful work, change the way we learn, and allow us to create unlikely new partnerships.

- **_Digital life will be tailored_** for highly individual experiences. Technology will assume a polite role of personal assistants, learn our behavior patterns, and appear upon command. Think of Jarvis, the voice-activated computer interface system in the _Iron Man_ movies. By Tony Stark's voice command, Jarvis helps in stations, from running simulations to making tea. Siri, Alexa, and Google are already making our lives easier from dimming our lights to changing our music. These technologies will keep a record of our personal lives. Every conversation, selection, and search will be kept, making our own memories less valuable.

- *A fully networked world will enhance* opportunities for real-time global collaboration, co-creation, and communities of practice. We will be unhindered by distance, language, or time. We'll willingly spend most of our lives in an augmented reality. Machine learning, fusion power, and quantum computing will dramatically amplify and accelerate our global reach, if not extraplanetary explorations.

There are specific subsets to our technological advancements. Richard Watson, in collaboration with Imperial College Tech Foresight,[10] has recognized the **five key mega advances in the timeline of emerging science and technology** (Figure 2.7) as:

1. **Digital** – This will be information technology in the use of computers to store, retrieve, transmit, and manipulate data.

2. **Bio** – This includes a broad area of biology, involving the use of living systems and organisms to develop or make products.

3. **Nano** – manipulation of matter on an atomic, molecular, and supramolecular scale.

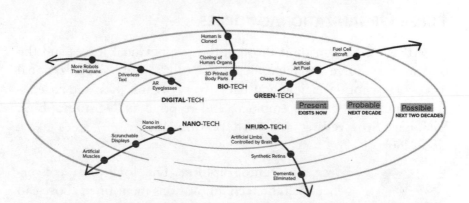

Figure 2.7 Five Key Mega Advances in Emerging Science and Technology

Source: Richard Watson, "Timeline of Emerging Science & Technology (2014 to 2030+)," What's Next: Top Trends, June 27, 2014.

4. **Neuro** – fundamental influence on understanding the brain, various aspects of consciousness, thoughts, and higher-order activities.

5. **Clean** – any service that reduces negative environmental impacts.

The timeline highlights three unique time frames, particularly relevant to our future living:

1. **Present** – defined as now or thereabouts.

2. **Probable** – defined as innovations highly likely to become mainstream by 2030.

3. **Possible** – defined as potentially available from 2030 onward.

After reading about Technology, grade (A, B, C, or F) both your current understanding of this force and its impact on your future success. Remember, technology will impact both your personal and organizational capabilities in the future. You can't abdicate it to the "IT guys"! _____

THREE ORGANIZATIONAL FORCES

Now that we have made it through the five personal forces and the transitionary force of Technology, we will explore organizational forces of disruption-facing industries. Every organization and its leadership must understand, embrace, and respond to **Demographics**, **Visionary Storytelling**, and **Co-Creation** (Figure 2.8). Let's take a closer look.

Demographics

Force 7: Demographics. The long-term convergence with the tech innovations mentioned above can reshape the future of work dramatically. BlackRock, an investment management company, believes that demographics will have the farthest-reaching impact on the global economy.[11] This will be important more

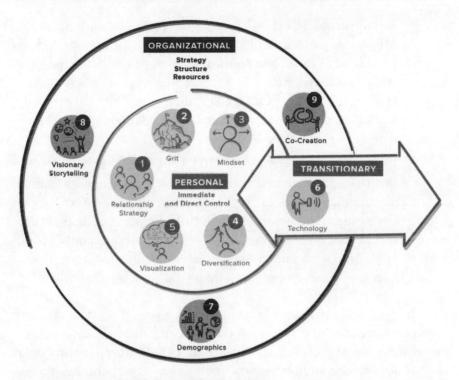

Figure 2.8   Three Organizational Forces

than rapid urbanization, emerging global wealth, technological breakthroughs, climate change, and resource scarcity. Over the next two
decades, our identity characteristics, birth and death rates, education
and income levels, and average family size will dramatically change.
Here are the contributing factors:

- *Aging population.* The population is rapidly increasing due to
  declining fertility rates. The U.S. median age is projected to
  reach 40 by 2030 and 45 by 2060.[12] In Europe, those 65 years
  or over accounted for 19.8% of the population in 2018. That
  ratio is predicted to grow to 31.3% by 2100.[13]

- *Future workforce.* Aging populations reduce the number of
  available workers. For the first time in recorded history, the
  number of working-age people in developed nations shrank
  in 2020.[14]

- **Immigration influx.** Global migration will steadily increase. Migration patterns will be influenced by a range of factors from serious issues like political turmoil to more hopeful situations such as better job offers. Some regions, such as Asia (130 million) and Europe (80 million), will see dramatically higher movements than others (Latin America, 43 million; Africa, 36 million) by 2030.[15]

- **Consumer spending.** Generational spending habits by youth in the future will reflect their distinct preference for digital assets and experiences over capital expenditures. However, the rise in the aging population will shift the purchasing power to older households. For example, in Japan, more than half of all household spending in the next decade will come from people over 65 – compared with less than 10% from people under 40.[16]

It is difficult to discuss demographics as a force of disruption without addressing the role of social change. Strong social change movements are the evolution of behaviors and cultural norms over time. They include ending poverty and hunger, expanding healthcare in developing nations, reforming education quality and accessibility, and closing the gap on gender and racial inequality.

After reading about Demographics, grade (A, B, C, or F) your current understanding of this force and its impact on your future success. Demographics forces are changing at an accelerated pace. In our networks and neighborhoods, diversity of gender, ethnicity, and thought will dramatically expand your horizons. _____

Visionary
Storytelling

Force 8: Visionary Storytelling. This is a fundamental strategy particularly relevant to your non-linear growth, but I see it as an incredibly disruptive force that most P&L leaders are not prepared to harness. Humans are born storytellers. Storytelling, by connecting with emotions, is how we exchange important information with others. The world will never stop wanting to hear stories of passion, heritage, or the testing of values. The best brands, leaders, and organizations must tell authentic, emotive, and compelling stories. Cultural anthropologists study how an organization's people who share a common culture come to shape their work environment. And, in turn, they are shaped by those ideas, behaviors, and environments.

To build on Scott Galloway's T-Algorithm and visionary storytelling from Chapter 1, here are a few critical topics on visionary storytelling that will force you to think and lead an organization differently:

- *Trust is the foundational value of every organization.* It underpins every form of communication. Every constituent who touches your organization – employees, customers, partners, investors, and suppliers – want to trust that you're going to deliver the experiences that you promised. Visionary storytelling must help your audience feel the emotions and the energy of your organization.

- *Authenticity becomes a sustainable differentiator in a world of endless content.* Every one of this chapter's forces will contribute to the future's clamor. Organizations will be lost in that din. That's where honest stories will help bond the target audience. You must use different media, be global, and try avenues that don't exist yet. You must speak your audience's idiom. This will be predominately digital, but the impact of stories well told will be the same.

- *Relevant stories are visual.* Organizations will produce more data from a multitude of sources, but they will find making sense of it increasingly difficult. At this point, it will become impossible to translate information, strategic priorities, and actionable next steps into a tangible ROI. Visual stories will make this effort dramatically easier because we process visuals better than other media. In fact, the human brain processes images 60,000 times faster than text[17]; 90% of the information transmitted to our brain is visual; it only takes 13 milliseconds for the human brain to process an image. If your organization wants to be relevant, it must cut what its audience won't remember.

Thriving organizations in the future of work are ones that study their target audiences and adjust each strategy to be relevant and authentic. Angela Ahrendts, former SVP of retail at Apple and former CEO of Burberry, shared in *HBR* that the leadership team asked, "How can we bring all that we're doing digitally to life in our stores?" So, along with brand czar Christopher Bailey, architects and tech innovators transformed the flagship store on Regent Street in London into a digital immersion, aka the store of the future. The makers integrated Burberry Acoustics, featuring young British talent on its website, into live concerts and streamed content into 150 other global stores, digital outdoor sites, and mobile-first experiences. They seamlessly integrated IRL with live offline. So, when they launched their first fragrance under their own ownership, they converted everything into a tightly integrated visual story – of music, emotion, digital experiences, physical worlds, and a hard product.[18]

Angela's visual storytelling over the past three decades has helped to create a definitive "Angela Ahrendts effect" that other retailers are desperately seeking.[19] Burberry saw sales triple and share price quadruple, as net income grew 236%, from $157 million in 2006 when she joined to $528 million in 2014, when she left the CEO position.

This approach to visionary storytelling will become increasingly pervasive in the future living. Leaders who invest in tools, talent, and capabilities will dramatically increase their organization's impact and their personal market value.

After reading about Visionary Storytelling, grade (A, B, C, or F) both your current understanding of this force and its impact on your future success. Remember, visionary storytelling sets leaders and organizations dramatically apart from their competitive peers. _____

Co-Creation

Force 9: Co-Creation. There are three traditional paths to net-new enterprise growth:

1. ***Build It.*** Where you invest the resources (time, effort, capital) to create something from scratch by your own labor.

2. ***Partner with It.*** Where you identify a joint venture, often complementary to yours and go to market together.

3. ***Buy It.*** Where you identify someone who has already created a product, a service, a new market, again, complementary to your portfolio, and you acquire it.

I would submit a fourth option, and the one most relevant to our increasingly dynamic world: *Co-Create it*. As I wrote in *Co-Create*, this net-new and highly sustainable competitive strategy is unusual. It differs from an alliance, a partnership, or a joint venture. Here are just a few strategic assets of co-creation in an organization's evolution:

- ***Co-Creation is predicated on a battle-tested relationship***. You can point to a past track record of great outcomes from the joint relationship. It's very difficult for any organization to co-create long-term value with a firm it has just met, one that doesn't have the battle scars of a lasting relationship.

- ***Co-Creation demands that two or more parties come together to create something that none could have done alone***. This new creation will be stronger, faster, better, and less expensive to co-create with others, through leveraging their unique insights, expertise, or particular assets.

- ***Co-Creation success demands a deeply rooted vested interest in the outcomes that are creating together***. The simplest example of co-creation is our children. If you're a parent, you understand that they never stop being your kids – at 10, 20, 30, or 50! We bring the best of ourselves to the child and invest in the child's long-term success. Most business partnerships stagger or fail in long-term value creation because one or both lack a sustained commitment.

- ***Co-Creation is a living, breathing, continuous process***. As outlined in the Co-Create Canvas, the process of co-create entails three unique phases: lay the relationship's foundation, design a unique joint value proposition, and execute on the common vision or an enemy. The Co-Creation is reinforced by a feedback loop to revisit the joint impact and course correct with newfound wisdom.

- *Co-Creation is governed by visionary executives of equal stature with sufficient organizational clout to sustain the process.* Strategists from both sides can set the direction, supported by tactical execution to bring the ideation to fruition. You don't need a battalion here; you need SEAL Team Six. Co-Creation is most impactful when it takes place away from the traditional corporate bureaucracy that masquerades as operational efficiency.

- *Co-Creation is transformative in its nature.* It's not another transaction. Co-Creation is disruptive as it challenges most organizational processes and business models at a deeper level, to the great discomfort of the herdsmen of the organization's outdated sacred cows.

After reading about Co-Creation, grade (A, B, C, or F) both your current understanding of this force and its impact on your future success. Remember, you cannot succeed in the future alone. _____

Transitionary Force: Economy

Like technology, the global economy is another transitionary force, as it bridges the individual organization's own efforts and the broader industry ecosystems within which it functions (Figure 2.9). Although you personally may not have much control over the direction of the economy or any of the subsequent forces, you must become proactive in understanding each force. You need to anticipate its future paths and devise a strategic response to each. Let's take a closer look at how:

Economy

Force 10: Economy. If you thought the economy in the last decade was eventful, you may use *turbulent* for the pandemic economy. One feature of the global economy is certain: there is seldom a return to whatever was called *normal* in the past. Interest rates, our evolving climate, deflationary pressures, our rapidly aging population, massive labor shifts due to unemployment in certain sectors, and the slew of recent bankruptcy filings (Figure 2.10) all point to several megatrends.[20]

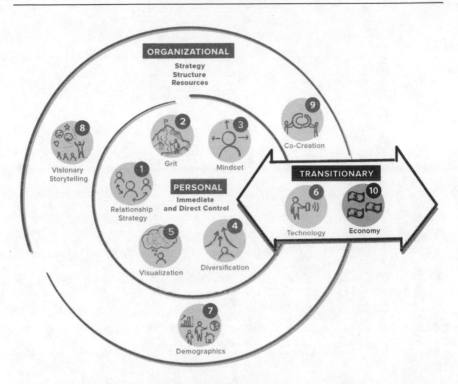

Figure 2.9 Transitionary Force of Economy

Over the next two decades, these factors will shape the global economy and economic policymakers will struggle to manage the implications:

- *Ultra-loose and unconventional monetary policy alone won't spur future growth.* According to the World Economic Forum's Future of Economic Progress, the world's four major banks alone injected $10 trillion into their respective economies between 2008–2017.[21] Yet, productivity has remained stagnant. This overreliance on monetary policy reduces growth because of the misallocation of capital. Banks will favor loans to businesses that are not credit-constrained, largely due to higher fees and trading activities. This will create a disproportionate disadvantage to smaller firms when it comes to capital to invest in their growth.

- *Beyond monetary policy, a broader toolkit is required: fiscal policy, reforms, and private investment incentives.* Our lives

The largest bankruptcies by asset in 2020 have been highly impacted by the coronavirus.

	Bankruptcy Date	Company	Actual Assets	Actual Liabilities	Industry
1	MAY 22, 2020	THE HERTZ CORPORATION	$25,842,000,000	$24,355,000,000	AUTOMOTIVE
2	MAY 25, 2020	LATAM AIRLINES GROUP S.A.	$21,087,806,000	$17,958,629,000	AVIATION
3	APRIL 14, 2020	FRONTIER COMMUNICATIONS CORPORATION	$17,433,201,422	$21,855,602,151	TELECOM
4	MAY 14, 2020	INTELSAT S.A.	$11,651,558,000	$16,805,844,000	TELECOM
5	JANUARY 21, 2020	MCDERMOTT INTERNATIONAL, INC.	$8,754,000,000	$9,863,000,000	OIL AND GAS
6	MAY 15, 2020	J.C. PENNEY COMPANY, INC.	$7,989,000,000	$7,160,000,000	RETAIL
7	APRIL 1, 2020	WHITING PETROLEUM CORPORATION	$7,636,700,000	$3,611,800,000	OIL AND GAS
8	MAY 7, 2020	NEIMAN MARCUS GROUP LTD LLC	$7,545,903,000	$6,786,722,000	RETAIL
9	MAY 10, 2020	AVIANCA HOLDINGS S.A. (2020)	$7,273,900,000	$7,268,700,000	AVIATION

10	APRIL 26, 2020	DIAMOND OFFSHORE DRILLING, INC.	$5,834,044,000	$2,601,834,000	OIL AND GAS
11	JUNE 14, 2020	EXTRACTION OIL & GAS, INC.	$2,926,957,000	$2,242,581,000	OIL AND GAS
12	MAY 19, 2020	HORNBECK OFFSHORE SERVICES, INC.	$2,691,806,000	$1,493,912,000	OIL AND GAS
13	MARCH 10, 2020	FORESIGHT ENERGY LP	$2,385,563,000	$1,877,628,000	MINING
14	MAY 22, 2020	UNIT CORPORATION	$2,090,052,000	$1,034,417,000	OIL AND GAS
15	MAY 18, 2020	CENTRIC BRANDS INC.	$1,855,722,808	$2,014,385,923	APPAREL
16	JUNE 24, 2020	CEC ENTERTAINMENT, INC. (CHUCK E. CHEESE'S)	$1,743,518,039	$1,998,548,744	RESTAURANT
17	MAY 10, 2020	STAGE STORES, INC. (2020)	$1,713,713,000	$1,010,210,000	RETAIL
18	APRIL 13, 2020	LSC COMMUNICATIONS, INC.	$1,649,000,000	$1,721,000,000	PUBLISHING
19	MAY 4, 2020	CHINOS HOLDINGS, INC. (J. CREW)	$1,599,300,000	$2,949,700,000	RETAIL
20	APRIL 7, 2020	QUORUM HEALTH CORPORATION	$1,574,100,000	$1,646,700,000	HEALTHCARE

Figure 2.10 The Largest Bankruptcies in 2020

will require substantial investments in infrastructure, human capital, R&D, the education system, healthcare, sustainable source of energy, and a unique public-private collaboration. In many global economies, these investments are funded by public debt, such as bonds. Many governments are not stepping up with these investments, largely because of their bloated debt as measured against the country's GDP.

- *Stability in global economic growth must come from public investments in all the Fourth Industrial Revolution ingredients.* Some advanced and emerging economies are adopting new technologies of the Fourth Industrial Revolution. According to the World Economic Forum's Global Future Council on Cities and Urbanization, two-thirds of the world's population is expected to live in cities by 2050.[22] The public and private sectors within each economy must invest in training the human capital to realize the full potential of these technologies.

- *Economic stability is predicated by living standards.* Sustained growth is a critical path out of poverty. Two factors heavily influence equality for growth enablers and poverty shifters: proactively building shared prosperity and a quantifiable commitment to a green economy. Growing income inequality and destabilization of the planet's ecosystem threaten viable and sustainable growth.

- *The shifting economic power winds are blowing from West to East.* In the next two decades, many believe that the aggregated GDP of the Emerging Seven (E7) markets of China, Brazil, Indonesia, India, Russia, Mexico, and Turkey will overtake that of the G7. The Asian middle class is growing at an accelerated rate. By 2030, it's estimated that Asia-Pacific will contain two-thirds of the world's middle-class population and 60% of the global middle-class consumption.[23]

Ray Dalio, founder of Bridgewater Associates, is arguably one of the brightest economic minds alive, leading one of world's most successful hedge funds. In a recent interview for a TED virtual session on the impact of the pandemic on the global economy, Ray equated it to a tsunami, with damage lingering long after the waves have subsided. When asked about who has the best prospects going forward, given the turbulent economic times ahead, he described two types of organizations ripe to succeed:

1. Those stable "meat and potatoes" unleveraged companies, such as Campbell Soup, and

2. The innovators/adaptors who have strong balance sheets.

The year 2020 clearly illustrated that the global economy continues to become more turbulent. Few of us can predict these changes. How can you become more adaptable and create recession-proof business models? Can you identify and prioritize a set of recession-proof skills? In a downturn, what will the market need that you could adapt to provide?

After reading about the Economy, grade (A, B, C, or F) both your current understanding of this force and its impact on your future success. Remember, the economy, like technology, is a transitionary force that impacts both your organization and industry; you must understand which levers will both minimize downside risks and maximize upside opportunities in a turbulent economy. _____

FIVE INDUSTRY FORCES

Of the 15 forces, I've covered five personal, three organizational, and two transitionary forces. It's time to think of the five macro industry forces that will have a strong overarching impact on our collective future. Although no one individual may control much here, we can all do our individual parts to understand each of these forces and create a lasting difference. While these remaining forces may seem insurmountable, I'm reminded of the advice my wife drove into our young children when they were faced with seemingly huge tasks: "How do you eat an elephant? One bite at a time!" Let's take a closer look at each.

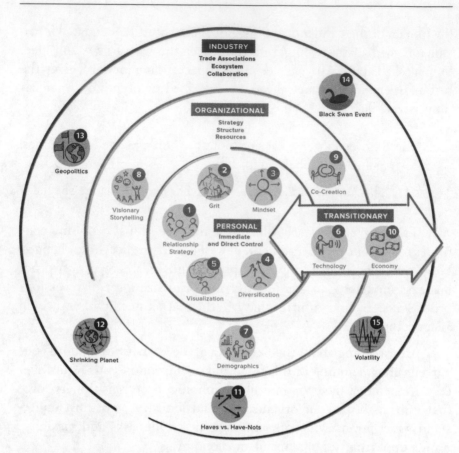

Figure 2.11 Five Industry Forces

The five industry forces are Haves vs. Have-Nots, Shrinking Planet, Geopolitics, Black Swan Events, and Volatility (Figure 2.11).

Haves vs. Have-Nots

Force 11: Haves vs. Have-Nots. The global pandemic and the ensuing economic recession have prompted discussions around the anticipated shape of a global recovery. Economists' various scenarios are defined by the shape of the recovery (Figure 2.12):

- The immediate and fast-paced *V-shaped* of a quarter or two where activities return to pre-recession levels in the same or less time as the duration of the downturn.

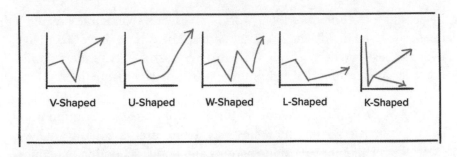

Figure 2.12   Five Shapes of Economic Recovery

- Intermediate, perhaps a year or two, *U-shaped*, similar to the global financial crisis of 2008–2009.

- The double-dip *W-shaped*, where the economy contracts, recovers, and then falls back into a recession, due to multiple factors.

- The drawn-out and most pessimistic, *L-shaped*, where the level of economic output drops almost vertically and remains essentially flat over several years.

For many organizations and industries, the pandemic is nothing more than a bump in the road toward greater growth. Thanks to various central bank liquidity measures and investor enthusiasm, some organizations have even benefited from a COVID tailwind, where their valuations – particularly in tech – have skyrocketed. Their access to the credit markets has also never been better. Amazon recently broke the record for the lowest interest rate for any bond in U.S. corporate history.[24]

For overleveraged organizations, the pandemic accelerated the end, as evident by many filed bankruptcies mentioned earlier.

Another shape of the potential economic recovery is deeply troubling and not often talked about: The *K-shaped* consumer experience. For the well-educated, often affluent workers who are able to work from home, the pandemic was an inconvenience. Although more remote work caused new tension to our technology and routines, our lives went on, largely unfazed by the outbreak. This inconvenience for the affluent was a disaster to those in a lower socioeconomic status who work in-person jobs. For the global working class, the pandemic created a deeper societal divide and a seismic shift in the way we'll work and live over the next two decades. Here are three concerns P&L leaders should consider in elevating their commitments to societal inequalities:

1. That the pandemic is hitting working-class communities hardest is hardly a surprise. There are vast disadvantages: challenging working parents and home-schooling dynamics, access to quality education, affordable healthcare, and professional growth opportunities. Those that *have* are largely returning to their previous prosperity trajectory, despite significant fiscal and monetary policy actions. However, the conditions of the *have-nots* have further deteriorated. According to the U.S. Bureau of Labor Statistics, only 20% of African Americans and 16% of Hispanics have jobs where working from home is an option.[25]

2. The Digital Divide will lead to an economic crater. Digital life is likely to improve the lives of people at the top of the socioeconomic ladder. This access and capabilities at a personal level will widen the economic divide.

3. Those we ignore will be pitted against our democracy and capitalism. According to the Pew Research Center, corporate and government agendas generally don't serve democratic goals. They serve the goals of those in power, often pitting the controllers against the controlled.[26]

If you're a knowledge worker with a good education, a professional pedigree, and multiple safety nets in your personal and professional ecosystem, it would be easy to dismiss these challenges, because they don't directly impact you – easy to dismiss, foolish to ignore. P&L leaders will be directly impacted by availability of front-line talent, diverse talent to develop and nurture up through the organization, and safety and security of their organization's supply chain, distribution, and go-to-market strategies if their organization's social responsibilities don't include the have-nots.

After reading about Haves vs. Have-Nots, grade (A, B, C, or F) both your current understanding of this force and its impact on your future success. Remember, the divide in our society will cause a direct threat to capitalism and meritocracy. _____

Shrinking Planet

Force 12: Shrinking Planet. From a supply chain perspective, the planet shrinks as global connectivity increases. Every organization can create a website and add a shopping cart logo. They can be connected to buyers and sellers at an accelerated pace. The complexity of continuously meeting buyer demands through the seller's global supply chain will only increase in the future of our lives. We understand how it works, but it is still amazing to buy something in Hong Kong one day and have it at our house the next day!

The longest rail link in the world is 8,111 miles from Yiwu in the Zhejiang coastal province of China to Madrid, Spain. The route crosses Kazakhstan, Russia, Belarus, Poland, Germany, and France. It's been dubbed the twenty-first-century Silk Road. The first train arrived in 2014 with 30 containers carrying 1,400 tons of cargo – mostly toys, stationery, and Christmas items for sale across Europe. It was a test run to assess the viability of Spain's adding to a route that had already linked China to Germany five times a week. Trains also link Chongqing, the largest industrial city in Southwest China, to Duisburg, Beijing, and Hamburg.

The train returned from Madrid with wine and olive oil in time for the Chinese New Year the following February. Yiwu is the world's largest wholesale hub for small consumer goods. Its two-square-mile market is home to tens of thousands of traders daily. The high-speed rail route takes just three weeks to complete compared to six weeks by sea. It's significantly more environmentally friendly than road transport, with an estimated 62% CO_2 emission reduction.

In the future, four business pressures on most industries will rattle the global supply chain and our shrinking planet:

1. ***Demand to launch products quickly before competitors.*** Let's begin with product development and innovation. Most organizations realize that they need to be first to market to maximize the profitability of a new design before fast

followers catch up. This pressures product development to collaborate with design locations and functions that are internal, as well as external, to the organization to minimize inefficiencies and delays. The customer's voice will gain greater strategic influence in product development. The Internet of Things (IoT) will enable demand to be driven by replacement signals from items already sold. Take, for example, your digitally connected refrigerator. It will signal back to its manufacturer in another country that a part will need to be replaced in the next three months. It will coordinate the shipment of that part to a field service technician and schedule preventive maintenance on your calendar for 90 days out.

2. ***Rising supply chain management costs.*** As service demands increase, costs will as well due to the incremental steps to provide those services and manage the complex logistics. In the future, sales and operations planning (S&OP) or integrated business planning (IBP), which manages the end-to-end view of the supply chain, will be increasingly driven by AI. Machine learning will enable incredible speed and access to signal changes, and both centralized processes will become continuous, real-time, living ecosystems. Predictive analytics will automatically calculate total landing costs and various fuel consumption scenarios.

3. ***Customer mandates for faster, more accurate, and more unique fulfillment.*** Amazon has been growing its own logistics operations over the past decade. According to a Morgan Stanley estimate, they deliver more than 50% of all Amazon packages in the United States.[27] "Customers love the transition of Prime from two days to one day – they've already ordered billions of items with free one-day delivery this year. It's a big investment, and it's the right long-term decision for our customers," shared Jeff Bezos on the earnings call in October 2019. For Amazon, it's not just about getting more packages to more customers at higher speed. It's also about owning everything from the arrival of the product at an Amazon factory to the last-mile delivery at a customer's doorstep. This control has historically been difficult for

most commerce companies to crack. The future of Amazon's retail success depends as much on its seller community as it does the buyers of its products. Shrinking planet is also clearly represented in Amazon's Seller Central. Its fulfillment metrics provide insights into everything from product ranking and seller rating to unit session percentage rate, units ordered, order defect rate, inventory performance, fulfillment performance, and supply chain fees.[28]

4. ***Growing complexity of global operations.*** Any organization's end-to-end global supply chain integration capability will also dramatically benefit from big data analytics. Chad Johnson, chief procurement officer at Humana, had to obtain 35 million masks for Humana members at the onset of the pandemic. Only through their best-in-class Enterprise Category Management were they able to cleanse, classify, and use their data for actionable insights to support a strategic sourcing process.

If there is a silver lining to the shrinking planet, it is that for astute P&L leaders, access to higher-quality relationships will be dramatically more valuable. As the above four business pressures continue to challenge global supply chains, the breadth and depth of the strategic relationships you can rely on will definitively set you apart from your competitive peers.

After reading about the Shrinking Planet, grade (A, B, C, or F) both your current understanding of this force and its impact on your future success. Remember, our expansive global reach has both advantages and dire consequences. _____

Geopolitics

Force 13: Geopolitics. Powerful curve-bending relationships will help P&L leaders not only better understand geopolitics, but their potential impact in the future of their organizations as well. Geopolitics are cyclical. From Brexit to political upheaval in Venezuela and continued human rights protests in Hong Kong, geopolitics are in a constant ebb and flow. It's harder to identify these cycles because they can last decades. Geopolitics have an immense impact on various industries, and the effects can ripple into your eco-system. The broader effects influence more than just your role, company, or industry. It causes shockwaves through policies on innovation, learning, and growth.

After World War II, U.S.-led global institutions, like the G7, reflected a new world order. Many believe these political juggernauts are unwinding, and that we're entering an interregnum where they are increasingly ineffective. Technology is catalyzing fundamental changes to the world order, and no train whistle will signal breakthroughs. Nor will we be able to predict how political forces will shape the implementation of technologies or vice versa. We do know that these shifts will change more than policies; they will change our values and beliefs. The wealthiest societies in the world will continue to have fewer children, which makes absolute population no longer the yardstick for wealth, bounty, and power. The transfer of power is seldom voluntary or equitable, raising concerns about how peacefully or willingly those transfers of power will occur.

Several key trends in geopolitics will dramatically impact our lives:

- *Climate change will continue to dominate the global narrative.* Continued global emissions and cheaper renewables are driving exciting new entrepreneurial endeavors. Certain difficult-to-decarbonize sectors like steel and chemicals remain vital to our infrastructure demands. Governments are announcing net-zero targets. Financial markets are under pressure to price carbon risks more accurately, further dividing clean investments from climate-deleterious ones.[29] Addressing climate change will require a vast nexus of boardrooms, public market investors, entrepreneurs, investors, and government leaders to launch a modern-day Manhattan Project.

- *Geopolitics will continue to fragment and result in greater conflict.* China's growing economic power and global influence is merely one example of the broader rise of Asia.[30] China is exporting its capitalism and authoritarian capabilities through its technology and across the One Belt, One Road initiative. India is on a trajectory to become the third-largest economy by 2030, approaching $10 trillion GDP. The world's three definitive trading blocs will exert their value in an effort to influence the rest of the world. The EU will continue to promote a citizen-centric model, while China a state-centered one. The United States at the time of this writing is challenged by racial injustice and a divided political atmosphere, which endanger its status as the home of endless opportunity and the world's moral guardian. Russia, Brexit Britain, and strong African and Asian nations are all demanding a seat at the table. If the fragmentation of the globally interoperable internet turns into four or more, we will lose the benefits associated with openness and democratization of technology.[31]

- *Social distancing may lead to nation distancing.* Globalization is in retreat. One of the lasting scars of the pandemic will be the diminished trust between nations. Countries are seeking to shore up the supply chain and production. State-sponsored investments will continue to be under scrutiny. Sovereign wealth funds (SWFs) and public pension funds (PPFs) are unusual as State-owned investors. They are embedded in the political and regulatory regimes of home and host nations. In the future, they may be asked to prove to the host countries that their investment intents are legitimate. News stories surrounding the provision of personal protective equipment (PPE) or vaccines helped to frame this problem. In the event of a global crisis, which nation's interest would a foreign investor in a PPE or vaccine production facility prioritize? Would the home or host sovereign have first call on the factory's output, granting them ultimate control?

- *Tech supremacy will guide many states to rethink their "social contract" for a new world of work.* AI and super-fast networks will reign supreme. What economist Mariana Mazzucato calls the *mission-driven* states will realize they need to take a more active role in directing investments in technology and shaping our societies.[32,33] This will take the form of DARPA-like research; smart nations will accelerate the entrepreneurial breakthroughs in semiconductors that are optimized for machine learning and the general availability of quantum computers. Optimization processes like routing in transit systems and renewable energy systems management will benefit. Nations will use machine information, path planning, and robotics across their geographic boundaries to build an increasingly accurate digital twin of the real world. Smart nations will bring intelligent and adaptive products into the real world. Facebook, Google, and Amazon will work aggressively to increase their global footprint as they push against regulatory restrictions that may limit their growth. New laws around the use of explicit and implied personal data will keep many tech companies from truly becoming global. TikTok, a video app owned by a Chinese company, run by an American CEO, was blocked in India after a heated border clash with China left at least 20 Indian soldiers dead. The global battle over 5G network infrastructure is another example. The UK has reexamined its decision to grant Chinese tech company Huawei the ability to help build the country's 5G network. That review came after the U.S.-imposed sanctions on the company that could prevent other firms from supplying it with the chipsets needed to build its next-generation technology.

- *Space will become the last geopolitical frontier.* Researchers at the Secure World Foundation (SWF) and the Center for Strategic and International Studies (CSIS) released reports suggesting that the biggest players in space have advanced their space military abilities. Their advancements range from anti-satellite weapons to technologies that disrupt spacecraft by blocking data collection or transmission.[34,35] Such power conflicts could be nonkinetic and not publicly visible, relying on cyber-based weaponry. Space-based conflict provides an avenue to deter adversary involvement by preemptively denying space-based capabilities, making terrestrial action more expensive or difficult for an adversary that needs to operate globally.

For example, prior to an invasion of the Baltic States, Russia could signal its will and launch reversible attacks against space-based assets that NATO forces rely on. This would slow operations and raise the cost of NATO and U.S. intervention.[36]

After reading about Geopolitics, grade (A, B, C, or F) your current understanding of this force and its impact on your future success. Remember, geographic distance is easily surmounted; political instability on the other side of the world is no longer someone else's problem. _____

Black Swan Event

Force 14: Black Swan Events. In 2007, statistician Nassim Nicholas Taleb defined a black swan as an outlier event from the realm of regular expectations. They are understood yet mostly unforeseen, rare, and often created by unexpected circumstances: geopolitical, economic, biological, terror, or other. Black swans are profoundly disruptive. In 2012, the U.S. National Intelligence Council published "Global Trends 2030: Alternative Worlds," which identified the following eight black swans capable of causing large-scale disruption.[37] All but two of these – the possibility of a democratic China or a reformed Iran – would have severely negative repercussions for the global economy, many industries, and our way of life. As evidenced by the first on the list, new terms like *flattening the curve* and *social distancing* have entered the popular lexicon.

- *Pandemics.* No one can anticipate which pathogen, when, or where will be next to spread to humans. As evident by COVID-19 (2019 Novel Coronavirus), an easily transmissible respiratory pathogen can kill or incapacitate more than 1% of its victims. In less than six months, we saw thousands dying in every corner of the world, while millions suffered massive economic losses. The recovery may be an economic crater. Massive carnage hits entire industries that are ill-prepared to maneuver with speed and agility.

- *Accelerated climate change.* Most scientists are alarmed by dramatic and unforeseen climate changes that are happening at accelerated rates. Many experts are not confident in predicting such events. Precipitation pattern changes, such as monsoons in India or painfully slow-moving hurricanes flooding streets of Venice, Italy, could drastically impact each of the impacted region's ability to function or feed its population. Record-breaking heat, wildfires, and unprecedented ice melt point to earth's temperature rising more than 1.5 degrees Celsius.[38] That's the threshold to maintain the Greenland Ice Sheet. Melting happens during warm cycles and balances out when new ice forms during cool cycles.[39] If the sheets are not regenerated, sea levels will rise. This threatens low-lying cities, such as Manhattan, Miami, New Orleans, Venice, Jakarta, and countries like Bangladesh and Vietnam.

- *Euro/EU collapse.* Greece's economic volatility and exit from the euro-zone could cause collateral damage. Amid the pandemic, the German French partnership brokered an $857 billion coronavirus recovery package. The wealthy northern European countries – the Netherlands, Denmark, Sweden, Finland, and Austria – were reluctant to send money to their southern neighbors and wanted strict spending oversight and labor market and pension reforms. Italy and Spain accuse their northern neighbors of "blackmailing" Europe and risking the bloc's future.

- *A democratic or collapsed china.* The per-capita purchasing power parity (PPP) in China was $19,504 – well beyond the $15,000 threshold trigger for democratization.[40] China's GDP is estimated to become 20% of the world GDP by 2050.[41] The unrest in Hong Kong is an example of the Chinese "soft" power dramatically boosted, setting off potential waves of democratic movements. Many geopolitical experts believe that a democratic China would become more nationalistic. On the other hand, an economically collapsed China would trigger political unrest and shock the global economy.

- *A reformed Iran.* This one hits close to home for me as I still have extended family there. A more liberal Islamic Republic regime could end the international sanctions and negotiate an end to Iran's isolationism due to growing public pressure. An Iranian leadership that abandoned its nuclear weapon ambitions and focused on economic modernization could create a more stable Middle East.[42]

- *Nuclear war, weapons of mass destruction, or cyberattacks.* Russia, India, China, Pakistan, and North Korea see nuclear weapon capabilities as a seat at the international adult table. This compensation for other political or security weaknesses only heightens the risk of their use. Additionally, chances of nonstate actors in various global theaters conducting a cyberattack or using weapons of mass destruction are increasing.[43]

- *Solar geomagnetic storms.* According to the National Oceanic and Atmospheric Administration (NOAA), a geomagnetic storm is caused by a major disturbance of Earth's magnetosphere. This occurs when there is an efficient exchange of energy from the solar wind into the space environment surrounding Earth. It can knock out satellites, electric grids, and sensitive electronic devices. Our global dependence on electricity would let this phenomenon cripple the world's capability to function.

- *U.S. disengagement.* Anarchy would ensue if the United States took an extensive retreat from the global stage. No leading power is currently willing and able to replace the United States as the guarantor of international order.

Despite the fact that none of us can control these events, they would have a tremendous impact on our personal and professional growth. You cannot ignore them. You cannot forecast them, but you must incorporate the potential for Black Swan Events into your Curve Benders Roadmap. Such events will continue to be part of our future. How can you prepare? Here are three ideas:

1. Create a strong and vast portfolio of strategic relationships to signal early potential signs of disruptions proactively.

2. Develop sufficient contingency and continuity planning so that the right response team can move quickly at the earliest signs of potential disruptions.

3. Create training simulations and development opportunities to stress-test your people and plans with consistent, clear, concise communication on potential disruptions.

After reading about Black Swan Events, grade (A, B, C, or F) your current understanding of this force and its impact on your future success. Remember, we may intellectually understand their disruptive nature and agree that they will happen; we just don't know when they may happen. _____

Volatility

Force 15: Volatility. Volatility refers to the amount of *uncertainty or risk* related to the size of changes in a security's value. Historically, fluctuations in firm's stock market prices creates stress. Similarly, those same fluctuations in our lives create uncertainty. When our confidence is shaken, we'll take defensive measures. Thanks to the coronavirus pandemic, the Congressional Budget Office (CBO) has projected an $8 trillion shortfall of the U.S. economy over the next decade.[44] This 3% decline in U.S. gross domestic product reported in June is largely due to a reduction of consumer spending and the closing of businesses.

In the future, industries and key companies must rearrange their capabilities and talent, maybe even business models, similar to the way investors rearrange asset allocation in their portfolios to diversify and reduce risk. Volatility occurs when trade is unbalanced between value seekers and value creators. Here are the top causes:

- *Economic crisis.* Every financial market is sensitive to major economic disruptions in what has been forecast. The worse the crisis, the bigger its influence on the market's overall performance. In the future, predictive analytics and AI in financial modeling will become dramatically stronger. Any anomalies will create even greater uncertainty and volatility.

- *Changes in national economic policy.* Driven by the Federal Reserve System (Fed), short-term changes in fiscal policy often cause sharp movements in the market. A good example is the U.S. Dollar Index: the relative value of the U.S. currency

against the majority of its trading partners. This index significantly increases when the U.S. dollar gains "strength" compared to other currencies.

- **Economic indicators.** Think of these leading drivers as windows into market trends. Economic reports such as monthly
job reports, inflation data, consumer spending figures, housing
prices, or supply chain dynamics of raw material are all forecast targets. When they exceed expectations, the market does
well; otherwise, it often tumbles.

- **Volatility in major global markets.** In our increasingly globally connected world, political unrest impacts trade on all
levels. What happens in a seemingly isolated part of the
world has a ripple effect on markets closer to home. Pay
attention to geopolitics, which will create significantly
greater unintended consequences in our future dependence
on foreign resources.

- **Political developments.** Government decisions on trade agree-
ments, taxes, and federal spending are all political moves that
directly affect market volatility. Political speeches, meetings at
large block trade conferences, and escalating trade wars cause
major indices to tumble. Furthermore, closer ties between two
nations can create rifts between outside countries. This is evident by the century-old Middle Eastern struggles between
Israel, Palestine, and the rest of the Arab world.

- **Public relations.** The public image of an organization or
industry affects market perceptions. Those perceptions and
the affected stock performance may be driven by PR-based
homeruns or strikeouts. Additionally, vertical integration scale
matters. The larger the organization, the more likely that its
performance will impact the entire industry sector.

Like people, market sectors may have unique personalities, with
some sectors being much more volatile than others. Large price swings
over time can influence investor emotions and depressed economic
conditions from inflation to deflation and bankruptcies of major
organizations.

Bottom line: volatility frightens investors and can dramatically impact your organization. It's a deviation from an expected pattern. Prudent investors prefer a stable, predictable market where stock prices move as expected, minimizing uncertainty and risk. How you steward your team and organization through volatility will dramatically enhance or dilute your brand as a crisis leader.

Some would argue that the world is more volatile today than during the Cold War. Every one of the previous forces leads to instability. Volatility impacts our mindset and behaviors. Stock market volatility is fundamental in the overall business ecosystem and reaches the broader volatility in our lives. We tend to move from prudence to anxiety. We invest less in ourselves.

After reading about Volatility, grade (A, B, C, or F) both your current understanding of this force and its impact on your future success. Remember, Volatility will increasingly continue to re-create our norms. _____

YOUR PRIORITIES SCORECARD

This section may seem to be an unreasonably broad list of faint market signals to track over time and prepare for in your future. My experience shows that ignoring these sources of disruption leaves organizations and their leaders vulnerable to unexpected change. If you listen harder for these faint signals and continuously recalibrate your organization's strategy, you'll uncover opportunities to refine and dramatically improve. That's iteration – doing the same thing better.

Iterate enough and you'll stumble onto opportunities to innovate – doing new things. Innovative products such as the Dyson bagless vacuum cleaner or bladeless fans come to mind. More interesting than innovative products or services to me are new business models, which adapt to dynamic market demands. Create a culture of innovation within your team or organization and you're much more likely to do new things, which make the old obsolete. Those are often opportunities for disruption.

Leaders who disrupt may lean into uncertainty. They methodically track these 15 forces early and often. They choose to challenge the status quo of their own mindset, their teams, and their organizations through their most valuable asset – their strategic relationships. That's where Curve Benders accelerate your traction with a strategic project. The key is to connect the dots between seemingly disparate observations and give space to ask questions others haven't thought of yet. How could a shift in one force lead to regulatory actions in another? Who would benefit from a shift in one force, while others could be harmed or impeded?

Here are two good ways to apply what you've read in this chapter to both your organization and your Curve Benders Roadmap planning as you grade yourself in the 15 Forces Scorecard (Figure 2.13):

1. *For your personal growth:* Transfer your grades from each of the forces in this chapter to the following table. It should help you become more familiar with and thoughtful regarding the impact of these forces on your future success. Then prioritize where you should invest resources (time, effort, and capital) to become more familiar with each force. Capture Curve Bender–centric actions that could accelerate your personal and professional growth journey. Ask yourself these questions: What profile of a relationship do I need to know in this topic, that I don't today? What type of relationships could help me learn more about, ask better questions, or capitalize on the opportunities impacted by this force? It's amazing how often Curve Benders can either fix a glaring challenge or help you capitalize on previously unattainable opportunities.

2. *For your organization:* Consider building an innovation sprint team – more on this in a later chapter where we'll discuss the organization of the future. It is comprised of a group of leaders from disparate parts of the organization, who commit to "owning" these forces. Their task is to dive deep into key trends driving that force and how that force could enhance or impede the organization. The innovation

Force	Grade	Prioritized	Curve Bender—Centric Action
9 Co-Creation			
10 Economy			
11 Haves vs. Have-Nots			
12 Shrinking Planet			
13 Geopolitics			
14 Black Swan Event			
15 Volatility			

© The Nour Group, Inc.

Force	Grade	Prioritized	Curve Bender—Centric Action
1 Relationship Strategy	*example* B	1	*Assess Your Current Relationship Bank*
2 Grit	C	4	
3 Mindset			*Consider a Mindset Bio*
4 Diversification			
5 Visualization			
6 Technology			
7 Demographics			
8 Visionary Storytelling			

© The Nour Group, Inc.

Figure 2.13   Fifteen Forces Scorecard

sprint team could meet virtually once a month, with each leader sharing their respective force knowledge and its potential impacts on the organization. Over time, these strategic conversations become more than interesting facts – they begin to shape the organization's maneuverability in its capabilities, talent, and business model. You could easily rotate the members annually, then ask them to invite a sharp, high-performing/high-potential subordinate. Suddenly, this environmental scanning of the 15 forces becomes a leadership competency program in disruption signal tracking and crisis resilience development.

CHAPTER 2 SUMMARY

1. 15 forces will dramatically impact the future of how you'll work, live, play, and give. Understanding and proactively planning your response to each are essential to your personal and professional growth.

2. These forces are of four kinds: personal, organizational, industry, and transitory.

3. You should be aware of and track where you are excelling and where you need outside support in internalizing, synthesizing, and preparing for the impact by each of these forces.

4. By seeking out Curve Bender relationships around each of these 15 forces, you can potentially reduce the disruptive nature of each force and elevate your readiness to respond.

5. Those who anticipate, plan, and prepare for the uncertainty will be more agile and hasten their personal and professional growth.

CHAPTER 3

Accelerated Relevancy

You cannot change your future. But you can change your habits.
And surely your habits will change your future.

> – A.P.J. Abdul Kalam, aerospace scientist and 11th
> president of India

So far, we've covered your personal market value, the growth grid, and the 15 forces that will dramatically impact your future. We know that Curve Benders will prevent you from becoming obsolete. We haven't yet discussed, however, *how to best prepare to make the most out of potential Curve Benders in your life*.

I'm going to break this chapter into two key sections:

1. The path to your Curve Benders

2. How to remain continuously relevant

Keep in mind that Curve Benders are more than just great bosses, mentors, or partners who help you elevate your performance and accomplish more. Curve Benders profoundly shape our future direction. What evolves is the person we become through a highly immersive learning and growth process. A Curve Bender isn't necessarily a high-profile author or content creator. Curve Benders may begin as people whose relationships we proactively seek and invest energy in. We give them a chance to get to know, trust, and buy in to our challenges and opportunities. Their knowledge, wisdom, and guidance are what shapes us into the contributors, managers, or leaders we aspire to become.

You must be humble enough to seek these people out. They often possess deep geographic, subject-matter, or domain expertise, which makes relationships with them incredibly valuable. They're likely extremely selective about relationships they choose to invest in. They have a tight inner circle and invest deeper in their portfolio of valuable relationships. Curve Benders often bring incredible emotional support, arising from their past experiences and wisdom and their successful track records. I've found Curve Benders to be well-read, well-spoken, and often well-traveled, which gives them a global perspective. They're intelligent, as they tend to experience more than most of us do. They're very intentional and show up with a zest for life, in whatever endeavor they've undertaken over the decades. They know who they are and who they're not and are unwilling to pretend or compromise one to become the other. Since they have already reached a certain level of success, they are more interested in *living a life of significance* in the fall and winter of their lives. If they are not already in our immediate circle, they are often within three connections from people we already know.

From hundreds of global interviews, I learned that Curve Benders often see the absolute best version of ourselves. Even as likely prospects come to know us, they see and hear the insurmountable obstacles we describe and challenge our assumptions to address how to overcome them. They open our eyes to new possibilities and push us to aim past our self-imposed limits.

Here are ideas to keep in mind as you search for Curve Benders in your life:

- **Curve Benders are not transactional.** They are highly *transformative* relationships. They're not a sales call, a quick buck, a checklist, a hit-and-run, or a drive-by-greeting. You must be willing to engage with them on insightful questions.

- **Listen intently and louder.** To learn from and grow through prospective Curve Benders, you must engage them with a set of core values and a succinct business outcome you seek. They will be particularly curious to learn *who you really are*, where and how you grew up, and the critical experiences that shaped your perspectives, challenges, and values. In their questions, they are trying to learn what you stand for and where your limits lie. They want to know if you're dependable and will follow through (a process), versus simply follow up (a transaction).

- **Curve Benders must be contextually relevant in your journey from now to next.** Most generous people you encounter want to help you: they simply don't know how. If you make others spend too much energy because you're not transparently yourself or don't know what you want or need, they'll disengage rather than spend too much time and energy, and deprioritize you.

- **Convey your credibility with the questions you ask.** In our hypergrowth business environment, we often rush to provide ideas to illustrate how smart we are. Yet we don't make space for inquiry. We seldom ask sufficient quality questions or invest in intellectual horsepower to make others think. With sufficient due diligence, you can develop a clear vision of where you want every potential curve-bending interaction to go. As such, your single biggest asset will be the quality questions you ask. When forming your questions, consider:

1. Are they intelligent, well-constructed, clear, and concise?

2. Are they directly relevant to what you need from the conversation?

3. What subsequent or follow-up questions will you pose?

4. How can you cast a wider net if the initial interaction with a potential Curve Bender is constructive and perceived to be mutually valuable?

5. Last, but certainly not least, a great question from an old mentor: "How will you get your return ticket punched?"

So, what do you need to know to identify prospective Curve Benders and access their transformative power? Here are the seven steps to pave the path to your Curve Benders (Figure 3.1):

1. **Personal Foundation:** Begin with a non-linear growth mindset – digital, entrepreneurial, and collaborative – to fuel your curiosity, creativity, and connections.

2. **Professional Commitment:** You must commit to mastering your craft or profession, and align your roles to quantifiable value creation.

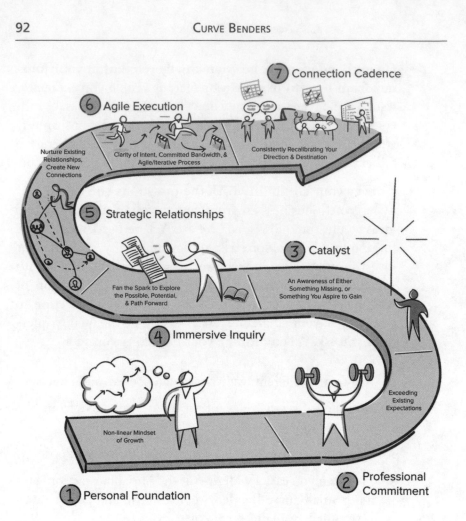

Figure 3.1   Seven Steps to Your Curve Benders

3. **Catalyst:** A spark can bring an awareness of something missing or something you aspire to gain to dramatically improve your condition.

4. **Immersive Inquiry:** If a catalyst whets your appetite, you must research how to challenge biases and assumptions and fan the spark to explore the potential and path forward.

5. **Strategic Relationships:** With a flame to pursue, think of your most valuable relationships as fuel. Now you must nurture existing relationships, create new connections, and gain access to an opportunity with those who may be your Curve Benders.

6. **Agile Execution:** Revisit the Growth Grid with your clarity of intent, committed bandwidth, and an agile/iterative process.

7. **Connection Cadence:** This final step will focus on keeping your strategic relationships updated and consistently recalibrating your direction.

Let's take a closer look at each step.

SEVEN-STEP PATH TO YOUR CURVE BENDERS

Non-linear Mindset of Growth

① Personal Foundation

Step 1: Personal Foundation. You must view your growth through digital, entrepreneurial, and collaborative filters. These are factors that will fuel your curiosity, creativity, and connections. To dramatically increase the chances of meeting potential Curve Benders, begin with a *proactive* growth mindset. If you become a lifelong learner, you'll begin to shift your growth trajectory to a non-linear one. Our research shows that many Curve Benders live at the edge of where constraints meet creative problem-solving. Alex Lazarow, a venture capitalist at Cathay Innovation, a global investment firm with over $3 billion in assets, believes this frontier of innovation is defined by three unique qualities:[1]

1. A nascent ecosystem of thinkers, explorers, and experimenters

2. An economic landscape with limited resources to support new business models

3. An environment that often highlights large macroeconomic shocks, such as political issues or infrastructure gaps

These ecosystems create *forced agility*, a drive to succeed regardless of the obstacles we face. According to Lazarow, "The Silicon Valley playbook of 'move fast and break things,' or 'scale at all costs' doesn't produce the desired outcomes at the frontier." Your personal foundation must focus on resilience and balanced growth.

Your foundation can dramatically benefit from admiring more camels and fewer unicorns. In recent years, business culture has begun to refer to companies valued at over $1 billion as "unicorns." As of September 2020, there are more than 400 of them across the world, including decacorns (firms valued at $10 billion+), and hectocorns ($100 billion+).[2] To create these companies, leaders are chasing ideas that can scale at all costs, aiming for rapid growth and a financial or strategic exit. The pursuit of unicorns brings incredibly high risk, often at a greater percentage of epic failures – Quibi's $1.7 billion squander comes to mind. Your personal and professional growth should be more like camels. You, too, can adapt to survive the harshest conditions. Your goal should embrace a balanced approach that inspires resilience, as a camel does. By weaving sustainability and resilience into your personal and professional growth, you'll be significantly more cognizant of your expenses, understand value creation from your growth, proactively invest in your growth, and look at your S-curve and Curve Benders Roadmap as a marathon and not a sprint.

When you live with a genuine sense of creative problem solving and connect the dots between your current relationships and the ones you need, your personal foundation is grounded in a non-linear growth mindset.

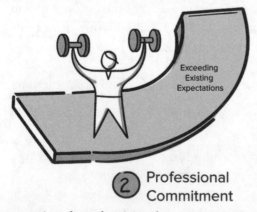

Exceeding
Existing
Expectations

② Professional
Commitment

Step 2: Professional Commitment. A strong personal foundation based on a non-linear growth mindset is half the equation. The second step in paving a path to your Curve Benders is a commitment to mastery in your work and life. True mastery means the aim to develop the intellectual, physical, emotional, and spiritual capacity to connect and inspire others. That power will allow you to unite your strengths into impactful roles, a broader realm of responsibilities, great teams you work with, and ultimately the organizations you choose to help in the future of your work.

Becoming world-class in your profession begins with personal mastery. You must master your emotions, behaviors, and prudent judgment to act congruently with a set of values. Staying positive, present, and grateful, independent of external circumstances, creates a beacon of inspiration that others will want to follow. When you demonstrate an innate drive to make a difference, you model the personal governance others should expect of themselves. In your role as a leader, you need to build a foundation of trust and appropriate behavior, with emotional and spiritual intelligence.

In any uncertain environment, trust becomes the glue that keeps high performers together in a team. Although countless articles, books, and podcasts have been produced around the topic, I have a simple formula for trust: **Trust = Credibility + Empathy**. Keep in mind that not everyone feels trust for the same reason. Beyond your expertise, understanding *others' dominant thinking style* will help you empathize with what others need to feel trust in working with you:

- A highly *analytical* colleague may feel she can trust you when she knows you have the right expertise.

- Conversely, a *creative* client will trust you when you allow them the freedom to be themselves and help them feel that their uniqueness adds value in your work together.

- You earn the trust with senior executives and highly *process-oriented* board members when they get the sense that you are consistently reliable and come through as discussed and planned.

- A supplier critical to your next product launch, who is a highly *relational* and intuitive person, needs to feel good about you as a caring individual and sense that you understand and respect her point of view.

Over the years, the most exceptional leaders I've coached committed to mastering these seven areas within their organizations:

1. **Human Motivation:** Learn the science of human motivation and inspiration to know what moves peak performers. Integrate findings into business value creation.

2. **Master Yourself:** Learn self-awareness and consistent behaviors to connect and inspire others to a higher level of productivity, performance, and resilience. Become the change catalyst others want to emulate and follow.

3. **Inspire Through a Noble Purpose:** Learn how to develop a noble purpose, a set of values, and a personal brand that inspire others and galvanize them into action.

4. **Expand Your Situational Awareness:** Operate as a conscious leader, surround yourself with independent thinkers to overcome your biases to gain a broader perspective, and develop astute situational awareness.

5. **Bridge Your Aspiration-to-Impact Gap:** Hold yourself and others accountable for consistent actions and expected results. We all have 168 hours in any given week; what we choose to focus on is what's accomplished.

6. **Practice EDGE Leadership:** As an Eagle Scout, I was taught early in my formative years the EDGE method: explain, demonstrate, guide, and enable others to succeed. Learn visionary storytelling, proactive conflict-based learnings, agile decision-making, energizing walking meetings, zero-based budgeting to improve growth, and cutting frivolous costs.

7. **Make "Exceptional" Fundamental Organizational DNA:** You've encountered my use of *exceptional* several times thus far. That's not accidental. In the future of work and your search for Curve Benders, average, good, or even great at times will prove to be your biggest enemy. Exceptional is the connective tissue to going above and beyond – in every business function, operational process, and daily interactions. Hustle until your haters ask if you're hiring!

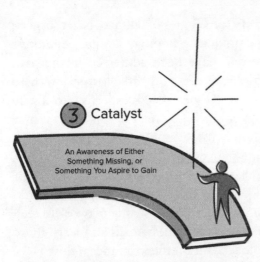

Step 3: Catalysts. Think back to one of your first chemistry experiments in grade school. You may recall when a *catalyst* was used. The teacher explained that this was a substance that acts to accelerate a chemical reaction, speeding up the change. In this step, a spark happens – an awareness of either something missing or a new aspiration beckoning in your life or work, which ignites action. As the saying from Darwin's life goes, *curiosity inspires; discovery reveals.*

A catalyst for change is the element that encourages you to adopt change. In your personal or professional life, a catalyst for change can be internal and/or external. And, importantly, they can be positive "pushes" in one direction or adverse events that "pull" you away from a route. These drivers have been described as the drive to achieve and the drive to avoid.[3] Complacency, arrogance, and inertia are anti-catalysts. They provide comfort that keeps you stuck in a rut. To produce change, you need to embrace pain points. We see the myriad restaurants-turned-retailers that, against all odds, are thriving in the midst of an epidemic that threatened their core business models.[4]

The following are three types of catalysts:

1. **Simple Catalysts for Change:** These are common in our daily lives; they require due diligence, but the path is well understood. You know what you need to do and how to do it. In changing a process or implementing a proven best practice, there is often a right answer, the cause and effect of the current state and the desired change are understood, and your ability to make that change has a high success rate. Although your portfolio of relationships will be useful in implementing the change, they will not warrant a mindshare from potential Curve Benders. You don't need relationships at Space X to help you get your car's oil changed.

2. **Complicated Catalysts for Change:** Think of heart surgery, building a rocket, or a unique technology design – definitive processes for change that have been addressed in the past. There are often multiple answers and paths forward in these scenarios, and you'll need specialized expertise to really understand what's happening. The effect of this catalyst may be subtle, but it is certainly discoverable. Success here is high with process and astute management of effort and resources. I've found strategic relationships to be particularly useful for your evaluation of potential options with complicated catalysts for change. For example, I have a strong network of tech execs where I can make a dozen phone calls and learn more about the impact of blockchain on the insurance industry.

3. **Complex Catalysts for Change:** These are the hardest for us to tackle but are ideal for Curve Benders to help us fine-tune our journey. Think of a child's growth stages. There is no single right answer, largely due to contrasting views, values, and sets of beliefs. You will need multifaceted and deep expertise, superb self-organization, and understanding of interconnected ecosystems. Real change in this area often results from a pursuit and does not come with a guarantee of success. The mindset required to succeed here demands that you become an explorer, someone who values the journey, inquiry, and experimentation over the destination.

Curve Benders behave as the connective tissue in highly complex environments for change. They crystallize our catalysts for change and show us how to remain steadfast in our pursuit of potential options. They become mentors, coaches, guides. Along the way, they bolster our fulfillment in progress versus perfection.

Fan the Spark to Explore the Possible, Potential, & Path Forward

④ Immersive Inquiry

Step 4: Immersive Inquiry. Immersive inquiry is when you deeply research the topic that was sparked by the catalyst. Einstein is famous for saying, "I have no special talents. I am only passionately curious."[5] Curiosity is a prerequisite to transformative change. By immersing yourself in inquiry, you get to see the possibilities for real, potentially lasting, and course-altering change. And, by being passionate in this endeavor, you identify the paths forward to achieving your desires.

You can immerse yourself in the intellectual ecosystem of your catalyst by diving deeper into a particular thought leader's idea, exploring tangential paths along the same direction of an idea, digging deeper into the root cause of a specific challenge, and consuming all the videos you can on the topic. This is where contextual inquiry is really valuable.[6] Think of this approach as literal inquiry of context.

Contextual inquiry is often one of the least-known tools user experience researchers use. User interface specialists derive it from the beginning of a design thinking process. I've long believed that it has dramatically deeper potential to address business challenges and opportunities. Contextual inquiry has primarily been used to uncover usability issues, reminiscent of anthropological research, which relies on participant observation.

If you take a semi-structured approach to obtaining information about the context of use, the immersive inquiry will allow you to observe and probe at the same time. You can document the process and capture significant details in their original settings. Over the years, I've found observable behaviors to be significantly more reliable than what people say in a survey or an interview. Don't tell me what you do – show me. Why are you doing it? Why that way? What happens next? What happens if you can't find what you need? I've taken videos, pictures, created sketches, and storyboarded countless processes. This way, I'm observing tools and practices under a social, technical, and physical umbrella.

Here are five principles of immersive inquiry to apply in your challenges or opportunities:

1. **Focus** – Create a targeted plan for your inquiry based on a clear understanding of your purpose. Ask tough questions early on to ensure that the problems you're pursuing are actual problems worth solving.

2. **Context** – Go to your target audience's environment and watch them do their work. Aim to understand what's

happening and why. Ask sufficient questions to understand possible inefficiencies in which the problem is framed, the solution is pursued, or options are considered today.

3. **Partnerships** – Talk to others who impact your target audience and their desired outcomes. Are there customers, suppliers, talent, or capital resources that you can engage with to uncover unarticulated aspects of what's happening and why? Are there individuals with expertise whom you could engage?

4. **Interpretation** – Develop a hypothesis and a shared understanding with those you engage about the aspects of the challenge or opportunity that matter. If you pull enough strings, you'll explore previously undiscovered paths. Diverse perspectives will help you fine-tune and solidify your thinking. I've found Peter Drucker's quote particularly relevant here: "The important and difficult job is never to find the right answers, it is to find the right question. For there are *few things as useless, if not dangerous*, as the right answer to the wrong question."[7]

5. **Leave Out Your Biased Solutions** – It is so easy for us to immediately jump into possible explanations we believe are perfectly obvious! Suspend that urge long enough to spend time in inquiry, exploration, and experimentation.

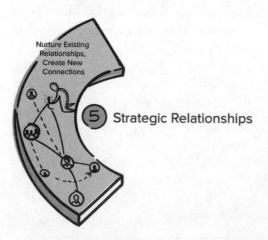

Step 5: Strategic Relationships. With a catalyst for change and immersive inquiry under your belt, it's time to activate an army that can dramatically propel you forward. The wealthy financier Baron de Rothschild was once approached for a loan by an acquaintance. He responded, "I won't give you a loan myself; but I will walk

arm-in-arm with you across the floor of the Stock Exchange, and you soon shall have willing lenders to spare."[8]

Regardless of what your situation may be, I'd submit that there are no new challenges! The only real challenges are the ones you haven't thought of before. Somewhere, somehow, someone else has explored a similar immersive inquiry, tried multiple solutions, failed, and tried again. Your challenge is to find these like minded kindred spirits. You've heard of the "Six Degrees of Kevin Bacon"? In the business world, we're typically only three degrees from almost anyone we need to meet.[9]

As such, the most valuable aspect of your inquiry is to engage your portfolio of relationships in search of *who* questions. Whom do you need? Whom do you know? How can you connect the dots between your existing relationships and your aspirational ones with a unique value-add? When we're faced with a challenge or an opportunity, we often ask *what* we should do, and *how* should we do it. But do we ask insightful *who* questions? Not very often.

It's important to reinforce the idea of strategic relationships here, especially in our business lives. Although this concept can extend beyond what we do for a living, most of us have three types of relationships:

1. **Personal** – They're discretionary, as you often choose many of the relevant attributes – where you live, where you send your kids to school or camps, and with whom you choose to spend time. Yet, you're never quite sure of their relevance to your professional life. Your personal relationships are a lot like you and have similar tastes in your material possessions, desired experiences, and behaviors.

2. **Functional** – These are some of your colleagues, clients, partners, investors, and market contacts. These are safe relationships because of the context of your work together. You may not care to spend any time with your colleagues or clients after work (although I'd submit that that's myopic at best and this mindset isn't serving you well). Nevertheless, they're highly relevant in your value creation efforts.

3. **Strategic** – These are your most valuable business relation-
    ships. They're current or past bosses, mentors, coaches, cli-
    ents, or other sources of wisdom. They elevate your
    perspectives. They challenge your assumptions. If you're
    managing 50 people today, they are your path to manage
    5,000. They're your Yoda. Unfortunately, most people
    I meet do not have enough strategic relationships they can
    capitalize on consistently in their personal or profes-
    sional lives.

Strategic relationships will be your single biggest asset to find
Curve Benders. Start by making a definitive list of your strategic relationships and make certain you're crystal clear as to why you believe
they are strategic. We're often eager to engage likeminded people,
referred to as the Halo Effect.[10] The danger zone is when we ignore
dissenting voices that are most valuable to us. Identify your weak ties,
those less invested in the relationship and, therefore, more willing to
offer valuable critique. Don't let your ego blind you to their value.
They're not firehoses to your brilliant ideas but quality elevators of
your initial experimentation. Prioritize cognitive diversity and muster
the courage to hear what you *need* to hear, versus what you may
want to hear.

Next, make time for introspection: consider whether you've made
significant investments of value creation to justify asking for their support. If you have not, you'll be hard-pressed to engage potential strategic relationships. If you have had regular interactions with each
individual and can point to a meaningful relationship, battle-tested by
time, formulate plans to approach them.

If your initial encounter creates relational gravity, your follow-
through process will cement it. I often like to get my return ticket
punched. So, I end the conversation with a request to return to them
with an update on my progress. By sharing my iterative progress with
them, not only am I demonstrating a real commitment to the pursuit,
but I'm also fueling their sense of curiosity and potential investment.
Keep in mind that if you're not open to criticism or modification when
appropriate, you'll soon see their support fade. They may perceive you
as incapable of the flexibility necessary for exploration.

The sad truth is that most people are unwilling to do the incredibly difficult work needed to tap into their strategic relationships. They "get" that relationships are important, yet are incapable of the heavy lifting to get to their full potential. It's simply too hard, too much work, and "they're too busy." They kid themselves that "I know a lot of people. I'm sure I can find someone to help." But, without a systematic and consistent process, they fail to bridge their relationship *creation* to their relationship *capitalization* efforts.

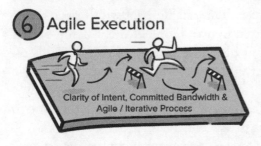

Step 6: Agile Execution. The next critical building block in the path to your Curve Benders is agile execution – staying focused on your desired outcomes, not drifting off on tangential ideas or paths, and resolving to overcome whatever obstacles come your way. I've found several attributes to be particularly useful in executing on my path forward with agility:

- **Clarity of Intent** – Say you want a particular model of a car. You've read various consumer review sites, spoken with friends who drive them, compared pricing on- and offline. Suddenly, you notice them everywhere. Ever wonder what is happening? Welcome to the Baader-Meinhof (pronounced badder mainhoff) phenomenon, otherwise known as frequency illusion or recency illusion.[11] You see that car more because of your heightened awareness of it. Two psychological processes are happening: first, your brain gets excited by learning something new, and second, your attention is skewed. Your brain subconsciously thinks, "Hey, that's fantastic! I'm going to really look out for more of them without thinking about it." This is termed *confirmation bias*; you see more of them "everywhere!"

    What if we used the same approach to tighten the aperture on our path of inquiry? What if we became crystal clear on the *why* in our quest? If we always learned something new and became more focused on that pursuit? I call this clarity of intent. You're crystal clear about why you're in this quest, and you're deliberate about all that you're doing. You understand that time, effort, and resources are finite. You don't get distracted and pursue your path forward with unparalleled gusto.

- **Committed Bandwidth** – In a frame relay, the internet service provider guarantees a committed information rate (CIR), the bandwidth for a virtual circuit, to work under normal conditions. Committed data rate is the payload portion of the CIR. At any given time, the available bandwidth should not fall below this committed figure. Think of this when it comes to your calendar. How will you prioritize all the demands on your time, effort, attention, and resources? It is ideal if the bandwidth committed to your pursuit does not fall below a certain level each week. You must commit to make the time to analyze, discuss, deconstruct, and reconstruct all the knowledge that you gain each week a priority. Then you must synthesize that knowledge into actions. I don't know about you, but if a priority isn't calendar-blocked in my world, it won't get done!

- **Agile/Iterative Process** – The key to agile execution is accelerated learning and applying what's learned to make immediate course corrections. In the business literature, this is called *failing fast* – recognizing errors quickly, and speedily making corrective changes to your course of action so as not to become irrelevant.[12] I'm not a fan of extensive analysis before I have sufficient data to pivot. If you create a checklist for the Growth Grid steps, you can follow a recipe and ensure you haven't missed any key lines of inquiry.

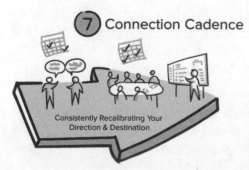

7 Connection Cadence

Consistently Recalibrating Your Direction & Destination

Step 7: Connection Cadence. The final step in the path to your Curve Benders is to keep your strategic relationships updated. I've found that one of the biggest myths in building and nurturing relationships is that you can neglect them, and yet, they'll somehow bear fruit when you need them! My motorcycle battery will die after a couple of weeks and refuse to start the bike if it's not connected to a battery tender. You need to think of your strategic relationships and a connection cadence in a similar fashion. Cold weather can drain your battery power. Distance lets your relationships get cold. If you don't create opportunities to add value to your relationships with regular touches, they'll become distracted with other priorities. Relationships established for a period of time because of a strategic initiative, and then allowed to fade, will be considered transactional and contextually relevant only to that initiative, and not a relationship of ongoing value.

A strong approach here is to separate your relationships into their respective strength buckets. I've found different relationships to be really useful depending on what I may need, or maybe struggling with. If you begin with a strong, foundational CRM, here are specific and practical ways I would create a healthy connection cadence with your most valuable relationships.

- **Visionaries** – Among all of your relationships, some will be long-term visionaries. Engage them early when you need to bounce ideas regarding your direction or destination in, say, three to five years. Visionaries pride themselves on their foresight, so send them the trends you've seen and ask questions about trends that excite and concern them.

- **Risk Collaborators** – These are your relationships in the startup world, the ones running incubators and accelerators, the angel investors, or venture capital firms. You know that many have a higher risk tolerance and will be great for gauging risk if you're exploring a job change or any type of a big leap. Similarly, ask for their deal flow and investment thesis. You can also add a great deal of value here if you introduce them to relationships they need for due diligence, roll-up, or co-investment opportunities to minimize their risks.

- **Signal Scouts** – These relationships are on the absolute bleeding age of new tech. These people were into Bitcoin years ago, attend the Consumer Electronics Show (CES), and are regulars at what is sure to become the next South by Southwest (SXSW) or TED gatherings.

- **Radical Candor** – These relationships are your brutally, borderline uncomfortable candor types. They have a heightened BS radar, and they have no problem (or, sometimes, filter) in sharing their views. You need their realism, so bounce ideas off of them, engage them in a heated discussion, and really understand the sources of their unique perspectives.

- **Innovation Sponsors** – These relationships have the professional acumen, and often very strong relationship portfolios, to support your ideas to think and lead differently. Gauge their opinions and perspectives, ask how they were able to accomplish their last remarkable success, and leverage their ability to distill the most creative ideas to those that will gain traction in your efforts forward.

Be mindful to never waste three of your strategic relationship's biggest assets: their time, relationships, or resources. Only when you bring a balanced approach to this pattern will you see real impact in your path. Too many interactions too fast indicates that you are desperate or unpolished. If you are too aloof, you'll seem uncommitted.

SUSTAINED RELEVANCE

While on your path to identifying and engaging potential Curve Benders, you want to ensure that you remain *sustainably relevant*. Steady momentum, engagement, and influence demonstrate your commitment to personal and professional growth and remaining top of mind to promising Curve Benders. You are not static; nor should your personal Growth Guide be. Rather, you need to make sure that your growth strategy is appropriate and connected to your ideal outcomes for the long haul. That comes with sustainable relevance.

Curiosity must become your spark plug that ignites continual questioning of *why* things happen, not just *what's* happening. Jordan Poppenk (PhD) is the Canada Research Chair in Cognitive Neuroscience at Queen's University. Poppenk focuses on what he calls *thought worms.* Each new thought creates new activity patterns in the brain, aka a new *worm.* He designed a method to pinpoint the beginning and end of a thought. This allowed him to isolate specific moments when subjects focused on a single idea. Poppenk and his team were able to measure 6,200 distinct thoughts, or worms, in a single day.[13]

What sets you up to be sustainably relevant is a thirst for lifelong learning. Lifelong learning is a conspicuous and valuable trait of the most successful leaders I've ever met. They seldom think of themselves as an expert in anything, but rather an eternal student of their passion. They thrive on the continual learning and growth process, which helps them create enormous value in their brands, organizations, and groups they belong to. Lifelong learners, driven by the outcomes of their learnings and growth, sustain their relevance. As Friedrich Nietzsche remarked, "The doer alone learneth."[14] While most professionals aim to grow linearly, sustainable relevance seekers are fundamentally after a non-linear growth trajectory. Let's discuss the fundamental differences between the two.

LINEAR VERSUS NON-LINEAR GROWTH

Linear and non-linear growth are profoundly different paths in your personal and professional development. Figure 3.2 illustrates the difference between linear and non-linear growth.

Linear growth, Path A, is straightforward. It is defined by adherence to the superposition principle and comprised of two attributes:

1. **Additivity** – When we add the output of two systems together, the result will be merely a simple addition of each system's isolated output. For all linear systems, the net response caused by two or more stimuli is also the sum of each stimuli's individual response. For example, if you learn a new skill and apply it to your job, you'll be that much better at it.

2. **Homogeneity** – The output to a linear system is always directly proportional to the input. So, if we put twice as much into the system, we will in turn get twice as much out.

For example, if I pay $50 for a hotel room, I get a certain quality of service. This principle states that, if I pay twice as much, I will get an accommodation service that is twice as good. If you learn a new skill and add it to what you already knew, you'll be more efficient at it.

In Figure 3.2, you see why linear systems are called linear. The result will always be a straight 45-degree line. These principles are, of course, intuitive to us and appear simple. But behind them are a set of assumptions about how the world works.

There are a couple of challenges with the linear growth model:

1. *It assumes that scale doesn't matter.* We know that economies of scale are more efficient.

2. *It fails to capture feedback.* Something new you learn may prove that another system is obsolete.

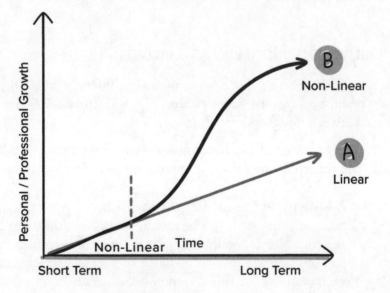

Path A – Linear Growth
Path B – Non-Linear Growth

Figure 3.2   Linear versus Non-Linear Paths in Your Personal/Professional Development

3. *Linear growth is static.* It points to your growth in a time vacuum, but our brains are always learning and creating new neural pathways. We never really stay still. That's the reality of our world and a unique attribute to our evolutionary capability as a species.

So, why use a linear growth model at all, if it's so flawed? First, it's intuitive to us. We can see that you've gotten better at using specific software after a training you attended. Static properties are real, like annual performance reviews. Also, tangible qualities of linear growth are easier for us to see and quantify. It is harder to quantify the intangible world of relationships between what we've learned and how we grow exponentially through others over time.

Second, linear growth captures the dynamics of cause and effect that we see in certain social and economic behaviors and organizational functions.

Last, and probably most significant, linear growth models remove any qualitative questions surrounding the relationships between the elements in the ecosystem. This makes them particularly amenable to questions about the quality of the training, the relevance to its applications on the job, and the enormous impact of strategic relationships in any role. For example, there couldn't possibly be a quantitative method that measures two equally educated and talented managers when one dramatically outperforms the other – unless there is a deeper dive into the applications of those assets when *combined with the relevance of each manager's strategic relationships inside and outside the organization!*

Path B is a voyage into the extraordinary world of non-linear growth. Non-linear growth is dynamic in its remarkable trajectory. Only when you understand non-linear growth's origins and embrace its inherent uncertainties can you see it when something as little as a butterfly flapping its wings influences the path of a massive hurricane. Seemingly small actions like attending an event or speaking with the presenter after having done your due diligence can result in something extraordinary. Most P&L leaders I coach have spent two to three decades building their teams, delivering financial results, and leading their organizations' strategic priorities. I wonder how much greater their impact could be if they were able to get there in half the time? This isn't about shortcuts. It's about the power of non-linear growth to accelerate their value creation timeline.

Random events will repeat themselves at various scales. When woven together, these events create the fabric of not just what we achieve, but also *who we become*. Like quantum physics, the world of non-linearity is inherently counterintuitive. It's a world where our basic assumptions start to break down, but we get incredible results. Although once the domain of obscure mathematics, non-linear systems theory and concepts are increasingly relevant in the twenty-first century.

Understanding non-linearity requires no specific knowledge of mathematics or science. Let Chaos Theory become an enabler of your growth.[15] It does require you to think less about individual transactions and more about transformations within ecosystems. In this case, think of an ecosystem as a group of related, yet independent, elements interacting toward a common outcome.

For your personal growth, interrelationships between an ecosystem's dimensions are like a kaleidoscope. The kaleidoscope's glass chambers are separate. When one looks though the lens, however, one sees a unique picture caused by the reflection of each glass chip. Twisting the tube creates a new perspective. Similarly, your vision of growth is comprised of different "chambers" or components. Those might be happiness, achievement, significance, or legacy.[16] The movement in one component, say achievement, causes new reflections in other components, like happiness, and on the sight as a whole.

When thinking about your non-linear growth, you want to look for opportunities with a straight line between a cause and its effect. The *superposition* in non-linear growth means that all the steps matter: what you're learning, how you combine and apply different modules, and the strategic relationships that guide your growth. When united, the interactions between elements create a new trajectory. This is contrary to the linear growth principles of additivity and homogeneity.

A fascinating aspect of non-linear growth is emergence. When two or more independent elements create novel and surprising new phenomena, you get out-of-the-box thinking. You might train in a new job and have a mentor from an entirely different industry. The external mentor may see the new manager, the training, and the role as ingredients. Together, these independent elements mold new approaches to past thinking or processes or challenge outdated assumptions.

Your trajectory is already set in a non-linear path once we deal with training, development, and growth through your relationships in the real world. Our interactions with our strategic relationships will become more robust and realistic the more we incorporate them into our growth model. The slope of that non-linear curve, I believe, is directly impacted by the quality of relationships you infuse into your personal and professional growth efforts.

FIVE STEPS THAT ACCELERATE YOUR RELEVANCY

The first step to accelerate your relevance is *intentional deep reflection*. I believe that most of us don't take the time or make the space for this. To succeed, you need a space for gratitude for all you have. Don't focus only on your shortcomings but make a fair of appraisal of them.

Specifically, asking meaningful and reflective questions such as:

- Where do I believe I am today in my personal and professional growth journey?

- What do I believe is going particularly well, and where are my growing edges?

- What do I enjoy learning, and what am I particularly curious about? How can I find reinforcement for learning and curiosity from my past positive experiences?

- Beyond passive efforts, how can I take part in highly experiential learning opportunities?

- How can I extend my learning beyond professional development to opportunities that bring me real jobs, help expand my horizons, and explore new hobbies?

- What am I doing to share those learnings with others and guide their growth journey?

With your preliminary personal reflections, it's time to explore a listening tour. I use this technique in coaching my clients. I've found a fundamental gap between our self-perceptions and how others perceive us. What we believe is a fundamental strength may be seen as a detriment by others. What we may discount as unconscious behaviors, others may notice and admire. Thus, I've found that listening to your most valuable relationships is worthwhile.

The key to an effective listening tour is to make a list of the top 10 to 30 relationships you like and respect. These highly valuable and strategic relationships should be potential Curve Benders. It is ideal if you don't feel obliged to impress these individuals and can ask them five questions:

1. What do you believe I am exceptionally good at?

2. Where do you believe are my growing edges?

3. Knowing me as well as you do, what do you envision this next chapter of my life or career to encompass?

4. If I were to invest in one or two areas of my personal and professional growth, what do you believe would be the highest ROI?

5. What question am I not asking if I really do aim to grow exponentially in the next decade?

Ensure that you create a safe space for their candid input and insist on it. Ask for specific examples when appropriate. Regardless of what they say, it's critical that you thank them for their time and insights. Even if you don't agree with their comments or perspectives, their time is a gift. Lastly, it's critical for your most trusted relationships to feel that you heard their input. You should show them the changes you're making if you ever want them to invest their time and effort again.

Here is the best way to capture your skills, competencies, and behavior gaps as they relate to your journey from now to next: put them on *one* page and share them with your prospective Curve Benders! This is a gesture of transparent reflection and a genuine ask for help.

Vulnerability is incredibly powerful with the right relationships to explore how they can help, support, or propel you to new heights.

The results of these conversations are often a new lens, question, or contact that I wouldn't have if I hadn't engaged my strategic relationships in this manner. That is my litmus test: Do I improve my questions, ideas, or relationships 1% each day from every interaction?

The second step in accelerating your relevance is to *examine your definition of success*. Not what your parents drove into you, your efforts to keep up with the Joneses, or other people's expectations. Detail a thoughtful, future-backward look at what it means to reach your full potential. During his 2005 commencement address at Stanford, Steve Jobs said, "You can't connect the dots looking forward; you can only connect them looking backwards. So, you have to trust that the dots will somehow connect in your future."[17] I see that notion through a slightly different lens: If I create a clear picture of what success means to me in the future, could I work my way backward to identify how I can get there? This to me is slightly different than future planning – taking a known present and extrapolating it forward. Instead, it's a nebulous future-backward lens that becomes clearer the closer I get to today.

Ask any of your potential Curve Benders their definition of success. You can likely describe most of their responses in one of two categories: personal or professional growth! When we learn, we often become more confident and diligent in our pursuits, which contributes to our growing competencies. When we grow, our realm of responsibilities expands, and our talent is directly correlated to value creation. When we apply the same growth to our personal lives, we similarly experience enhanced value creation.

I believe that discretionary time is the real definition of wealth and success. Discretionary time to do *what* we want, *when* we want, *how* we want to do it, and, most importantly, *with whom* we want to experience it makes us happy and improves our condition without financial constraints or considerations.

Curve Benders also have an interesting way of teaching us that we don't fail; we learn. This rephrasing makes our inquiry, experimentation, and exploration dramatically less prone to fearing failure. Curve Benders make time for us and often introduce us to other brilliant people we would not have had a chance to meet otherwise. Many of these new connections have accomplished unbelievable personal and professional triumphs. Curve Benders encourage us to create incredible value in what we're working on, not the job we're tied down to.

Use extraordinary caution with relationships that you can identify, nurture, and sustain so that the ones you choose can become truly strategic. Additionally, use a trusted sample of those strategic relationships – those that demonstrate true curve-bending potential – to redefine your personal and professional success metrics.

The third step in accelerating your relevance is to *leverage your refraction points* I mentioned in the Introduction (repeated here as Figure 3.3). Refraction is when light, sound, water, or other waves bend as they pass from one transparent substance into another. This bend makes lenses, magnifying glasses, prisms, and rainbows possible.

It is normal to feel more discomfort and discontentment at the critical refraction points. At these negative events, you have reached a personal plateau in your role or realm of responsibilities. In my

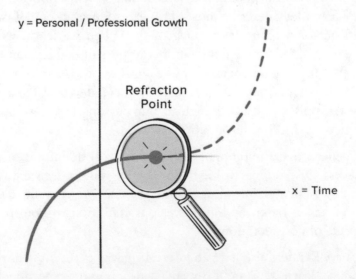

Figure 3.3   Figure I.1 from Introduction – Refraction Point

executive coaching work with global leaders, when we've closely exam-
ined a plateau, we've uncovered signs of burnout that had been present
for some time. If not addressed, burnout can lead to a professional or a
personal downward spiral.

It's important to point out that not all refraction points are negative. Some are fortuitous or incline you toward a new exciting
path forward.

The fascinating aspect of refraction points is that they seldom
surprise. Whether positive or negative, most of us have foreseen this
crucial point coming for some time. However, we have ignored the
leading drivers or postponed the inevitable. We've been bored, distracted, or otherwise uneasy about the accelerated pace of external
change around us without recognizing the same adaptation
from within.

When you change your angle and accelerate your journey through
a challenging time, your path will refract and show you alternative possibilities (Figure 3.4). That's where your strategic relationships come
in. I've found these select relevant individuals to be phenomenal
sounding boards when I share my seemingly insurmountable obstacles.
I'm always amazed by the questions they ask or the perspective they
share that I hadn't thought of. Suddenly, I see a crack in my obstacle,

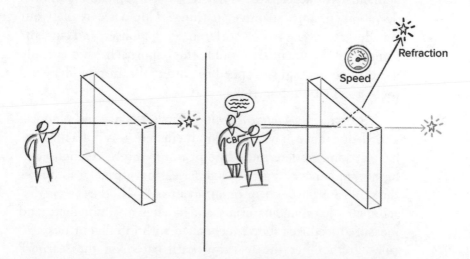

Figure 3.4   Change Your Angle and Accelerate Your Journey

ways to work around it, or alternatives to consider and explore. Behind every refraction point is a relationship that triggers a change of state.

The fourth step in accelerating your relevance is to *adapt and accelerate your learning*. One fundamental enabler of non-linear growth is the speed with which you approach your refraction points in your personal S-curve. Adaptive and accelerated learning is your rocket fuel.

We must embrace acceleration of internalizing, synthesizing, and applying ideas. We can no longer afford to learn-learn-learn and then maybe look for possible applications. Work in the future will move too fast for us to apply this lethargic development approach. We must learn-try-fail-adapt-try again. We need to grow through this accelerated process, accept setbacks, and rebrand failure as growth moments. A critical step here is to destigmatize failure.

Let's take a closer look at what must happen differently in each key enabler of this transformation:

- **Adaptation** –The learning challenges around new knowledge that professionals face today include disengagement, lack of customization, the forgetting curve, and too little time. In the future, time pressures will continue while changing skill demands will accelerate. What if we reorganized traditional development into adaptive learning? Could we realign our learning according to our preferences, responses, and current/ future role demands? Could this approach dramatically increase absorption and speed the internalization of ideas and their systematic application?

  So, what is *adaptive learning*? First, it is narrow, practical knowledge that can be applied immediately. It is not a nice-to-have at some undetermined point in the future. Second, it's a highly immersive, digitally led series that directly addresses the skill gap. Through automation and AI/ML, the system disseminates learning materials and creates an immediate and measured feedback loop mechanism with intelligent business rules. It modifies the learning path based on the learner's unique learning preferences. It's dramatically more accessible to an increasingly remote and global audience.

Why should you prioritize adaptive learning in your own personal and professional growth journey?

1. It addresses the single biggest challenge we all face: lack of time for L&D.

2. It keeps you engaged in your learning experience.

3. It's an antidote for the forgetting curve. *HBR* noted that we forget 75% of new information in just six days if it isn't applied in the real world.[18] That's why blending adaptive learning into your workflow will help maximize absorption and retention.

4. Adaptive learning is the connective tissue to successful collaborations with your multigenerational workforce.

5. Adaptive learning modifies your path as you learn and grow. This means that your workplace learning will evolve as fast as your expectations.

• **Acceleration** – We must also accelerate the speed with which we internalize and apply new ideas. But how? Can we train our brains to soak in and retain new information faster and better? How can we apply it automatically when and where we need it? If you understand how you learn, the answer is yes.

Scott Young is the author of *Ultralearning: Master Hard Skills, Outsmart the Competition, and Accelerate Your Career* (Harper Business, 2019). Young gained fame for teaching himself the four-year MIT computer science curriculum through their Open Courseware platform in just 12 months. He asked whether he could pass the final exam and do the programming projects for each of the 33 classes he took. His journey was close to what an MIT student would take. Could he do it more effectively than going to school? Like binge-watching an entire season of a show, he watched the videos on his own schedule at 1.5 times the speed. When he became confused, he paused and hit rewind. Instead of struggling through an entire assignment, he'd work on one problem and double-check his understanding of it against the solution. He would gauge whether he learned the concept sufficiently enough to move on; otherwise, he'd investigate his shortcomings.

He believes that anyone can use his fast, focused learning style, whether to master coding, become fluent in a foreign language, or excel at public speaking. Instead of cramming or speed-reading, Young advocates teaching yourself by finding people who have acquired impressive skills through self-directed learning projects. His research concluded that the right recipe was to focus on exactly what you most need and care about instead of mastering an arbitrary curriculum developed by someone else. By figuring out exactly what skill you want to acquire, how others have learned it, and what resources are available, you can accelerate your path through the process.

So, how can you combine both adaptation and acceleration in your learning? Prioritize the most relevant skills, knowledge, and behaviors that you need to learn right now. This is where Curve Benders are brilliantly helpful. By sharing your key challenges and growth opportunities and why you believe this next path is your best option, you can benefit from their experiences. Since most Curve Benders will be several steps ahead of you in their personal and professional experiences, the investment in a relationship with them will further clarify your journey from now to next.

One final note about adaptation and acceleration of your learning: it's critical that you practice your new skill or knowledge quickly. It is tempting to accumulate as much knowledge as possible for mastery, but skills can only be honed with practice.

Let's bring accelerating your relevancy home with the fifth and final step that has injections and inquiry: *relational relevance*. Relational relevance is about staying top of mind with your strategic relationships and elevating your personal brand above the market noise. Staying sharp is a byproduct of this campaign.

I refer to it as a *campaign* because:

- It must be deliberate, strategic, and quantifiable. Only your most strategic relationships will be curious enough to question what you do with their input and expect you to follow through (vs. simply follow up) in your interactions with them.

- Relationship nurturing requires a consistent communication strategy and frequency for each person to catch up on the other's progress. Your strategic relationships will be curious about your journey – the successes or missteps you've learned from.

- It's a lot like creative problem-solving, fueled by six unique reinforcers of its ultimate success:[19]

   1. You must remain continually curious about every element of your challenge/growth opportunity.

   2. You must be willing to tolerate imperfection and have a high tolerance for ambiguity.

   3. You must see the same challenge/opportunity through multiple lenses.

   4. You must be willing to pursue multiple options and experiment with each relentlessly.

   5. You must tap into your broader relationship ecosystem for unique perspectives.

   6. You must engage others in visionary storytelling to influence their thinking and call to action.

Randy Seidl launched The Sales Community in September 2020. His *global pandemic moment* was the realization that a global technology sales community of front-line contributors, managers, and executives didn't exist, unlike communities for legal, accounting, or other professional roles. After some 150 conversations over the summer with sales friends and colleagues, he identified that *learning* was the single biggest motivator among this community. Learning from his relational relevance, he focused on learning from the best:

- Sales and CEO executives

- CXO clients the industry sells to

- Channel partners to sell with

- Sales and methodology experts

- Peers calling on the same or similar accounts or verticals
- Executive coaches who would attract his ideal community members

So far, Seidl and his team are off to a great start with over 200 members in a global Advisory Board and thousands of community members. I'm not sure if he would have gotten the community off the ground without relational relevance.

CHAPTER 3 SUMMARY

1. This chapter was all about how you can make yourself appealing to potential Curve Benders; it takes a lot of active work.

2. Seven steps pave a path to your Curve Benders: personal foundation, professional commitment, catalyst, immersive inquiry, strategic relationships, agile execution, and connection cadence.

3. A love of lifelong learning ensures that you will cultivate sustainable relevance on your personal and professional growth journey.

4. There are two kinds of growth: linear and non-linear. Following non-linear growth will have substantially larger, and longer-term impact on your growth journey.

5. There are five steps to accelerate your relevancy: reflecting for relevance, redefining success, leveraging refraction points, adaptive and accelerated learning, and relational relevance.

CHAPTER 4

Curve Benders as Risk Mitigators in Your Personal S-Curve

> Risk is like fire: If controlled, it will help you; if uncontrolled, it will rise up and destroy you.
>
> – Theodore Roosevelt, 26th president of the United States, 1901–1909

In a future clouded with uncertainty, your strategic relationships become a lighthouse to help you see and act clearly. In this chapter, we focus on the strategic value of Curve Benders as risk mitigators, and the fundamental need for your continued reinvention via your personal S-curve.

The risk landscape for global leaders is rapidly changing in its composition and impact. Risk management, as a discipline, is evolving, affecting how leaders identify the early stages of potential risk and manage the risk profile and its ultimate consequences. P&L leaders no longer simply aim to minimize risk, but view risk as a value-creation tool to achieve higher performance levels, accelerate their execution, and drive greater results.

Curve Benders serve as risk mitigators by helping you continuously ask yourself: *Will I be able to quickly harness trends to increase my market value, expand my portfolio of relationships, and become more resilient in the face of uncertainty?* (See Figure 4.1.)

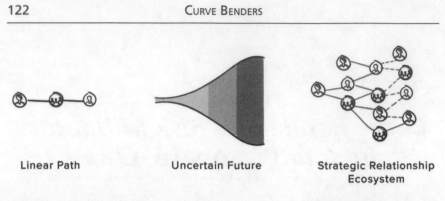

Linear Path   Uncertain Future   Strategic Relationship
                                                        Ecosystem

Figure 4.1   Which Approach Do You Believe Would Most Help in Anticipating Risk?

RELATIONSHIP INTELLIGENCE

In our past, reports of reduced or eliminated jobs have been greatly exaggerated. In fact, in many industries, technology has created more viable, higher-wage jobs than it has wiped out. Nevertheless, some of us have feared these technological developments. The "Luddite fallacy" refers to the thinking that new technology leads to job loss; this belief led some nineteenth-century textile workers to smash a new weaving machinery that made their skills obsolete. In *Humans Need Not Apply: A Guide to Wealth and Work in the Age of Artificial Intelligence*[1] (Yale University Press, 2015), Stanford University professor Jerry Kaplan stresses that automation is "blind to the color of your collar." Regardless of your role, automation and advanced technologies will dramatically impact the future of how you'll work, live, play, and give.

It has been almost a decade since Deep Knowledge Ventures, a Hong Kong–based venture capital firm, appointed a software algorithm, VITAL, to its Board of Directors.[2] Just like other members of the board, VITAL gets to vote on whether the firm should make specific investments in portfolio companies or not. The VITAL algorithm scans an estimated 50 variables, including the prospective company's financials, clinical trial data, intellectual property portfolio, competitive landscape in the market, and previous funding rounds. VITAL possesses exponential brainpower. The board won't move on an investment decision without their "colleague's" corroboration. The CEO credits VITAL with saving the firm from multiple investments that went bad after it recommended passing on the offers.

In the face of uncertainty, strategic relationships provide invaluable insights. Where business intelligence data focus on unique company-centric metrics, relationship intelligence focuses on interpersonal interactions between individuals. Recent research shows that in fast-moving turbulent environments, individuals who can tap into their social relationships are best placed to turn uncertainty into innovation.[3] When captured, analyzed, and used fully, strategic relationships can help dramatically elevate your capacity for understanding, planning, problem-solving around, and communicating to drive your desired outcomes.

Although relationship intelligence is not based on emotional intelligence (EQ), they're highly correlated: how you identify and capitalize on your strategic relationships will directly impact your success.

In the previous chapter, I outlined seven steps to pave your Curve Benders path and we discussed how to accelerate your relevance. Let's combine those into the five key areas Curve Benders can provide relationship intelligence (Figure 4.2).

1. **Catalyst** – As you explore new frontiers, it is critical that you have a clear and succinct vision for a different future and the path to get there. You should combine this vision with a strong personal foundation and a commitment to deliver your current role's expectations. Your catalyst for change could be simple, complicated, or complex. Nevertheless,

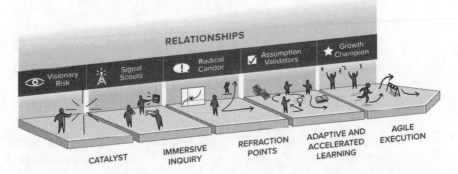

Figure 4.2 Five Key Areas Curve Benders Can Provide Relationship Intelligence

these different catalyst paths all include the risk of the unknown journey. To discover your catalyst for change, you must explore overly optimistic risk assessments. Only the confident change the status quo with a "nothing to lose" or "no choice" mindset.

Curve Benders can serve as your *visionary risk* guide. Unpredictable or inconsistent reactions to outside forces scatter your thinking, waste valuable efforts, and hinder your ability to move key ideas forward. Curve Benders can help recognize your shortcomings and fill in your gaps. They can serve as brilliant thought partners for introspection and self-awareness. They can help push beyond possible shortcomings in skills or knowledge. If your catalyst for change is overly impractical and unrealistic about market changes and outside threats, Curve Benders help you establish and communicate a clear vision and direction, as well as remind you to reinforce it repeatedly.

2. **Immersive Inquiry** – Once you've homed in on your catalyst for change, immersive inquiry becomes your deep consumption of that topic. This contextual inquiry requires a targeted plan. You must be in a relevant environment with necessary ecosystem attributes, input from multiple stakeholders, interpretation of your raw data acquisition, and the maturity to leave out your biased solutions.

In this vital phase of risk exploration, Curve Benders serve as your *signal scouts*. In my experience, the trends that dramatically impact our lives tend to leave breadcrumbs. They begin as *faint signals*. They appear as anomalies that people observe, stumble upon, or proactively discover. From a highly diverse portfolio of relationships, at least one person will provide an early warning. We knew what a pandemic was, yet warnings of a pandemic were typically ignored, despite the evidence of SARS and Ebola. Globally, we have an early warning system (EWS) for volcanic, earthquake, tsunami, and flood hazards.

An effective EWS requires an extensive observation and communication system. It must integrate vast areas of expertise, thresholds, tipping points, and reliable communication media.[4] The same goes for your network of strategic relationships. In this phase, Curve Benders can convey risk levels in an easy-to-understand format, ensure credibility, and be honest about a risk's potential consequences. On top of that, they can provide lessons from their experience and translate their observations into alerts and responses.

3. **Refraction Points** – These are unique points of discomfort or discontentment in your personal and professional growth. They're your impetus to reinvent a key part of your work or life. You realize that you've reached a plateau in your role, have outgrown your team or organization, and need to make a real change. Not all refraction points are negative or a downward pressure in your professional track, whether triggered within or external to your organization. They can also lead to a highly optimistic and inspiring new chapter in your life.

Curve Benders are an excellent source of *radical candor* in this phase of your risk evaluation. In its most basic form, *radical candor* is a framework to facilitate kind, clear, and sincere discussions.[5] They function well here because they can simultaneously care for you personally and directly challenge your key assumptions. During your refraction points, you experience heightened anxieties and may exaggerate the discomfort of uncertainties. Curve Benders in this phase usually focus on gauging your input and encouraging feedforward without false pretenses. Their honesty becomes invaluable around your fear, avoidance, competing priorities, and compliance-driven reasons to change. As your risk becomes more tangible, Curve Benders can assess upside value of risk very accurately and encourage the desired level of risk-taking behavior. They aim to balance your potential risk with possible rewards.

4. **Adaptive and Accelerated Learning** – In the previous chapter, we discussed accelerating your relevancy, and I highlighted the need to adapt and accelerate your learning. The speed with which you approach your refraction points is fueled by your ability to adapt to your challenges to learn. This accelerates internalizing an idea and applying it immediately. When it comes to risks in your life, the same fuel gets you beyond the intellectual understanding of the need for change and leads you to action. In the face of a risky or ambiguous situation, individuals exhibit a curiosity that leads them toward closing those knowledge gaps.[6] Similarly, in this phase of exploring risk, you'll make plenty of assumptions about key pieces of information and individuals, whether each one moves you forward or is an anchor in your path.

   Curve Benders serve as strong litmus tests here and become your *assumption validators*. Isaac Asimov, a Boston University professor of biochemistry, warns, "Your assumptions are your windows on the world. Scrub them off every once in a while, or the light won't come in." You'll make many assumptions in your adaptive and accelerated learning about the facets of the risk you're facing. They may be shortcuts to navigate the uncertainty around you. Neuroimaging data show that our brains are masterful in convincing us that the facts we've gathered fit into a pattern. It's an energy preservation effort to avoid extra analysis.

   Curve Benders validate or void the assumptions on which we base our actions. If your adaptive and accelerated learning around a potential risk is based on false assumptions, you'll spend time and energy moving away from your desired outcomes. I call those relationships Fender Benders – more about these later in the book. Curve Benders help you minimize the opportunity costs of a risk not pursued!

5. **Agile Execution** – The final area in which Curve Benders can provide relationship intelligence is when you must focus on your acceptance and reaction to risk. Agile execution through risk requires clarity of your intent, a committed

bandwidth, and an iterative process. You can certainly choose to go at it alone, or you can leverage your network of internal and external stakeholders. Crowd-driven or sharing-based initiatives have gained broad acceptance. Growing up, our parents drove into us to never speak to strangers and certainly never get into a car with one. Yet, the vast majority of us would get into an Uber anywhere on the planet!

Curve Benders serve as your *growth champions* as you learn to share data, broadly use leading-edge technology, and are more vulnerable in revealing your uncertainties. In the future of your work and life, you'll manage risk in a manner that reflects the ecosystem around you.

POWER OF LEARNING MOMENTS

"G'day, I'm Garry!" That's Garry Ridge introducing himself at a Marshall Goldsmith MG100 gathering. Ridge is the CEO and Board Chair of the industrial lubricant and degreaser company WD-40 (NASDAQ: WDFC). Beyond his affable Australian demeanor, Ridge has an incredibly successful track record at WD-40 since becoming CEO in 1997. The company's beloved products are found in eight out of 10 American households and sold in more than 176 countries. In fact, there's a saying, "You only need two tools in life: duct tape and WD-40. If it's not stuck, and it's supposed to be, duct tape it. If it's stuck, and it's not supposed to be, WD-40 it." No wonder WD-40 enjoys a $2.5 billion market cap, and its stock has gone up 475% in the past 10 years. Ridge is equally proud of a 93% employee engagement score among his global workforce. Compare that to the most recent Gallup poll finding that an estimated 66% of people who go to work every day are either not engaged or actively disengaged.[7] He attributes consistently high engagement metrics and the employees who love working there and are optimistic about their future to a culture obsessed with learning and fearless employees.

"We want to reduce the fear of failure among our people. We say that we don't make mistakes, we have *learning moments*," Ridge told a room full of seasoned executives, coaches, and thought leaders. Ridge and the other WD-40 leaders pride themselves on building a culture where employees feel safe to express opinions without the fear of retribution. The same goes for receiving criticism, the importance of which is outlined in WD-40's company values.[8] They call their employees tribe members, not team members. They share common tribe attributes such as values, knowledge, celebration, and a strong sense of belonging. Ridge argues passionately that what keeps people in most organizations from learning is that they perceive mistakes as career-limiting events rather than opportunities to learn, and he encourages to openly share these learning moments with others in order to avoid similar errors in the future.

What's important to understand is the fundamental difference between bruises, *small failures, and* bleeding, *big failures*. For many companies and even entire industries (airlines, space, weapon systems, and emergency medicine immediately come to mind), bleeding isn't an option. The good news is that few of us work in an environment where someone could die if we make a mistake! If you can keep mistakes in perspective, you'll quickly see that most are bruises. What I've learned from over a decade of riding motorcycles is that both bikes and bodies heal. Similarly, bruises to our egos, confidence, and reputation also heal, and there's more wisdom gleaned from riding motorcycles: it's not a matter of *if* you're going to fall, but *when* and what will you learn from it.

Bruises and bleedings both heal. One can be lethal; the other aching. Foresight and perspective become invaluable when facing failure. If you can sharpen your foresight and anticipate setbacks and learning moments more accurately, you'll waste less time, effort, and money in recovery. Similarly, if you can maintain a calm, collected mindset, even amid the bleedings, you'll quickly move from the sting of the big failure to mitigating the risk of lethal damage. As I've learned in riding motorcycles, slow is smooth, and smooth is fast.

If you understand the reasons for your perceived or actualized failures, can you think of preventive measures earlier in the process? How can your Curve Benders help you turn failures into an advantage?

Actual, not actualized, is the opposite of perceived. If a businessperson can't tell if he failed or not, he's pretty bad at it.

Most people are terrified of risk because they fear trauma, adversity, and the associated stress from them. Unfortunately, our futures don't come with a roadmap. There are inevitable twists and turns from everyday challenges to traumatic events with long-lasting impacts. The perception, planning, and mitigation of risk affect people differently. Yet, research on lottery winners and paraplegics after accidents finds that people adapt over time to life-altering circumstances and highly stressful situations. In fact, failure can intensify learning because the mind focuses on the unfinished task. This results in improved future performance, thereby raising the probability of future success. For this reason, accepting failure as part of the journey helps individuals become better prepared to face adversity.[9] We learn to manage the pressure, the barrage of personal and professional demands, and the setbacks, thanks to resilience.

Resilience is an interpersonal quality that describes tireless determination in the face of challenge or high-stress situations. It is the ability to overcome and learn from failure. Back in Chapter 2, I identified Grit as one of the 15 forces that will dramatically impact our future. Grittier individuals don't give up when they bump up against blockades; they find an alternative path.

Psychologists consider that the "bouncing back" from threats, adversity, and trauma is fundamental to personal growth. Resilience is key in mitigating painful and difficult circumstances that may determine the outcome of our lives. The development of a resiliency helps us survive difficult experiences and empowers us to improve our lives along this journey.

The key to solidifying your resilient mind and mitigating risk is to prioritize your strategic relationships. A P&L leader who proactively builds an informal board of advisors comprised of members from within their organization, as well as external to it, creates a sounding board to openly discuss risk variables, mitigation options, and their real fears. When going through a difficult phase, personally or professionally, this board of advisors helps develop the leader's perspective of the validity and potential impact of any risk. Hence, P&L leaders who have been through hardship often let crisis roll off their backs. Suffice

it to say that a strong ecosystem of empathetic and understanding relationships will remind you that you're not alone amid challenging times.
Compassionate individuals who reinforce your belief in a brighter day
ahead will keep you from isolating yourself, reinforce self-compassion,
and help you in moments of adversity. I cover this in more detail in the
next section.

Strength is shown when, facing risk, you *suspend judgments* and
use radical candor with your relationships. Speaking objectively and
openly can reduce the impact of risks. Our society is increasingly con-
ditioning us to think in terms of strict dichotomies. Your political ideology exclusively belongs to the left or the right. Forcing to choose
between two extremes has led many to believe that a refusal to endorse
one position is tacit support for its opposite position. Could our primi-
tive struggle for power at work lurk just beneath the surface of polite
behavior in most meetings? I've witnessed first-hand how potentially
brilliant responses to risk become lost in agenda-laden, underground
conflicts. Great ideas are attacked and destroyed before they're even
slightly understood. Useful risk mitigation strategies are prematurely
cut off by interruptions that are completely unconnected to previous
statements.

When we suspend judgments long enough, something magical
happens. We begin to listen intelligently, think, and discuss the implications of a risk. Instead of wasting time in subversive ego-boosting
and power struggles, we show authentic vulnerability. We begin to
interact with mutual respect and stay focused on the desired outcomes
of our collaborative efforts.

Respect for yourself and relationships important in your life
begins with an open mind, curiosity, suspending judgment and, most
importantly, the willingness and ability to give others the benefit of the
doubt. Curve Benders are often precisely the nudge we need. With
their radical candor, they can create a space for us to be vulnerable.
Particularly when the stakes are high, they remind us to remember to
suspend our judgments. Our resilient minds allow us to learn and grow
despite threats, disappointments, and setbacks. We adapt and move
forward with resolve.

Bending Your Growth Curve While Avoiding Fender Benders

So far, in this chapter, we've discussed the impact of Curve Benders as potential risk mitigators. But when is the right time to call on your Curve Benders for help? As previously mentioned in our discussion of your refraction points, I've found approaching one of those to be particularly opportune. Here is what I mean:

As you can see in Figure 4.3, there are three options when your work or life approaches a refraction point:

- Path A – Accelerated Climb
- Path B – Static Recalibration
- Path C – Unfortunate Falloff

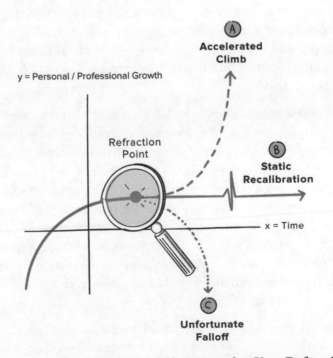

Figure 4.3   Three Options When Life Approaches Your Refraction Point

Path A: Accelerated Climb. Curve Benders have infused sufficient insights, perspective, and their strategic relationships into your journey. They have dramatically bent your growth curve in a non-linear and positive manner. You feel energized as you make significant progress to clarify your milestones; your metrics accelerate, and you're in a better condition. Doors are opening as you engage others in valuable collaborations. Your ideas are gaining traction; you're getting buy-in and support from unlikely sources. Your star is on the rise. Curve Benders have become a springboard to your success.

Path B: Static Recalibration. Staying still isn't necessarily a failure, because I believe every instance is a learning moment. If you're not learning, you're not growing. Perhaps you had anticipated being at a different place at this moment in your journey. You aspired to reach a height that hasn't hit yet. You invested time and effort, but those investments haven't yielded a return. As mentioned in the section on learning moments, here is your opportunity. Break it down and take a step back to see the refraction point with a clear head. Codify what didn't happen and why. Introspection is useful here as I seek to uncover what I could have done differently. I also engage my most valuable and relevant relationships.

Path C: Unfortunate Falloff. As is evident from its shape, things are clearly headed in the wrong direction. You can't help but feel like you're struggling in quicksand. What used to come easily to you is suddenly incredibly difficult. Similar to a baseball player who's in a hitting slump, you just can't turn things around. Financial conditions like being overleveraged and needing to file for bankruptcy may cause such situations. The key here is not to wallow in your sorrow. Grieve, learn, and quickly move forward. It'll be important for you to assess why your plans didn't work, but you may never figure it out. Some situations are simply unavoidable. Sometimes we blame external factors for the problems of our own making.

Path C has another unfortunate attribute, in that not all relationships are uplifting. In some scenarios our excitement or desperation regarding circumstances affect our judgment. We may be attracted to people who hold us back, challenge our faith in humanity, or betray our confidence. Worse, they may lie, cheat, and steal from us. These individuals cost you time, effort, and resources. Above all, they become incredibly damaging to your personal brand and reputation. If iron sharpens iron, these people are the mud.

How could so many intelligent, reputable – dare I say, world-class – people have been so spectacularly gullible when it came to Bernie Madoff's $65 billion Ponzi scheme? Or Elizabeth Holmes's improbable Theranos fraud to the tune of $9 billion?

Bernie Madoff's deception goes back decades. Legal documents disclosed that some of his closest associates turned a blind eye to early warning signs. The 70-year-old man bullied most of them. The Fairfield Greenwich hedge fund, with $14 billion under management, was among the biggest "feeder funds" to Madoff's investment scheme. Their profit was $100 million annually from their involvement with Madoff, and they made little effort to monitor what he was doing with their customers' money. Jeffrey Tucker, the co-founder of Fairfield, was a former Securities and Exchange Commission (SEC) official.[10]

In another field, investors were blinded by the inspiring story of Elizabeth Holmes. Holmes was a 19-year-old Stanford dropout with a vision: create a revolutionary way to test for illness and disease with a single drop of blood in minutes. This technology would have been a game-changer. She won the trust of corporations like Walgreens, respected leaders such as Henry Kissinger, and former Defense Secretary Jim Mattis. She was on the cover of reputable publications such as *Forbes* and *Fortune*. Then, the world discovered that none of the technology worked. To me, the fascinating psychology behind her deception is that in multiple interviews, Elizabeth didn't think she was doing anything wrong and showed no sign of guilt.[11]

The easiest way to describe these toxic relationships is to refer to them as *Fender Benders*!

Here are three distinct phases to detect, disengage, and discard Fender Benders from your personal and professional life. Pay close attention to warning signs (Figure 4.4) in each phase. Don't walk away – run as quickly as possible!

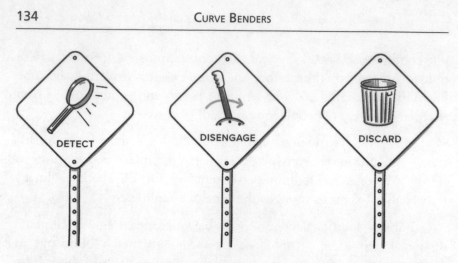

Figure 4.4 Three Phases in Dealing with Fenders Benders in Your Personal/Professional Life

- *Detect* – Let's begin with several yellow flags early in your interactions:

  - Fender Benders are typically disorganized, scattered in their initial interactions, lazy, or indifferent to doing any real work.

  - They have a complete disregard for the time, effort, or resources of others.

  - You perceive their modus operandi to be inconsistent, with no real digital footprint or mixed reviews.

  - You don't understand their brand, or they're vague in the value they create for others.

  - You don't sense much intellectual or professional depth in a business setting, credibility in their chosen field, or a positive repute online.

  - You may have multiple interactions before ever meeting in person, and you realize they tend to exaggerate, bend the rules (or the law), and conveniently forget or outright disregard societal norms.

  - They seem to be void of a moral compass, and you can't nail them down to specific answers, timelines, or processes.

- If you've read any of my work on relationship economics, you'll recognize them as classic relationship takers. The only time they reach out is when they want something, and every conversation inevitably becomes about them – interestingly, this is also the classic definition of a narcissist.

- They seldom, if ever, offer to help you or add value to your world.

- They may also be polished, buttoned-down, and present an odd story that seems too miraculous to be true.

- They may come across as overbearing, bullying, or having a time-sensitive proposition that "everyone is interested in."

Thankfully, most people have the means to nip this pseudo-relationship in the bud. Others, reluctantly, or influenced by a recommendation from someone they appreciate, agree to meet or otherwise further engage with these individuals.

- *Disengage* – When you meet, their offline presence is consistent with their online persona you discovered in advance.

  - It's normal for them to cancel calls and meetings or just not show up.

  - When they do show up, they're incredibly scattered.

  - Their ideas are half-baked, and it's clear that they've done zero homework or synthesizing of your previous discussions.

  - I put incredibly arrogant people, know-it-alls, and unprofessional name droppers in this bucket as well.

  - Inauthenticity oozes from their every word, and the way they carry themselves gives you an uneasy feeling.

  - Your intuition says, "This person is more likely to dilute my brand than to enhance it."

  - In interactions with others, their demeanor is embarrassing or uncouth. At a business dinner years ago, I actually had one "colleague" grab the final shrimp off of someone else's plate while the waiter was clearing the table! I wanted to melt into my chair around other executives I had invited to our group dinner. Needless to say, we weren't colleagues for long.

- They seem to have no filter between their brains and their mouths, and are often their own worst enemy.

- The kiss of death is when these individuals bring up financials that don't add up. They mention an economic model that greatly benefits them without an equitable position commensurate with others' efforts and way too early in your discussions.

You need to find an exit ramp from these types of individuals as quickly as possible. Be extremely cautious in sharing any confidential information about yourself, your business, organization, or aspirations with these individuals. Their lack of integrity makes them incredibly unreliable confidants.

- *Discard* – After your initial interactions, they seldom follow up or follow through.

  - It's nearly impossible to nail them down to deliver on their commitments.

  - They have more excuses for why something didn't/doesn't/can't happen than resolutions for obstacles.

  - They're unreliable and noncommunicative.

  - They make you chase them to get things done via multiple requests.

  - They have selective hearing in each conversation and selective memory of key discussions.

  - It's clear that their integrity or value system shifts with the direction of the wind.

All of these characterizations highlight a deeper truth: these individuals promise the world, but they're incapable of delivering it. Most are unwilling to do the difficult work necessary to succeed. So, they're always looking for shortcuts in life, without any of the hard work, commitments, or investment of their own resources. All these factors signal degrading the relationship's value.

My counsel is to always be cordial but firm with your boundaries and disengage.

Your Personal S-Curve

Curve Benders, in many ways, are similar to the evolution of bridges, from the simple stone arches of our past to the swooping suspension bridges that run for miles. They go beyond their inherent ability to help us mitigate risk like falling in a river or off a cliff. Curve Benders can also create unparalleled access to new opportunities and get you to the other side faster than you could before.

The deck, the central horizontal platform of a bridge, has no support directly beneath it. Yet, bridges tend to last for years due to two large forces that stabilize its function: *compression* and *tension*.

Compression is a push or a squeeze inward, and *tension* is a stretching force pulled outward. These two forces channel the bridge's total weight alone or when rolled on. Compression and tension counteract gravity, which is why so few bridges fall (Figure 4.5).[12]

Gravity, that pervasive force in the universe that tugs objects down, acts on our personal and professional growth – except in business and life, what pulls us down from our growth is *complacency*. We

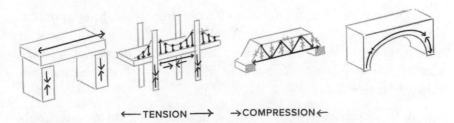

← TENSION →   → COMPRESSION ←

Figure 4.5   The Impact of Compression and Tension on Bridge Design
Source: Inspired by 10 of the world's most incredible bridges.

need to stay challenged to avoid becoming complacent. Educationist Nevitt Sanford argued that challenges are one of the keys to personal development. Sanford believed that the best way to grow is to experience psychological disequilibrium, an unsettling stimulus that alters or disrupts one's existing beliefs or understanding.[13]

Likewise, I've long believed that no growth comes from a place of comfort. Don't confuse complacency with contentment. You can be incredibly content with your work, but when complacency creeps in, you are reluctant to build bridges to extend your growth. Further, you may build them poorly or neglect to maintain them. These various forms of inaction all imperil your future success. In order to grow, you need compression and tension in your personal and professional growth.

Compression and tension can be correctly applied when you understand your personal S-curve, also known as life cycle thinking or the "sigmoid curve." This is how you'll measure your non-linear growth practically. This was first used by management thinker Charles Handy, who applied the S-curve to organizational and individual development in the mid-1990s.[14]

The S-curve is fundamentally based on the theory of the *diffusion of innovation*: explaining how, why, and at what rate new ideas spread. Everett Rogers popularized this in his book, *Diffusion of Innovations*.[15] Initially published in 1962, Rogers insisted that four distinct elements heavily influence the spread of a new idea, with a need to be widely adopted to self-sustain: *the innovative product or service itself, communication channels, time,* and *social systems*. His focus here was to highlight that these elements are combined, and they create total influence on a potential adopter.

Within the rate of adoption over time, there is a definite moment where the innovation reaches a critical mass. According to Rogers, in the diffusion of innovation, clusters within social networks, be they individuals or organizations, become adopters based on their risk tolerance (Figure 4.6).

With successive groups of consumers adopting the new technology (darker curve), its market share (lighter curve) will eventually reach the saturation level. The dark curve is broken into sections of adopters.

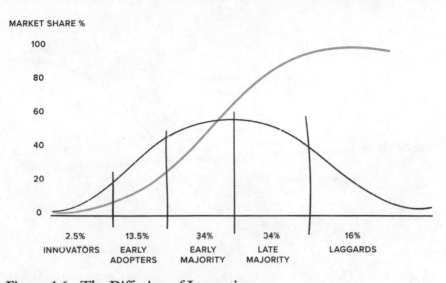

MARKET SHARE %

Figure 4.6   The Diffusion of Innovation
Source: Everett Rogers, *Diffusion of Innovations*, 5th ed. (Free Press, 2003).

The fundamental challenge in our current understanding and application of the personal S-curve is that it's *two-dimensional and static*. I believe that, in the future of how we'll work, live, play, and give, two critical forces will dramatically reshape our current perception of the S-curve:

1. **A Third Dimension in the Personal S-Curve.** Through work–life blending, discussed in Chapter 1, I believe the skills, knowledge, and behaviors we learn in one part of our life will become increasingly relevant and blended into other facets of it. For example, if learning about the physical dynamics of motorcycling around a racetrack is directly relevant to my agile cloud app development cycle at work, won't that create a more in-depth investigation on that topic? I've also met incredibly valuable relationships on the racetrack, who have definitely accelerated my professional growth on the job as well. So, now my static curve in Figure 4.6 has a 3D view of contextual relevance and depth in a topic, not just the lean sprint up the ramp (see Figure 4.7).

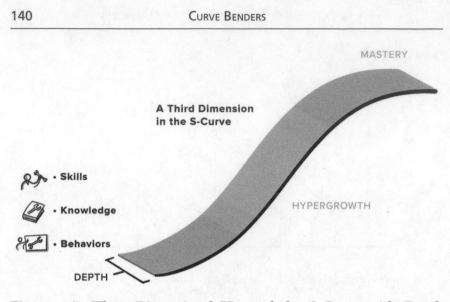

Figure 4.7 Three-Dimensional View of the S-Curve with Depth of Knowledge

2. **Continuously Shortened S-Curves.** In many industries, especially in the high-tech and digital sectors, the rate of innovation adoption is accelerating, making innovation curves steeper than ever.[16] Considering the 15 forces from Chapter 2, the ones that create a measurable tailwind will increase the accelerated change and adoption. This will force your personal S-curve to shrink continually (Figure 4.8). We're learning at an increasingly faster rate, immediately applying that learning to address complex challenges or opportunities. Multiple input sources are giving us more clarity on the skills and knowledge renewals necessary to reach the next milestone in our path.[17] If you recall adaptive and accelerated learning back in Chapter 3, Scott Young taught himself a four-year MIT degree in 12 months. In the words of the business theorist Arie de Geus, "The ability to learn faster than your competitors may be the only sustainable competitive advantage."

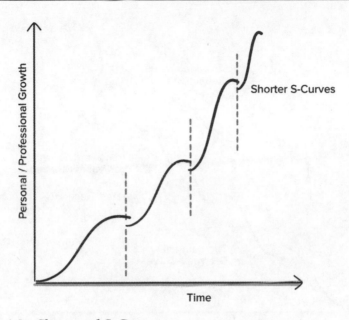

Figure 4.8 Shortened S-Curves

Now, let's apply these two fundamental shifts of an *S-curve to your personal and professional growth* (Figure 4.9):

A. **Your Current and Future Market Value:** As discussed in Chapter 1, a good starting place is to capture your current market value and estimate its future. Let's say today that the market value of someone with your expertise in your unique industry is $150,000/year. Your current compensation would go in the bottom-left corner. Next, do some research and create milestones of your estimated future market value points, say in 18, 36, 48, and 60 months out. My supposition here is that, if you're truly reinventing yourself and increasing your skills non-linearly, your market value is one possible measure to reflect your growth.

B. **The Sequential Growth S-Curves:** These curves are your projected growth journey over time in a new role, a realm of

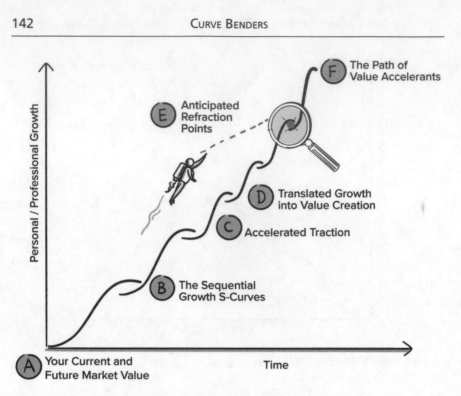

Figure 4.9   S-Curves in Your Personal and Professional Growth

responsibility, or a realignment with value creation in your organization. Each growth S-curve is moving you along a continuum of enhanced knowledge, skills, and elevated behaviors. Along the way, you're also heavily investing in your portfolio of strategic relationships. You are consistently connecting with your thought partners, collaborators, and co-creators. Completion of each individual S-curve should also enhance your market value over time.

C. **Accelerated Traction:** Your initial traction may be slow when you develop competence and deliver results within a new area of expertise. This is where Curve Benders can be an enormous asset in accelerating your traction, helping you better assess and enhance the quality of each new team, and focusing on selective, forward-thinking initiatives.

D. **Translated Growth into Value Creation:** When your initiatives are aligned with the overarching corporate strategy, and you deliver the desired outcomes, you begin to correlate your impact into organizational value creation. When combined with the right strategic relationship ecosystem, your performance, execution, and results propel you in a non-linear path forward.

E. **Anticipated Refraction Points:** Each S-curve will reach a plateau. By anticipating them, you identify these refraction points much earlier in their typical maturity cycle. You won't stay in a role where you're not learning, growing, or reaching for new heights any longer than necessary.

F. **The Path of Value Accelerants:** Your path begins to escape the traditional linear journey when you deliver on your commitments, immerse yourself in the next inquiry, and leverage your portfolio of strategic relationships. This will help you consistently learn, grow, and deliver value. This path begins to take a dramatic non-linear shape over time.

RELATIONSHIP ON-RAMPS, GROWTH BOOSTS, AND EXITS

The breakdown of refraction points earlier in this chapter helps better explain what happens at that unique point in your personal S-curve. In this section, I depict the three unique paths from the same refraction point and how relationships will direct each path (Figure 4.10).

A. **Relational On-Ramps** – Proactive opportunities to seek out and give relationships a chance to come along with you on your growth journey.

B. **Growth Boosts** – Infusions of other relationships, often through your Curve Benders, who dramatically propel you forward.

C. **Relational Exits** – Appropriate exits of those relationships that are not relevant to moving forward.

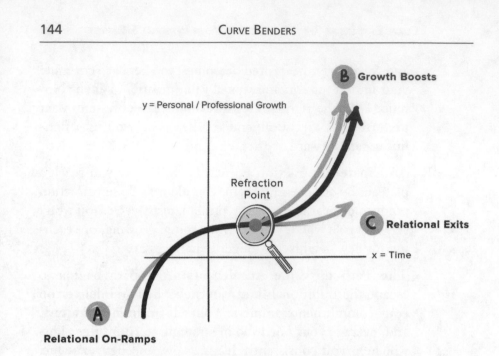

Figure 4.10   Three Possible Paths at Your Refraction Point

Relational On-Ramps – It's rather difficult to start a refraction point conversation with anyone out of the blue. As such, in the relational on-ramps, you'll need to think about three key attributes:

1. *Target Relationships* – Who's your most valuable, strategic, and relevant relationship, the one you want to invite into your personal S-curve? Who has demonstrated genuine care and interest in your success? Who has direct and relevant subject matter expertise in your refraction point? Who has a giving heart without an agenda and will serve as an enabler of your journey?

2. *Your Desired Outcomes* – What do you want these target relationships to do differently to support your thinking or behaviors? If they are to serve as a viable sounding board, shaping your new perspectives, challenging your concreteness, and leading you toward the conceptual, you'll need to capture and communicate those desired outcomes succinctly. Relationships can't help you if they don't understand where the ship is headed.

3. *Your Story* – What narrative will engage their thinking, entice their extended relationships, and influence their call to action? They don't need to know your entire life story, just what they need to know to help. They'll want to know how you've arrived here. What was your immersive inquiry into your challenge or opportunities, and what are the possible paths you're exploring?

When you create relational on-ramps, you immediately make yourself more accessible, likeable, and approachable. Brilliant ideas inside and outside of your organization find their way to your radar, and you develop a brand for uncovering or inspiring the best in others. A couple of years ago, in my keynotes at global company, industry, or academic events, I began sharing one or two pictures of my motorcycles. Some 200 people approached me in one year alone to share pictures of their bikes, stories about great bike adventures, or invite me to ride with them.

When you have the above attributes, you make an A-B-C list of the most relevant relationships, based on your depth and relevance to the refraction point. With a clearly defined set of desired outcomes, you reach out with a succinct narrative. In the pre-pandemic world, I always preferred these conversations over a meal. In a relaxed environment, I'd still feel the need to prepare to defend my positions without the crutch of a presentation. During the pandemic, I recommended my clients use virtual engagement, something I did myself, but to avoid canned presentations. I like simple visuals, like those by my friend and our creative director, Lin Wilson, in this book. One or two illustrations should depict your specific challenge or opportunity. The key is to let the relationships decide where and how much they wish to be involved in your journey. You'll learn that some simply want to provide ideas or ask you a handful of pertinent questions. Others are much more hands-on and may want to read up on your circumstance. Give them those options.

Relational Growth Boosts. Growth boosts are the express lanes. These relationships dramatically help you refine your path. Clay can't become a beautiful vase without direction, continuous refinement, and molding. Growth boosts are your guide. Not only can they help you avoid unnecessary pitfalls and serve as your guardrails against risk, but they also elevate and accelerate your journey.

Here in Atlanta, where I live, several express lanes are raised platforms. It's incredibly liberating to ride the ramps up to these express lanes and fly by above the horrendous gridlock traffic below. Growth boosts can potentially do the same: they can dissect your steps, accelerate divergent paths, and bring other critical resources/relationships into your personal S-curve (Figure 4.11).

This is all to improve your perspective, efforts, and forward impact dramatically. In *Relationship Economics*, I refer to these as Pivotal Contacts, because they can often make a single phone call or email introduction and save you hours, if not days and weeks, in the path to your desired outcomes.

But, just like our highway express lanes, they require a toll. They're only available at certain times, and exits are limited in between. Similarly, the toll you'll need to pay is often a deeper, more intimate relationship that requires more time and effort. Their available time may not align with your times of need. Possibly, they're exclusively focused on the longer-term, transformational outcomes instead of transactional next steps. So, be careful not to let your exuberance blind your judgment on when, where, and how to embrace growth boosts in your journey.

Growth boosts are able to bridge your growth from one S-curve to another. This superpower comes from their own personal journey. Think of an entrepreneur who successfully raised several rounds of capital and exited their firm, helping another entrepreneur follow in their footsteps. They may provide everything from angel capital to serving on the startup board to making vital introductions to a CTO

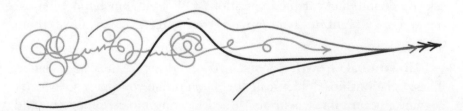

Figure 4.11   **Relational Growth Boosts Propel You Forward**

partner. They can bring in early customers and other investors and support a strategic buyer's exit. That journey doesn't happen overnight; growth boosts often deserve an equity stake in the startup. Yet, they're the classic example of how a watermelon slice is always bigger than the whole grape. That's what growth boosts do: they help you turn your grape-sized idea into a watermelon of a team or company!

Relational Exits. When does it make sense to end a relationship? This is less about diminished value than it is about diminished relevance. The exit could be from one path you may be considering, where the progression of your direction is no longer in their wheelhouse. You both know there is no point in taking up any more of the other's bandwidth. Ensure that you periodically keep them updated on your progress. I would also make sure that you never forget their kindness and generosity. Every contribution to your personal/professional growth is a gift you accept with gratitude. Finally, don't forget the fundamental law of business relationships: reciprocity. Maybe not today, tomorrow, next week, or next month, but if any of these relationships, who were instrumental in your personal S-curve, *ever* need your help, you must move their request to the top of your list and support their journey. That's how you earn the right to come back to them the next time you reach a refraction point.

A final note about your personal S-curve: it's never a linear path. You never have just *one* relational on-ramp, one exit, or one growth boost. Just like our 16-lane highways in Atlanta on I-285, you'll have multiple sources of relationship input, insights, and outcomes. The key is to learn from every single interaction every single time. It won't always be a smooth ride. Your path will get potholes, so fix them ASAP. There's always construction; that's how you'll expand and repair bridges and overpasses. Detours will force you to find another way.

The richness of your interactions increases along the journey.

CHAPTER 4 SUMMARY

1. There are five key areas Curve Benders can provide relationship intelligence: catalyst, immersive inquiry, refraction points, adaptive and accelerated learning, and agile execution.

2. We need to rebrand failure as a learning moment. We cannot be afraid of failure, and in fact we may succeed better once we do fail.

3. There are three routes for refraction: accelerated climb, static recalibration, or unfortunate falloff. Each bends your growth curve in a different direction.

4. Your personal S-curve is life-cycle thinking or the "sigmoid curve." Three-dimensional and shortened S-curves are two critical forces that will dramatically reshape the S-curve.

5. At the same refraction point three unique paths begin. The role of relationships will direct each path: relationship on-ramps, growth boosts, and exits.

CHAPTER 5

Organization of the Future

'The organizations that will truly excel in the future will be the organizations that discover how to tap people's commitment and capacity to learn at all levels in the organization.

– Peter Senge, American systems scientist

Most knowledge workers yearn to work for a company that they believe values innovation. According to research, Millennials in particular vastly favor startups over traditional corporations because they are seeking company cultures that prize innovation.[1] Did you know that there are an estimated 70,000 books on innovation available for purchase right now? A Google search returns with no fewer than 2 billion results. *HBR* alone offers some 5,000 digital articles and 10,000 case studies. In PwC's most recent Annual Global CEO Survey, 55% of the participants said, "We are not able to innovate effectively." They place innovation at the top of the talent gap.[2] The Conference Board, in its 2020 C-Suite Challenge Report, surveyed 740 CEOs globally. They listed "building an innovative culture" among the top-three most pressing internal concerns.[3] From classrooms to newsrooms and boardrooms, innovation is *the* buzz. It has become the global darling and is on every CEO's go-to playlist.

Over the past two decades, I've consulted with hundreds of executives under a broad spectrum of industries. When asked what an innovative culture looks like, most leaders in mature companies in mature industries are fairly predictable in their response: *entrepreneurial, collaborative, fun, a high tolerance for failure, with great candor among the team members*. More recently, desiderata like *psychological safety, hearing all voices, a willingness to experiment, leaning in*, and *flat organizations* have entered the popular lexicon. Who wouldn't want to work in a company with these attributes? Yet, for most people, this is a flowery wish list.

If everyone wants to work in a company that values innovation, why is it so hard to create a culture where the personal S-curve can equally be developed in teams and organizations?

There are a handful of insights I've captured regarding mature companies in mature industries and the mindset of the leadership when it comes to real innovation versus innovation theater (Figure 5.1):

- They focus and thrive from a highly transactional core business.

- They've garnered a great deal of success from perfecting their execution model.

- The business fundamentals are based on a sound business model where steadfast leadership is rewarded, like in legacy manufacturing and distribution companies.

- They've benefited from flat to moderate organic growth because of their maturity and known market dynamics. They perhaps have a fixed set of current and prospective customers and have the fundamentals it takes for flawless execution. Their overall growth and profitability are fairly predictable in

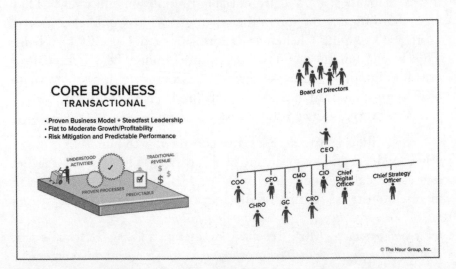

Figure 5.1 The Mature Organization's Core Business and Governance Model

light of acquisitions, divestitures, or access to abundant, cheap capital that may enable financial engineering.

- Risk mitigation is their accepted norm, primarily to avoid any surprises in the forecasting and production planning efforts.

- The governance model consists of a CEO, a capable C-suite, and board members who are typically conservative, elder statesmen and -women. In member-based organizations or trade associations, you can exchange the C-suite for an executive committee.

CORE BUSINESS BLIND SPOTS

Following are a handful of fundamental business model challenges and opportunities with the core business model and leadership/governance model as depicted in Figure 5.1:

1. **What it *really* takes to innovate.** I define iteration as doing the same thing *better*. Real innovation is about doing things *differently*. This is why it's often grossly misunderstood and mismanaged. Since none of us can pick the winners, fear and doubt circle any attempts to create new technologies, design new business models, or explore co-creation opportunities with others. People don't know what they don't know. Leaders may say that learning comes from failure, but their actions demonstrate a clear success bias. Nonetheless, failure is the oil in the invaluable lessons that move ideas forward.

However erroneously, as most mature companies see it, heavily funding a venture arm or a new innovation initiative yields speed and creativity. They'll put a tenured "insider" with decades of deeply rooted beliefs, experiences, and relationships in charge of transformation, digital, or reinvention. This insider is wedded to a raft of behaviors that inhibit the transformation he is supposed to be leading. Regrettably, many of the same mindsets fast track the organization toward obsolescence.

2. Due to many organizations' sheer size, complexity, and lack of courage from key leaders to nurture exceptional talent, **incompetence and coasting is excused, tolerated, or simply transferred**. That person didn't make it in sales? "It wasn't his fault; let's transfer him to HR or IT." "She didn't make it as a manager in this region? No problem, let's promote her to a district manager in another region." "Maybe he just needs more training or time" or "Let's get her a coach to fix her" are often the organizational Band-Aids to deflect conflict. Did you know that companies hire A-players, those high-performing unicorns, around 25% of the time?[4] Bad hires or hiring good people for the wrong needs are incredibly common in core businesses. Mediocre technical skills, an inability to critically think, a poor work ethic, and woefully inadequate management behaviors are all met with indifference. In many organizations, a high-quality standard is never set for employees.

Recently, I learned of a practice group in one of the Big Four professional services arms that hasn't hit its target performance numbers in close to a decade. Despite this poor performance, the senior partners responsible have made no real changes in the group's leadership or personnel. Sadly, thanks to their compensation system, the consultants in this practice receive the same salaries and bonuses as consultants in dramatically more productive practice groups. The unspoken truth is that the firm seldom terminates anyone for mediocre performance, short of ethical or legal violations. They can coast for decades into retirement! Even more stunning: the recent announcement that one of the leaders in the nonperforming practice made partner and ousted two levels of other leaders to take their national role. It is a dangerous precedent to keep people who clearly are out of their depth, much less promote them. It was no surprise to learn recently that an entire crop of seasoned leaders had chosen to retire.

What many leaders in these organizations fail to recognize is that it's *nearly impossible to train people to be intelligent*. Innovation, first and foremost, demands competent, intelligent people. Failure here does not come from valuable lessons that move ideas forward. It comes from flawed research and analysis, careless designs, lack of transparency in what's going well, and outright negligent management in seeking or providing timely help.

There is a dirty little secret most leaders don't want to admit: **innovation for many employees is perceived to be "extra work," or worse yet, "lost jobs."** A research team at the University of Toronto surveyed 1,000 American and Canadian knowledge workers to assess attitudes toward innovation, grit, and openness to risk. Drive for innovation broke 25% in only two of the six groups. The willingness to take risks was at 19%, as low as 11% in some groups.[5] Employees hear "innovation" and alarm bells ring in their brains with "Danger, danger! Avoid at all costs!"

3. **Experimentation is ad hoc at best.** It is shoved deep down in the bowels of most organizations. There is no discipline in how the process is initiated, resourced, or documented. It's seen as a "nice to have" and "someday" in many organizations and pushes against more pressing quarterly financial metrics. Fear of failure is institutionalized in some organizations, often derived from past painful emotions such as hurt, anger, shame, and even depression. Projects are structured, so no resources (time, effort, capital) are available for experimentation, while recognition and rewards go to those who deliver against a predetermined plan. Findings of ad hoc experiments can seldom be reproduced. These one-off tests are often dependent on a skilled tester with extensive subject-matter expertise. When it can't be replicated by others, the opportunity for broader learning and growth from the experiment is lost.

Without discipline, almost every initiative is somehow justified as experimentation. When the results are negative, this "bad news" is spun by various teams. It is described as an aberration of some kind, just to keep zombie projects going. Having your initiative canceled is terrible news for you, personally. It is a "career-limiting" black-eye status. You can even lose your job, as I was told at one client company. So, keeping your initiative alive is just a smart career move, "if you want to stick around this place for a while."

4. **Brutal candor is seldom the modus operandi** because it's incredibly uncomfortable for most people. Candid debate is viewed as uncivil. There is little to no training, development, or coaching for a culture that's unafraid of retribution. Its expectations are unclear. Speaking up is seldom celebrated among the rank-and-file. My friend and Harvard Business School professor Amy Edmundson, author of *The Fearless Organization: Creating Psychological Safety in the Workplace for Learning, Innovation, and Growth* (Wiley, 2018), has spent decades researching the organizational climate where people feel they can speak truthfully about problems without fear of reprisal. Small minds crush big ideas when people are afraid to criticize, openly challenge superiors' views, debate the validity of others' ideas, or even raise counterperspectives.

In some organizations, people are too polite. They are restrained in how, when, and with whom they disagree. Words are carefully chosen, and critique is peppered with accolades to avoid offending. Assertively challenging an idea gets you labeled offensive, condescending, or not a team player. Team members care more about being nice than right, even when the data indicate need for change. Although no one complains about a culture that's too polite, I've long believed that respectful pushback is healthy! It enhances the idea or initiative and mitigates risks because those who challenge the idea have stress-tested it in advance. If everyone is afraid of offending others, much-needed views that would help ideas are never brought up.

5. **Collaboration takes a second chair to individualism**, accountability, commitment, and results, as if they're somehow mutually exclusive. Shifting technologies and/or business priorities can make a competent individual in one context be utterly incompetent in another. That superstar sales rep, loved by clients, is now stuck in the office trying to figure out the new AI-based CRM system. He doesn't get out as much; his numbers crater, so he's let go.

Collaboration is often mischaracterized as gaining consensus. Cross-functional task forces become poison for urgent decisions.

Navigating complex problems suddenly becomes kryptonite and paralyzes any transformative efforts. Eventually, someone must make a decision, often without accountability or ownership of the consequences.

6. **Reduced bureaucracy takes courage.** Abandoning old habits takes a new purpose, and flattening the organization takes a commitment by strong leaders. The modern-day organizational structure dates back to Adam Smith, the father of modern capitalism. In 1776, he wrote about the division of labor.[6] Although the division of labor may illustrate the flatness of the company, it neglects to illustrate its culture: how people behave and interact regardless of their position.

Who stands out in these environments? Leaders who bring their personal S-curves to lead their organizations.

Imagine an organization where individuals are held accountable for their decisions. You own it, for better or worse. In these scenarios, visionary leaders who have worked on their personal S-curves are more than eager to solicit input, embrace cooperation, and encourage others to collaborate. Inside and outside the organization, everyone welcomes improving the value of an idea. So, what does bringing your personal S-curve to lead in your organization mean? It's about helping others in your team or organization challenge their assumptions through the quality of the questions you ask. It's about introducing new ideas, processes, and perspectives into the organization to dramatically, if not exponentially, help others leap beyond their current challenges to reach their future possibilities. It's about creating micro-learning sprints to immediately learn what we need to apply to that next project to improve its results.

As a board advisor to the sales community, I've interviewed well over 100 chief revenue officers, chief customer officers, CEOs, presidents, and senior executives in the technology sector. I'm fascinated by the increased migration of extremely seasoned executives from large companies (EMC, Dell, VMware, Oracle, Cisco, IBM, or HP) into smaller, venture capital- or private equity-backed, hypergrowth start-ups. These executives are leaping to operate in a more entrepreneurial, collaborative, and innovative manner. They want to attract exceptional talent, grow it, scale it, and put their stamp on a high-performing culture. It's in these smaller, venture-backed firms that they can more proactively bring their personal S-curves to their company cultures, whereas in the much larger organizations they were a cog in the wheel.

Senior leaders who clearly differentiate between valuable and useless failures set the right tone in creating a culture that balances learning and growth with performance and results. Valuable failures produce incredible insights relative to the investments to gain them. Useless failures consume millions on a product that no one wants but still launches 18 months later. All the organization discovers is that the product is an expensive and costly flop. Valuable failures come from quick prototypes that fail to perform due to a previously undiscovered technical roadblock, which is ameliorated immediately for the next iteration.[7]

Like your personal commitments in the S-curve, an organization desperately needs a culture of competence defined by a clear standard of performance. I refuse to believe that anyone wakes up, on a given day, deciding to fail. In fear of slowing down the growth of the company, hiring standards are not raised. If those standards are not communicated clearly or consistently, they're not well-understood. When performance falls short of senior leaders' expectations, the difficult decision to remove people is misconstrued as punishment for failure.

P&L leaders have a great opportunity to model innovative behaviors. They can begin by mustering up the courage to critique others' ideas constructively without being abrasive or abusive. A great way to set the tone would be to insist on criticism of their own ideas and proposals. I've been on several leadership business plan reviews for one of my favorite CEOs. He openly asks, "Here is what we've come up with that I believe in. Shoot holes in it. What am I not seeing or thinking about?" Talk about a leader who's dedicated to uncovering his own flaws and aiming for the best results. He does this through constructive and forward-thinking criticism, almost like a solemn duty by his direct reports. That is not only intentional and proactive S-curve learning and growth, but he's also demonstrating to others that he doesn't have all the answers and that the team is dramatically better off through surgical collaboration. He's not asking for grandiose ideation or some vague corporate-speak; he wants specific questions or statements to uncover his blind spots.

THE SANDBOX ENGINE

Let's compare and contrast some of the challenges of the core business with the Sandbox Engine (Figure 5.2).

In the Sandbox Engine, individuals bring their personal S-curve mindset to work every day. In their disciplined experiments, they work in small teams to research "hair on fire" problems, a term coined by my friend and longtime mentor, Charlie Paparelli, for problems that someone desperately needs to have fixed. Back in the Sandbox, they identify key target segments, often currently underserved by the core business, willing to pay a premium to solve these unique problems. They extensively research the market for alternative solutions that exist today. They simultaneously engage with a broad portfolio of internal and external relationships to conceive new insights. Their explorations are initially unconstrained and entertain a broad spectrum of ideas. They formulate testable business model hypotheses. Regardless of stature in the organization, psychological safety is bidirectional: it's as safe for me to criticize your ideas as it is for you to do the same with mine.

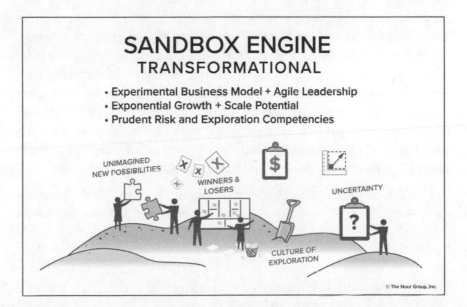

Figure 5.2   The Transformational Sandbox Engine

Leaders who embrace experimentation are comfortable with ambiguity, prudent risk, and uncertainty. They know they don't have all the answers and can only make the best available decisions with the information and insights available now. They see the incredible value of experimentation as a learning tool, rather than a producer of hit products and/or services with immediate market acceptance.

Agile and nimble cultures in the Sandbox Engine are disciplined in developing and executing their experiments. They consider the potential of the learning value, and they design a rigorous yield that balances the production of information and insights with the allocation of resources. The team members agree to emotionally detach from any single idea. They decapitate the zombie initiative even if it's someone's pet. They subject experimental data to incredible rigor. Conclusions could range from admitting flaws in the original hypothesis to execution missteps or significantly redirecting resources to other more viable experiments. From the outset, they are willing to kill 999 flowers to grow a single oak tree.

In previous references to radical candor, the subject has always been you and your personal and professional growth. The same unvarnished candor is critical in Sandbox Engine exploration. That's how ideas are nurtured, challenged, and modified. Here, people are comfortable debating and confronting internal relationships to move ideas, approaches, or business models forward. Criticism is crisp, sharp, and directed at the idea – *never* the person presenting it. It's expected that people will defend their positions with data or logic, not simply regurgitate an opinion. In the Sandbox Engine, candor is preferred over niceties every time. Here experimenters value respect more than politeness. They understand that they have earned the respect of their peers only when they provide and accept constructive criticism.

Keep in mind, people's capacity for this honesty varies dramatically. Outsiders or newcomers may consider the discussions hard-edged. For some, the debates only become invigorating when every facet of a business model design is challenged. Some are excited when strategies unravel, assumptions are voided, and perceptions of key competitors or market dynamics are disproven. Unfortunately for others, it may take some time, or they'll move on.

The Sandbox Engine also demands a culturally flat organization, where people are given wide latitude to think, make decisions, solve problems, and voice their dissent. Deference is earned with competence, not titles. These teams respond with incredible speed because decision making is decentralized and at the edge of its most direct impact on the outcomes. They're rich with diverse ideas because cognitive diversity is equally celebrated. The wide variety of ideas are created by a broad spectrum of contributors in gender and ethnicity.

Experimentation is critical to the Sandbox Engine exploration process since that's where ideas are curated, reformulated, and modified. Unlike most experiments designed to validate an idea, the Sandbox Engine explorers pursue experiments to discredit or kill an idea by uncovering the flaws in its business model. Instead of heavily funding any new experiment, they create "go/no-go" gates based on data-driven validation. They give ideas six months to survive a barrage of attacks to uncover its flaws. This rapid-cycle experimentation not only allows the team to test more ideas, but its trim structure accelerates the process, making it psychologically easier to walk away from bad ideas. The goal here is to fail in a day versus a week, a week versus a month, a month versus a year. The speed at which they fail and apply new learnings directly correlates to the acceleration of multiple S-curves chained together.

In the Sandbox Engine, data from every experiment is invaluable. When any idea yields negative data, the teams are expected to recalibrate their business models or kill it and move on. Ignoring or justifying experimental data is against their core value of transparency. Not even the most promising business model ideas survive or scale if they fail at the small level. This is why Sandbox Engines need continuous reinforcement of scientific and business acumen, prudent judgment, and the ability to discern the right time to move forward with or reformulate a business model.

Lastly, each member of the Sandbox Engine has the right metrics and incentives to adhere to discipline and consistency. There are no financial gains in staying with a flawed business model longer than necessary. The opposite is true. The real opportunity costs of pursuing a dead-end business model instead of investing in a compelling one are obvious. The real recognition comes from designing, testing, and launching a successful business model that gains market traction.

UNLOCKING REAL INNOVATION

Steve Blank, serial Silicon Valley entrepreneur, adjunct professor at Stanford, and senior fellow at Columbia, describes most organizations' efforts in innovation as one of three exercises in futility:[8]

1. *Organizational Theater.* The organization hires big-name management consultants who roll out their twentieth-century playbooks. They reorganize the company from functional groups into a matrixed one. It keeps everyone busy for a year, provides a new focus or two, but is inadequate for any type of rapid innovation.

2. *Innovation Theater.* There is a mass adoption of innovation activities, such as hackathons, design thinking classes, innovation workshops, and innovation labs. These activities often shape cultures, but they don't win wars or create useful product or service for the market.

3. *Process Theater.* The lightbulb goes off! The organization's current processes – procurement, hiring, security, legal, and the like – created for optimizing execution are impediments to innovation. So, they embark on well-intended and massive efforts to reform processes. My favorite is when they throw massive tech infrastructure upgrades as big ERP implementations; but without an overall innovation strategy, they might as well build sandcastles on the beach.

What does it take to jump past these efforts and unlock real innovation potential? How can leaders overcome the sobering statistics on the difficulty of creating serial innovation? BCG's annual top-50 most innovative companies list has featured 162 companies over the past two decades. Almost 30% have made it just once! Another 57% have only appeared two or three times. Eight companies, only eight, have made the list every year: Alphabet, Amazon, Apple, HP, IBM, Microsoft,

Samsung, and Toyota.[9] What do these eight companies have in common? A sustainable construct to unlock real innovation.

Real innovation is difficult and complex. The ripple effect guarantees unintended consequences. Shifting the culture is often the most challenging aspect of a leader's effort to transform the organization. In their efforts to lead along a different path, they're challenging the social, if not legal, contract between employees and employers. When understandings around the core business are challenged, those who thought they joined one organization and see a new one taking its place will resist. "I didn't sign on for this," is the mantra of every resister.

In their efforts to battle the onslaught of disruptive forces, many organizations simply aren't nimble enough to mobilize the innovative talent and technology they need to make it a fair fight. So, they play a form of whack-a-mole to swat at problems that keep popping up, without a real understanding of what's happening and why. In many organizations, their great management processes are seen as their biggest strength. Yet, those same processes become their biggest obstacle and hold them back from responding to new challenges. They are anchored by the idea that leadership is always at the top.

Rapidly shifting patterns of supply, demand, market behaviors, and business model maneuverability make the Sandbox Engine imperative for serial innovation. I coach my CEO clients and their board on the aspects of the required mindset shift:

1. **Courage** – It takes courage to set an ambitious agenda and fund promising opportunities.

2. **Commitment** – It takes size to transform opportunities into real sources of net new revenue growth.

3. **Construct** – It takes a well-defined innovation system to rinse and repeat for serial success.

Courage from any CEO in exploring new frontiers requires a combination of contradictory behaviors. They risk creating confusing messages up, down, and across the organization. Should they celebrate if an early investment in a promising startup fails? Should the CEO be held accountable? Was the failure preventable? Where was the team transparency, and so on? It's easy to see why people could get cynical about the CEO's intentions, vision, and direction. Courage, when combined with the other attributes, wins the day. Most of our clients report a rising percentage of revenues coming from products and services launched in the past three years. Courageous CEOs will bet on AI and increasingly use external innovation channels such as incubators and co-creation opportunities with academic institutions. They will digitize innovation processes and prioritize a handful of innovation challenges to address them more effectively.

The Sandbox Engine also takes enormous courage in the form of unparalleled discipline. Before we ever begin a client engagement, we gain the commitment from the CEO to create a moat around the Sandbox Engine and protect it "from all enemies, foreign and domestic." This type of innovation isn't a free-for-all. Members of the Sandbox Engine should emulate SEAL Team Six, officially known as the United States Naval Special Warfare Development Group. They are a highly trained, elite, special mission unit that performs various clandestine and highly classified missions worldwide. They focus on advanced analytics, digital design, increasingly mobile capabilities, and technology platforms (Figure 5.3).

INNOVATION TYPE	ADVANCED ANALYTICS	TECHNOLOGY PLATFORMS	DIGITAL DESIGN	MOBILE CAPABILITIES
NEW PRODUCT	Insurance Medtech	Chemicals, Pharma	Durables, Industrial Goods	Wholesale & Retail
NEW SERVICE	Public Sector Telco		Transportation	Finance
GO-TO-MARKET	Travel & Tourism	Consumer Goods		Media
INTERNAL PROCESS	Materials	Software	Technology	
BUSINESS MODEL	Automotive	Energy		

Figure 5.3   Top Innovation Priorities by Industry
Source: Michael Ringel, Ramón Baeza, Raholl Panandiker, and Johann D. Harnoss, "Successful Innovators Walk the Talk," Boston Consulting Group, June 22, 2020.

Commitment is walking the talk on innovation. Research consistently shows that when organizations double down on innovation during downturns, leverage the crisis to invest, and position themselves for the rebound and recovery, they greatly benefit from the long-tail gains of those investments.[10]

At the onset of the global pandemic, many organizations immediately took a defensive posture in their efforts to preserve cash. They cut business travel, entertainment, advertising, conferences and events, training, and development. There were many initiatives in their problem stacks at the time. Rightfully so, as the uncertainty loomed large. Yet, I don't know of an organization that can cut its way to growth. The pandemic continued for months without solution. When the second wave came, many leaders, whose products and services created newfound fortunes in a "COVID tailwind," recognized that living with the pandemic requires an offensive strategy.

Even before the pandemic, the uncertain economic outlook amid geopolitical upheaval discouraged an innovation commitment. Recent BCG research categorized most companies into three distinct positions regarding innovation (Figure 5.4):[11]

- *Committed* – Innovation is a strategic priority and is invested accordingly (45%).

- *Confused* – Commitment and resource investment are indifferent or inconsistent (25%).

- *Skeptical* – Innovation is clearly not a strategic or investment priority (30%).

In the future of work, every industry will largely be technology-led. The blurring of industry boundaries will make cross-industry innovation a critical capability. Some companies have done this for years. 3M regularly innovates in multiple industries, from consumer products to chemicals, manufacturing, and medtech. More recently, Sony, Nike, Tesla, Xiaomi, and JD.com have joined the party. Our research points to software and services, tech hardware and equipment, media, and entertainment to be the most cross-industry disruptors.

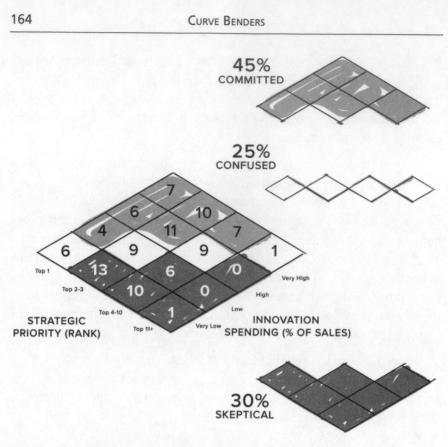

45%
COMMITTED

25%
CONFUSED

			7	
		6		10
	4		11		7
6		9		9		1
	13		6		0
		10		0
			1	

Top 1
Top 2-3
Top 4-10
Top 11+

Very High
High
Low
Very Low

STRATEGIC
PRIORITY (RANK)

INNOVATION
SPENDING (% OF SALES)

30%
SKEPTICAL

Figure 5.4   Walking the Talk on Innovation
Source: Inspired by Michael Ringel, Ramón Baeza, Raholl Panandiker, and Johann D. Harnoss, "The Most Innovative Companies 2020," Boston Consulting Group.

COURAGE, COMMITMENT, CONSTRUCT

There are three enablers of courage, commitment, and construct. They will contribute to the organization's efforts to play more when battling disruptive forces. They are the first three steps in creating a culture of experimentation (Figure 5.5).

Let's take a closer look at each and how they contribute to a fundamental shift in leading the organization of the future.

1. **Strategy Visualization.** Visual storytelling of a vision and the organization's strategic path forward. It's no surprise that the biggest barriers our team continues to encounter

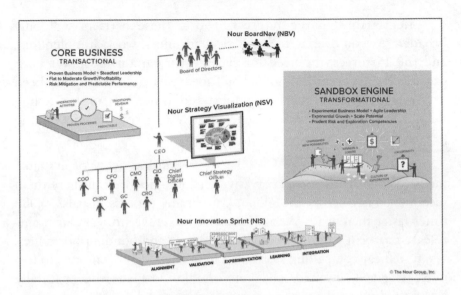

Figure 5.5 Nour Culture of Experimentation (NCE)

surface when global leaders attempt to bridge brilliant strategies with the actual implementation of their ideas (Figure 1.3 from Chapter 1, repeated here as Figure 5.6).

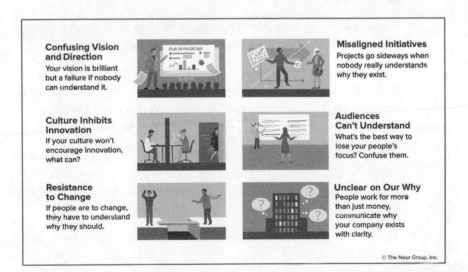

Figure 5.6 Figure 1.3 from Chapter 1 – Six Barriers to Strategy Execution

Regrettably, in the future of work, these barriers will only broaden. As you overlay technological advances, work–life blending, and the 15 forces, the need for clarity of intention has never been greater. From cave paintings to YouTube, visual storytelling has been extremely pervasive over geography and time. Visual storytelling helps you share ideas and influence others with your conviction and perspective.

In the future of work, we'll have a limitless array of available media. With expansive and pervasive technologies, we can share them instantaneously across the globe. Our brains process visuals 60,000 times faster than text.[12] We are hardwired to crave stories. Our brains release oxytocin and dopamine, the pleasure and bonding hormones, when we hear compelling stories.[13] These chemicals prompt us to feel more engaged, inspired, and comfortable. The audience naturally wants to immerse themselves in the journey ahead.

So, how do you make *Strategy Visualization* particularly useful? Five key considerations:

- **Why** – *Why are you doing it?* If you don't have a compelling enough reason, don't do it. It's too much effort for it to go to waste.

- **Audience** – *Whom are you engaging?* Who's your primary target audience that you need to engage and influence?

- **Outcome** – *What do you want them to think, feel, or do differently?* Unless you're clear on your ask, the outcomes, or what's next, the message you're trying to send will be different from the signals they'll receive.

- **Story** – *Which story do you want to tell?* In my experience, many stories can help the audience connect the dots. Which is your most powerful and engaging one? If you have one chance to move them, don't leave them indifferent.

- **Rollout** – *How will you communicate and cascade your path forward?* The story should be a theater to invite your audience and your desired outcome "into" for greater explorations and opportunities to collaborate. If you tell them everything they want to know, what questions are you leaving them to ask? How you'll roll out this vision and manifest it throughout the organization will be a critical consideration upfront.

2. **Innovation Sprints.** If Strategy Visualization creates a compelling vision of the future, why wouldn't it resonate with a broader audience and become a living guide in the organization's journey from now to next? We've uncovered a glaring challenge: most organizations lack innovation capabilities, competencies, and a systematic, disciplined process to replicate. As mentioned earlier, every free-for-all initiative, regardless of its validity, is labeled as innovation. Yet, most are an exercise in futility.

Hence, the opportunity to introduce an *Innovation Sprint*: disciplined learning, design, and testing capabilities developed in a highly controlled, adaptive, and accelerated ecosystem (Figure 5.7).

Think of the Innovation Sprint as your organization's innovation enabler. The goal is to unlock new growth pathways with a sharp focus on iteration, innovation, and disruption. Through a rigorous 12-week

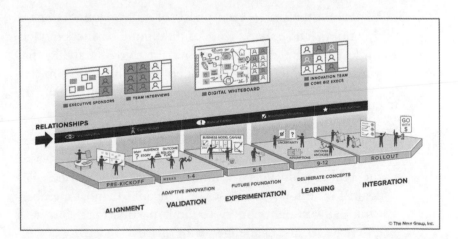

Figure 5.7   Nour Innovation Sprint (NIS)

process, you can have an innovation team immersed in the five disciplined phases:

1. **Alignment** – This is the opportunity to gain a shared understanding with an executive sponsor who is willing to support the Innovation Sprint team. Once others become aware of this effort, questions will be asked about how and to what end it will function in the organization. In this critical step, you're reinforcing the Strategy Visualization path and using it as a guide for the exploration. Using an ideal participant profile, various business units and geographies nominate candidates for the intensive program. They're interviewed and assessed. A cohort is selected from the candidate pool, best representatives with a Whole-Brain® Thinking team.[14] You also establish the tech infrastructure to streamline the journey.

2. **Validation** – This phase is for adaptive innovation. It includes a kickoff, onboarding the cohort, introducing them to various eLearning subjects, and coaching their early learning and growth efforts. It is critical that, in the early weeks, the cohorts establish a solid foundation of knowledge in innovation fundamentals.

3. **Experimentation** – This phase of future foundations is designing. The cohorts will design unique business models. By leveraging the cohorts' dominant thinking styles, they synthesize and test business models that solve a fundamental problem. They explore financial viability and outline the exceptional talent required to make it work.

4. **Learning** – With "getting it" and "designing it" under their belt, the cohort members are now ready to test their ideas in the real world. This learning phase tests empirical data against intuition and focuses on concepts. Cohort members explore investment options (build it, partner for it, buy it, or co-create it), and challenge teams' biases.

5. **Integration** – The final step is the opportunity to showcase all that the cohorts have worked toward in the past quarter.

The most fun is the "Shark Tank" presentation, where the cohort presents to key members of the core business leadership and competes for sponsorships of their ongoing journey. Past clients have included everything from financial support to the next milestone and much-needed resources. They have channel partners and end customer relationships. They possibly have access to the core business's global supply chain, suppliers, and innovation facilities.

We've found the end of one Innovation Sprint to be an excellent opportunity to promote some cohort members into the Sandbox Engine. Invite guest faculty or mentors as you launch the next cohort group. Imagine a dramatically different culture in your organization when there is an established farm program for training open-minds innovative capabilities in new business model innovation.

3. **BoardNav Innovation Committee.** The final enabler of your courage, commitment, and a construct to unlocking real innovation, is one of a *Board Innovation Committee* – stewardship of exploration and advocates for foresight investments in the evolution of the organization (Figure 5.8).

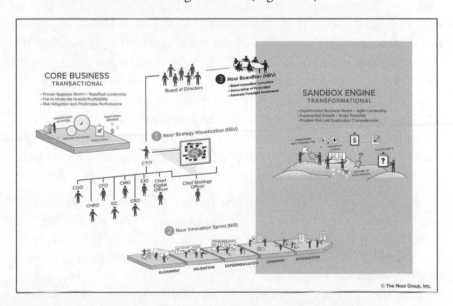

Figure 5.8   Nour BoardNav Innovation Committee (NBV)

Innovation is a slippery risk for most boards of directors to consider. Invest in innovation and increase your chances of failure; fail to invest in innovation and risk obsolescence. Like most innovation initiatives, the traditional big-three focused committees on most corporate boards (audit, compensation, nomination and governance) have missed the mark when it comes to their forward-thinking governance of real innovation. As technology becomes an increasingly strategic facet of an organization's evolution, many board chairs find themselves and their colleagues woefully unaware of the right questions to ask the management team. So, they bring in expert board advisors, academics, and guests to accelerate their steep learning curves. They create Technology Committees as a popular new adjacency to the big three. They begin to ask about cybersecurity, innovation, and, more recently, digital transformation. The Audit committee also participates in these discussions, as they bear the risk associated with cyber.

At Ford, they have even created a charter for their Sustainability and Innovation Committee. It "shall evaluate and advise on the Company's pursuit of innovative practices and technologies, as set forth in Section IV of this Charter, that improve environmental and social sustainability, and that seek to enrich our customers' experiences, increase shareholder value, and lead to a better world."[15] Anyone else wondering what that means, exactly? Research shows that most board members' attention in innovation is directed at improving the organization's capacity to execute its current strategy: extending its product line, reducing cost structures to improve operating margins, improving customer-centricity to battle rising customer expectations, and responding to new regulatory requirements and cyber threats. Although valuable, many of these are the core business's efforts at iteration. And its blind spots toward real innovation and disruption of its current business model.

Interestingly, board members acknowledge the courage CEOs need to make bold moves to keep their companies relevant in the next decade. This is due to the growing demands by activist investors. Boards who haven't done enough to encourage management to pursue risk in a Sandbox Engine will seldom see the CEO stick around long enough to reinvent the business. According to a Korn Ferry analysis, the average tenure for today's CEOs has dipped to 6.9 years, down

14% over the past five years.[16] Numerous experts anticipate an accelerated path ahead.

The executives celebrated on *HBR*'s 2019 list of best-performing CEOs had an average of 15 years under their belts, more than twice the average S&P 500 CEO's tenure of 7.4 years back in 2017. A team of researchers at Spencer Stuart tracked year-by-year financial performance of 749 S&P 500 CEOs to illuminate the pattern of five stages shown in Figure 5.9.[17] Only CEOs who outperform in their years 6 to 10 (the complacency trap) recognize the need for reinvention, stay focused on the business, and continuously challenge the status quo. Even for many CEOs who recognize the need for greater maneuverability, inertia on the board kills any meaningful and lasting exploration.

Research overwhelmingly shows that most directors will say that their organizations have an innovation vision and features in their strategic plan.[18] Far fewer, however, have innovation as a regular board agenda item. Not many board committees are innovation focused.[19]

With the Board Innovation Committee, you can create focused and relevant stewards of the Sandbox Engine. This includes the CEO's vision for a different path forward and the protected consistent investments necessary to explore new competencies. The National Association of Corporate Directors (NACD), through its

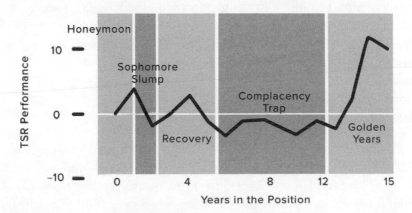

Figure 5.9   Five Stages of CEO Value Creation
Source: "The CEO 100, 2019 Edition," *Harvard Business Review*, November–December 2019.

Board Professionalism curriculum, drives the prevailing notion of "nose-in, fingers-off" governance model – board members aren't there to do; that's the role of management. Board members are there to ask compelling questions, guide key discussions, and support management's vision. The nose-in, however, isn't asking sufficient questions about business model innovation, objectives and key results (OKRs), and management's efforts to make VC-like bets – where you know that eight out of 10 may yield no financial return. But the two that are viable will gain market traction and can scale into profitable growth. Those two could in fact redefine the future of the core business.

To succeed here, the Board Chair must address generational and mindset differences. The highly curious, under-50, next-gen board members and their over-70 counterparts will think differently about revolutionary tech, disruptive business models, and innovation. Broader board refresh is critical to encourage innovation. The UK encourages board rotations with a law that stipulates that board members are no longer considered independent once they've served over nine years. As such, they are disallowed from voting on certain matters, like compensation.[20] The Spring 2019 *MIT Sloan Management Review* disclosed that, in a study of more than 1,200 publicly traded companies with revenues over $1 billion, 24% reported that they had "digitally savvy" boards. A comparison showed, "Those businesses with digitally savvy board members significantly outperformed others on key metrics such as revenue growth, return on assets, and market cap growth. Interestingly, a cohort of at least three digitally savvy directors was needed to have an impact on performance."[21]

It would be very tempting here to simply give a P&L leader a practical, step-by-step summary of creating your own Sandbox Engine. Usually, the truth is that restraints — your current realm of responsibilities, reporting structure, annual performance reviews, how you're measured and compensated, and much of what defines your role within the core business — will prevent you from even getting one off the ground, much less succeeding. Particularly if you function within a mature company or an industry, your world is comprised of cross-functional task forces, procurement policy compliance, and complex decision-making authority. These attributes are the lifeblood of the core business. Unfortunately, they're not in the vernacular or the DNA of the Sandbox Engine.

It is incredibly difficult to attempt to manage your present circumstances while you invent the future of your team or organization. The two camps (core and sandbox) require diametrically opposed skills, organizational values, strategic priorities, and a fundamental shift in mindset and roadmap. The combination of the Strategy Visualization, the Innovation Sprint, and the Board Innovation Committee reinforces the CEO's courage and commitment with a construct that gives the organization of the future the best possible chance to succeed.

CHIEF ENTREPRENEUR

If the Board of Directors, the CEO, and the entire C-suite is predominantly focused on the core business's predictable performance, whose responsibility is it to explore new frontiers? I believe many who operate a core business lack the right structure and long-term focus, diverse investments, and visionary stewardship of its next-gen drivers of growth in most mature organizations. I'm not discrediting the success many organizations have uncovered in an iteration of their existing business models, innovation in various products and services, and venture funds to co-invest in promising new startups. However, the organizational structure of the core business is unlikely to produce dramatic and sustainable new growth – in essence, a repeatable and highly disciplined *organizational S-curve*.

Although improving various facets of the core business model is important, a different lens is required for net-new growth. Researchers have identified that entrepreneurs who continually innovate and build up novel portfolios of businesses differ significantly from other types of entrepreneurs in their ambidexterity.[22] Serial innovation will require an entrepreneurial instinct of inquiry toward entirely new target market segments, value propositions, and a portfolio approach to business model innovation. Exploiting the core business and exploring new frontiers, at the same time, by the same team, is extremely difficult. Most chief strategy, chief innovation, chief transformation, and chief digital officers are already pressed for bandwidth.

If CEOs are concerned about their known competitors, as well as unknown new entrants into their industry, they should prioritize how their own organizations can disrupt their business models before someone else does. With the plethora of new and innovative business models we've seen in the market in the past decade, how can any organization's core business model not be at risk? After a decade of failed innovation centers, flavor-of-the-week innovation campaigns, and billions in investments, only to see most produce no significant value, maybe the current organizational structure just isn't conducive to real breakthrough growth.

Hence, the introduction of the Sandbox Engine.

Running a successful Sandbox Engine is a balancing act. The leader must crusade for a team of explorers who test hypotheses and explore uncommon ideas. Even so, when hard data confirms the flaws in a business model and forces its revision or demise, the leader must guard that squashing that idea or approach does not squander the team's creativity and willingness to go at it again. Especially here, it's crucial for the leader to model the right behaviors in disciplined exper- imentation. When the rest of the team witnesses their leader, who per- sonally championed an idea, terminate the business model, they recognize the willingness of one they respect and trust to change his mind in the face of results.

Welcome to the new role of a *chief entrepreneur* (Figure 5.10).

Although the visionary structure would be a peer to a CEO reporting to the Board Innovation Committee, most CEOs aren't quite ready for this leap to equal power. While the CEO has developed his reputation through the established core business, he remains under pressure to deliver immediate business results, a problem known as short-termism.[23] He often lacks the understanding of what's required for serial innovation. Leading the core business and the Sandbox Engine requires dramatically different skill sets and organizational structures.

It's important to highlight the crucial nature of the chief strategy, digital, and innovations officers. They are the ambassadors between the core business and the Sandbox Engine. They deeply understand the core business and can apply the resources, inventions, and

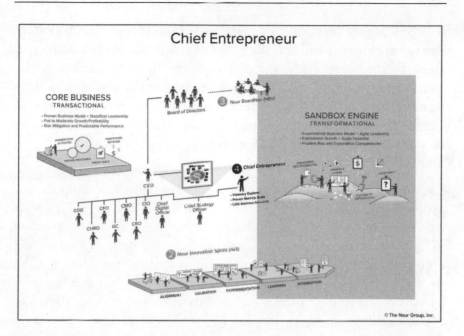

Figure 5.10 The Role of the Chief Entrepreneur as the Steward of the Sandbox Engine

exceptional talent of the core business with the unique business models emerging in the Sandbox Engine. They ensure that the chief entrepreneur and the Sandbox Engine benefit from the strength and the scale of the core business by negotiating invaluable access to customers, distributors, the sales force, the brand, and the deep village knowledge. They bridge the core business and its future innovations.

So, reporting to the CEO, the chief entrepreneur will focus exclusively on the Sandbox Engine and the invention of the company's future. What is important to understand is that, as I have said in countless conversations with past CEOs and boards, this is not a chief technology, chief commercial, chief innovation, or chief transformation officer, or the head of R&D position.

So, what are the key attributes of the chief entrepreneur? What jobs will be aligned with value creation in the organization? The chief entrepreneur is the steward of the company's curiosity-led innovation culture. He is leading a team of entrepreneurs responsible for a portfolio of business model experiments. The role will bridge the gap between highly unpredictable and experimental business models. These experiments will transform the organization, with incremental and efficient iterations by the core business. For example, while the core business optimizes cost-cutting measures and business process reengineering, it can also introduce new product model expansions, extend the lifecycle of an existing service, or pursue a new market segment to drive short-term revenue growth.

Those in the Sandbox Engine don't seek fame. These quiet professionals discreetly explore great new market segments, unique value propositions, and innovative business models. They often lead with tech enablers because they fundamentally understand the digitization of both business processes and customer engagement. The chief entrepreneur often protects core business and transactional leaders from the emotional turbulence of risky innovation. Just as a financial advisor protecting you from erratic investment decisions, the chief entrepreneur is investing in your future. They are less deterred by failure, while the transactional business drives revenue with their core business model.

Here are the top-three attributes they bring to the role:

1. **Entrepreneurial Mindset.** The chief entrepreneur has previously developed, raised capital, and strategically sold a company to a larger public entity. Post-acquisition, they have learned how to function within a large, complex business. But their path hasn't always been paved with one success after another. They will have failed and have embraced the rapid and adaptive learning process. They often have an incredibly giving heart and act as a servant leader. They have a battle-tested process for developing exceptional talent and can help the team of entrepreneurs focus on solving the most complex and rewarding challenges through his coaching and mentoring.

2. **Highly Relevant Experiences.** The chief entrepreneur is a serial innovator with successful strategic exits and expertise in your industry. They've uncovered various facets of inefficiencies, neglected market segments, or a unique partnership to build and exit a highly valuable ecosystem. They

have raised angel investments through series D rounds of capital. Perhaps they have taken a company public, merged, or rolled up several to build a compelling scale. They have a deep portfolio of entrepreneurial, financial, mergers and acquisitions (M&A), and legal relationships that are all independent of the core business. They have developed these relationships over the years in the four paths to value creation: building, partnering, buying, or co-creating. They have a strong and often idiosyncratic view. They have intellectual curiosity to learn and emotional intelligence to listen and grow with others around them.

3. **Translator of the Conceptual into the Concrete.** Ultimately, the fundamental value in exploration is the ability to move a business model that gains market traction (read: paying customers) from the Sandbox Engine into the core business. This is a highly delicate process of timing, testing, talent, and tension. Timing because the chief entrepreneur must discern between viable ideas ready for the full force plus the effect of the core business and those not quite ready for prime time. Testing because they must also serve the Sandbox Engine as the chief idea killer (a product or a service alone is not a company). Early on, promising ideas must be killed to make others stronger. They must prioritize exceptional talent because the Sandbox Engine's biggest asset is the portfolio of entrepreneurs that it's able to attract and promote. They must identify enablers who can help fledgling businesses scale. This could be inside or outside of the Sandbox, through the Chief Strategy or Digital Officers of the Core Business, as well as external resources to uncover strategic opportunities for new initiatives.

The chief entrepreneur is the harvester of hope in building the future of the company. They will plant seeds with their team of entrepreneurs, unique value propositions, and promising business models. They will nurture this fragile ecosystem with a culture of experimentation, fertilize it with an infectious culture, learn processes, incentives to go above and beyond mediocrity, and metrics that reward meritocracy.

Three herculean challenges stand in their way:

1. **Inventing an Innovation Accounting System.** I agree with Eric Ries in *The Lean Startup* and Alex Osterwalder at Strategyzer that a new process is required for quantifying the value of the Sandbox Engine. Innovation accounting can range from the chief entrepreneur using a simple dashboard of objectives and key results (OKRs) – a goal-setting framework for defining and tracking objectives and their outcomes – to testing key assumptions in a well-thought-out business plan, all the way to managing investment decisions, measuring success of specific innovation initiatives in the Sandbox Engine, and accessing the impact that innovation has back into the core.

2. **Establishing Deeply Rooted Trust and a Long-Term Partnership with the CEO.** The CEO is the steward of the core business. He will be responsible for ensuring that the resources, assets, and talent are available for the Sandbox Engine to design, test, and scale a portfolio of business models. This is not an easy or inexpensive undertaking. The CEO will be challenged by all the naysayers, including the board, for allocating resources when the global economy suffers a down cycle or a bad quarter affects the core business's financial metrics. Communication, trust, and a long-term vested interest in their respective success will be key in the CEO financing future experiments, while the chief entrepreneur delivers promising and validated new business models into the core business.

3. **Protecting and Supporting the Sandbox Engine at All Costs.** In order to innovate, the CEO and the Board Innovation Committee must create a moat around the Sandbox Engine and the chief entrepreneur's decisions. They can serve as an investment committee in supporting the incredibly difficult decisions the chief entrepreneur must make in creating and nurturing a portfolio of business models. As the Sandbox Engine grows, it will be crucial to create an "innovation dream team" by adding several unique roles to support the chief entrepreneur (Figure 5.11):

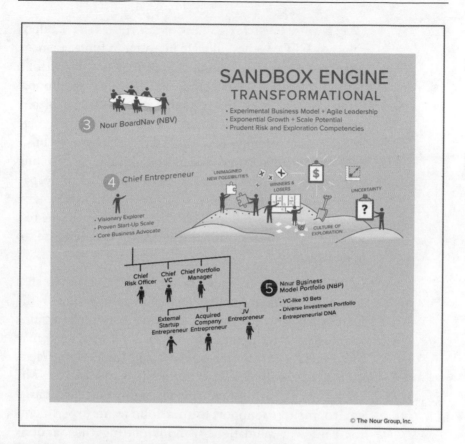

Figure 5.11   Nour Business Model Portfolio (NBP)

- *Chief Portfolio Manager* – This person scans the market for vast opportunities, business models, and entrepreneurial diversity. They ensure a broad portfolio and aim for a balanced approach between potential and guaranteed yields in investments. By understanding the core business, they can scour the market for disruptive technologies, key trends evolving a market sector, engage with others who are seeing the potential, and find opportunities to co-invest with other trusted sources. They establish a strong portfolio of signal scout relationships in the market, scanning for faint signals, and ensure that the core business is well-positioned to take early steps in its future direction.

- *Chief Venture Capitalist* – Think of this role as the Sandbox Engine's CFO, as they allocate investment funds, manage financing rounds, and gauge the progress of the portfolio entrepreneurs for the next milestone to release additional resources. I've long believed that an abundance of any resource is a recipe for disaster. This is particularly true in early-stage funding of a promising yet unproven business model. Few things are more painful than building something no one wants or doesn't want enough to pay what it costs you to provide it. That's not an experiment. That's an expensive flop. The chief VC is the litmus test for business model validation before they choose to invest more.

- *Chief Risk Officer* – They are the adult supervision in a group of brilliant minds. Unfortunately, some of the team's experiments could dilute the Sandbox Engine's brand or expose it to legal liabilities. Where legal may often behave as a business *inhibitor* in the core business, within the Sandbox, they must be the team's *enabler*. The chief risk officer must come from highly entrepreneurial environments to support the portfolio frame experiments for sufficient validation, without putting the Sandbox Engine or core business at unnecessary risk.

- *Entrepreneurs* – At the epicenter of the Sandbox Engine are the entrepreneurs who are building future business models. They are more than product or program managers in the core business. They are entrepreneurs with a fundamental focus, highly vested interest, and a clear incentive in the design, development, and deployment of a proven and scalable business model. They can be a highly diverse group from internally sprung entrepreneurs, acquired startups, or external entrepreneurs the Sandbox Engine invests in (similar to an incubator). They could even be a joint venture with an entrepreneurial venture where the Sandbox Engine holds an equity stake in an early-stage venture and a board seat.

An interesting opportunity for the chief entrepreneur is to consider the CEO and the chief strategy, chief digital, chief innovation, and chief transformation officers (if they exist) as an advisory board with regular communication on the two sides' progress.

ENTREPRENEURIAL IMPACT AT WALMART.COM

Here's the truth: transformative innovation to drive future growth cannot succeed in the twenty-first century through a 1950s organizational structure. The focus on flawless execution and excellence in iteration will serve the core business well, as it exploits its proven current business model. The design of the organization of the future must embrace an aggressive S-curve of prudent investments by a portfolio of entrepreneurs who will test or disprove unique value propositions and business models through a series of experiments.

The chief entrepreneur is the visionary leader and the steward of the culture necessary to move the organization in a dramatically different future direction.

One such example is Marc Lore (pronounced Lori), former president and chief executive officer of Walmart U.S. eCommerce. He was appointed to this role as a member of the company's four-business-unit-leader Executive Committee (others are head of International, U.S. Stores, and Sam's Club), in September 2016, when Walmart, Inc. acquired his company, Jet.com, for $3 billion to compete more effectively with Amazon. Marc had founded and grown Jet.com to a $1 billion gross merchandise value run rate in its first year. Previously, he had co-founded Quidsi (comprised of several websites such as Diapers .com, Soap.com, Wag.com, and more) and sold it to Amazon in 2011 for $550 million. "The way you've described it, I was basically the chief entrepreneur at Walmart," he said in our interview. When I asked him why he sold Jet.com to Walmart, he directly referred to his entrepreneurial reputation and a relationship with Doug McMillon, Walmart CEO. "Doug and I had the same mission," he added – to give Marc and his team the keys to the Walmart eCommerce business, access to a lot of capital, and the great Walmart brand.

Marc understood that the path to building something meaningful at Walmart.com required his ability to attract and retain exceptional talent. Where Amazon wanted to leave Quidsi alone to operate autonomously, McMillon and Marc agreed to integrate, carefully and intentionally, the Jet.com and Walmart.com teams. As a serial entrepreneur, Marc was able to change the Walmart.com external narrative as Walmart's Sandbox Engine. "Early on, we made several small acquisitions, started an incubator called Store No. 8, to develop leapfrog capabilities to transform the future of retail, think virtual reality, augmented reality, drones, and conversational commerce," he added. Visionary leadership, combined with deliberate explosive growth in year 1, suddenly made Walmart.com attractive to the best and the brightest e-commerce and tech talent. "I'm a big believer in VCP – vision, capital, people – being 90 percent of where most of the damage is done," Marc commented.

One of Marc's more exciting opportunities was exploring Walmart's long-term strategy, innovation, and the push for the organization to think bigger. "I led a project we called Walmart 2040 – instead of five years, which is nothing in retail, how can we think 20 years out?" Increasingly his colleagues recognized the different mindset it takes to think 20 years out and the impact of their decisions today. "The buy-in came when the top 40 executives in the company saw a very transparent report from a 32-question survey, with the range of what we think the future will look like, with their names attached to their responses. Fascinating when you see how your colleagues think, what they believe, and why they believe it – it really helps in getting everyone on the same page in the long-term direction of where we need to go," Marc commented.

Beyond exceptional talent, changing the external narrative, and getting buy-in on the company's long-term vision, Marc also created a more unified and collaborative organizational structure. "When I got there, the eCommerce and U.S. Stores groups were two separate organizations: separate merchandising teams, separate supply chain teams, different strategies, focus, and hiring of very different types of talent." All were trying to serve one customer. Since then, they've created one omnichannel organization, merging teams, including the supply chain, to move faster with less political friction and greater alignment. "We got a lot more done, we were nimbler, and this was critical to our success," Marc concluded.

Marc was also instrumental in recruiting Janey Whiteside, EVP, and Walmart's first chief customer officer. "We needed someone who would be solely responsible for thinking about the end-to-end customer experience, customers and products, and marketing to the lifetime value of a customer," he added. Whiteside is one of four critical leaders within the U.S. organization, filling a crucial role previously divided between merchandising, supply chain, and store operations.

Empowered and inspired over the past four years, Marc felt that they've made much progress and yet have a long way to go. Walmart is making many more investments in the future than they ever have. Marc believed they're still just scratching the surface. "I think we needed to be way more aggressive on making bets that don't have a known high probability of success. Big companies, generally speaking, and Walmart is not alone here, don't have an incentive structure for individuals to take a low-probability swing, even if they have big potential outcomes." If I'm an executive moving up the ranks, I'm less likely to support an opportunity with a 30% chance to have a 100x return because of the optics. Large company optics tends to highlight the 70% chance that the initiative could fail on my watch, diluting that P&L leader's brand and jeopardizing their upward mobility. If the P&L leader does take the 30% chance of success and sees it through, he or she is often called lucky. If it fails, the naysayers come out with "I told you so!" This is also consistent with the compensation structure and the inherent conflict of interest of most P&L executives. Their bonuses are tied to profitable growth and not in the VC-like investments such as Store No. 8.

Even though large enterprises are in the best possible position to take these diversified shots, and a 100x return would equate to enormous value, the core business mindset, metrics, and incentives are too much risk for many leaders to bear. "Give that same 30% probability of success to any entrepreneur, and they're all over it," Marc commented. Imagine the potential for any core business to take 10 or 20 shots and move three of them ahead with enormous success.

Store No. 8 is a good example. Many believe that the investments Walmart is making, in the context of its size and scale, are a fraction of what's necessary to drive sufficient experimentation and exploration of innovative ideas and business models.

What would be incredibly exciting is to allow someone of Marc Lore's caliber to incubate startups within the Walmart ecosystem, raise external capital and spin them out, with a 49% interest in each. This way, you invent your future out of the Sandbox Engine without utilizing the core's management bandwidth, recruit exceptional talent to each startup, run fast, and even if they become a competitor, your ownership stake would increase Walmart's market cap. I've always believed that a slice of watermelon will always be bigger than the whole grape.

When I asked Marc what gets him up every day, particularly since he doesn't need the money, and serial entrepreneurs who have built successful startups can attest to the absolute daily grind, he told me of wanting to be a farmer since he was 10 or 12 years old. "Because farmers grow stuff from nothing, and that summarizes me. I like creating something from nothing to create a more positive impact in the world," he added. In our interview, I got the impression that he's a big advocate of creating a great culture, a great work environment, hiring great people, and watching them grow and flourish as they learn and then do great things. And that's the case with all his past startups. He loves hearing about his past colleagues' or stakeholders' success or stakeholders they've made happy and proud of the investments they've made.

"I also made a commitment to Doug when he bought Jet.com that I'd be here for five years and get it (the acquisition and integration) right. That handshake, our mutual respect, and trust mean a great deal to me. I have incredible loyalty to Doug and the board. I wanted to leave them in really good hands," he concluded.

That is how a chief entrepreneur brings his or her S-curve to impact the organization's long-term viability.

CHAPTER 5 SUMMARY

1. Everyone wants to work in a company that values innovation, yet it's hard to create a culture where the personal S-curve can equally be developed in teams and organizations.

2. The Sandbox Engine extensively researches the market for alternative solutions to problems that exist today. They engage with a broad portfolio of internal and external relationships to conceive new insights.

3. Companies need to be fostering a culture of experimentation. That includes Strategy Visualization, Innovation Sprints, and a BoardNav Innovation Committee.

4. Companies need to invest in a chief entrepreneur position. The chief entrepreneur will report to the CEO but will focus on the Sandbox Engine and inventing the company's future.

5. The chief entrepreneur brings three unique attributes the role: entrepreneurial mindset, highly relevant experiences, and translator of the conceptual into the concrete.

6. Branching off from the chief entrepreneur, there needs to be a team that adds several unique roles to support the chief entrepreneur: chief portfolio manager, chief venture capitalist, entrepreneurs.

CHAPTER 6

Curve Bending in the Lives of Others

From what we get, we can make a living. From what we give, we can make a life.

– Arthur Ashe, professional tennis player

There is an old Persian proverb about a man who walks into a village. He asks three men who are weaving a basket what they are doing. The first replied that he is weaving. The second says that he is making a basket. The last one says he is helping feed a family by making a basket to carry bread. The story's moral breaks down the fundamental difference between a task, an output, and a purpose.

I'm often perplexed when I meet brilliant, highly educated, and successful-by-all-measure leaders who cannot articulate a compelling life purpose. Years ago, I read John Maxwell's framework of the challenges we face as we evolve. We go through five phases: survival, security, stability, success, and, finally, significance.[1]

Early in most of our professional lives, we're in survival mode like hunter-gatherers. We focus on extending our educational foundation, developing our professional pedigree, starting a family, and passing our beliefs and values to our children. In the security and stability phases, our drive is to regularly accumulate, achieve, and accelerate a path forward. We're busy building our homes, raising our kids, and climbing the ladders of our careers. We sacrifice time with loved ones in the constant pursuit of "success" in our professional lives. We miss out on the parts of life that are important and matter if you're playing the long game.

Thus far in the book, I've focused on how to search for a Curve Bender and the transformational impact they can have on your future non-linear growth. But how can you become a Curve Bender in the lives of others?

When you think of the individuals who have dramatically changed your trajectory, are there some common traits between them? How did those relationships shift your direction and ultimate destination? What was the context and cadence of your interactions? How did they find the right needle to strike the right nerve to transform your life?

The global pandemic made many of us take stock of our success. While quarantined with our families, we listened to their stories and reconnected with them in incredibly meaningful ways. It caused many executives to reassess their approach to work, regroup with valuable key relationships, and commit to a different path moving forward. In the past, our titles, bank balance, cars, or exotic vacations mattered. Conspicuous consumption and these self-centered status symbols were tied to fulfillment. Uncertain about what to do, some people considered a career change. The answer to feeling unfulfilled is seldom a job or a career. When people are self-centered, they believe that the remedy must be an external change. "Happiness will come in my next career," they think.

Most conversations I'm having with true servant leaders are increasingly around how they want to be remembered and where they're seeking inspiration. We've talked about their mentors in the fall and winter of their careers. We've touched on how they will achieve a higher quality of life in the future of how they'll work, live, play, and give. Most importantly, these leaders don't want their children to spend their entire life climbing a ladder of success only to reach the top and realize that the ladder is leaning against the wrong wall.

In the past three seasons of my Curve Benders podcast, I've had meaningful conversations with over 100 executives, leaders in thought and practice. I've interviewed those who have had success in their careers, lives, how they show up, and give of themselves. I asked each one about the Curve Benders in their lives and what they believe it takes to become a Curve Bender to others. This is the single most consistent answer to date:

They saw the potential in me that I somehow couldn't see or believe possible myself!

Beyond their kindness to listen, wisdom to guide, and a unique value-add to the relationship, most executives thought of several unique archetypes:

- A past undergrad or grad school professor who took a real interest in them as a student

- A boss they deeply believed in and followed in several jobs spanning a decade or more

- A startup founder with a successful exit subsequently becoming an investor in other promising entrepreneurs

- A board member who was the CEO's advocate early in his tenure and remained so for a decade

- An adversary or a direct competitor who pushed them to deliver their full potential consistently

I believe the future will compel us to identify, sustain, and capitalize on relationships that energize us to do things that are bigger than just a job. We will invest in people who invite us to make truly meaningful work that is bigger than ourselves. In the future, the urgency to prioritize our purpose will increase with each passing day. We'll move from asking what you do to what are you working on and whom you are impacting. That mindset shift is about playing a bigger game in your future and long-term non-linear growth.

We're all wired to be meaning-makers. If we lack positive Curve Benders in our lives, we often gravitate toward negative Fender Benders, as I shared earlier. If our purpose is an organizing force in our lives, your relationships portfolio is its delivery engine. Some of the intangible benefits of Curve Benders in your life are to foster optimism and hope and to increase your life satisfaction. Researchers have found that access to social support can improve cognitive function over the life course and drive higher satisfaction in older age.[2] As such, you must be driven to prune Fender Benders from your life consistently and relentlessly.

As a P&L leader, you're in a uniquely qualified position to give back and ensure that those you lead don't experience feelings of frustration and regret about the direction of their career, or, worse, their lives. By definition, your P&L stewardship means that you have both the responsibility for certain organizational outcomes and the authority to lead its prioritized pursuits. Where and how you choose to invest says a lot about your personal values, strategic vision, and the impact you create on your biggest asset: your talent. With experiences, you develop more academic, **relational, and emotional intelligence**. "Am I aiming for or reaching my potential?" is distinct from "How do I get promoted?" or "How can I succeed in this role?" The former is a deeper, wiser, more transformational inquiry about your impact; the latter are highly transactional and short-term concerns about your progress.

Your wisdom delineates the questions above in helping others better define *what* success means in their heart and *how* to explore a path to get there. You've seen that non-linear growth dramatically raises the market value of others and brings enormous satisfaction and joy in their work. In return, they show boundless gratitude in paying those learnings forward. You demystify the notion that it's never too late. Consistent evaluation and immediate course corrections are the keys to non-linear growth.

With a vested interest in their long-term success, your independent lens sees who they really are. While reflecting on your past, you realize that supporting them to proactively manage their growth journey will require a commitment to three behavior changes in their path ahead:

1. Knowing themselves

2. Excelling at what really matters

3. Demonstrating character in how they lead

Becoming a potential Curve Bender in others' lives begins by supporting their efforts to go through a candid assessment of their current skills, knowledge, behaviors, and performance. Can they hone and validate their own, as well as the market's, perception of what they do exceptionally well, and where their growing edges may be? Sadly, most bosses' and organizational assessments aren't useful here. This is an opportunity for meaningful reflection and a **listening tour**. Encourage them to solicit perspectives of their most valuable, trusted, respected, and strategic relationships, who will tell them the brutal and often uncomfortable truth. People can almost always rattle off their strengths in spades. Their fundamental weaknesses and even some of those strengths, when amplified, become stumbling blocks. Their growing edges tend to be their blind spots.

Curve Benders are the enablers of our resilience: the will, belief, and ability to bounce back from losses, failures, and disappointments. They become our source of compassion, grit, courage, and motivation. When they help us focus our life's purpose, they give us reasons to weather setbacks and sustain efforts that we didn't realize we had in us. With Curve Benders in our lives, our sense of resolve, patience, persistence, fierceness, and even physical vitality tends to show up in abundance. When our purpose is based on impacting others' lives, it helps us weather future risks, tackle uncertain opportunities, and navigate unpaved paths in our personal and professional growth. And because they support our non-linear growth, our lives move from impact that's transactional to impact that's transformational.

CURVE BENDING MINDSET AND CADENCE

Almost two decades ago, when I wrote *Relationship Economics*, I delineated three unique relationship development styles: givers, takers, and investors. I've found that givers get something euphoric by providing to others. Obviously, relationship takers only call when they want something. Unfortunately, most of us, certainly the givers, enable takers' behaviors. Those who fundamentally understand and consistently practice investing in their most valuable relationships will see a long-term return on their Relationship Currency® deposits, Reputation Capital® accrual, and Professional Net Worth® analysis – about which I've written extensively in *Relationship Economics* (Wiley, 2012).

Helping others see their blind spots takes time, humility, and the willingness to confront. Most of us fear our blind spots, which maybe we are unaware of, incredibly credulous or defensive about, and would rather ignore altogether. When you give time, share incredible humility and generosity, and have the courage to face the uncomfortable with those you genuinely care about, this shifts your mindset. You shift from a constant and relentless aim for success to one of significance.

There lies the Curve Bender mindset: the wiser you get, the more your efforts shift from your own financial and status upgrades to tangible impact in other's lives. After reaching material milestones, you begin to reflect on your legacy. Beyond what you have accomplished, how did you change the direction and destination of others? Listen closely to how your colleagues or leaders you admire describe individuals who have had a profound impact on what they've achieved, whom they've become, and how they lead. You soon realize that true success is lived through others.

Don't take me wrong: helping others achieve and be more is admirable and praiseworthy. We all stand on the shoulders of giants. Yet, the reason we typically show up for others is highly transactional.

Shaping their future path toward non-linear growth has an unfathomable and transformational impact on their lives. A Chinese proverb says, "If you want happiness for an hour, take a nap. If you want happiness for a day, go fishing. If you want happiness for a year, inherit a fortune. If you want happiness for a lifetime, *help somebody*."[3] Beyond that next promotion, what if you were able to help shape successful marriages, parents, leaders, and human beings? A successful career, team, or company is the icing on the cake of a life well-lived.

People build relationships for three purposes:

1. *A Reason* – Often a transaction. Think of a vendor relationship, an investment banker, or a client you support for specific reasons.

2. *A Season* – Several relationship reasons strung together. Think of a highly reliable vendor you have worked with over several years. Or the same investment banker who helped you with multiple M&A transactions. Don't forget that one

fabulous client who buys consistently from you over the years.

3. *A Lifetime* – The few meaningful relationships we nurture over our lifetime, ones bridging one aspect of our lives to the others. That vendor you engage in multiple jobs in several companies becomes a strategic asset to your supply chain success. The investment banker who moves to an advisory firm and consummates the transaction and supports the acquired company's integration. Or the client who attends your daughter's wedding, long after you've worked together.

The curve bending mindset shifts from a transactional relationship to something more lasting. It starts by working with someone for a reason, deepening their relevancy over a season, to finally shaping their non-linear growth over a lifetime. Authenticity, aligned expectations, and reciprocal value pave the way for this evolution in your relationship. They become genuine and deeply rooted personal friends.

One of the keys in becoming a Curve Bender in the lives of others is to show up consistently, often in small ways. When you create a regular cadence for interacting with, engaging, influencing, adding value, or simply listening to your most valuable relationships, you create more chances to be in the right place to create impact when the opportunity arises. To understand fully the lives of others you want to impact, you need quality opportunities to see their struggles as well as the highlight reel of their successes.

It's nearly impossible to build a successful track record if you don't excel at the tasks critical to your chosen role, realm of responsibilities, or the industry your company serves. The second behavior in bending the curve of someone's path is to help them excel at what really matters. If someone you want to help is assessing a fundamental shift in their life stage, a Curve Bender would help them understand what will drive success in the new position and learn as much about those shifts as possible before they make the leap.

Mark Stephenson is the chief customer officer at Evisort. He has become passionate about helping early-stage tech ventures gain traction. During our *Tech Sales Insights* podcast interview for The Sales

Community, he mentioned the four operating principles that he uses to run every global sales organization he has led:

1. Solve critical problems for ideal customers in large markets. Stephenson and his teams focus on high gross margin, double-digit growth customer targets.

2. Hire great sales talent. Enable and empower them, as it's incredibly difficult for a small, new player to gain traction in any market with critical mass.

3. Create market alignment. It is painful and yet necessary to align the problems you're trying to solve with what the target audience is willing and able to pay for solving those problems.

4. You can't improve what you don't measure. This is your standard revenue operations best practice.

Stephenson needs to add similarly passionate leaders to his team who value what he values and believe in the same four operating principles. If he doesn't, his team and company won't survive.

The curve bending cadence is any time, all the time, anywhere, and everywhere. The potential to bend someone's curve is like the dye in the fabric of our favorite shirt. The dye permeates the fabric, and the texture of the shirt feels great against our skin. Most importantly, we look good wearing it. Stop thinking transactionally and start putting a process toward your investment in your relationships. Create a weekly or a monthly cadence where you help people who are on lower floors than you. If your career has you working on the 40th floor of a building, create opportunities to help those on the 39 floors below. Make room for those waiting in the lobby, and those who can't even get into the building. By the way, this could also be an answer to our struggle for real diversity, inclusion, and equity. For example, let's go recruit inner-city kids for summer internships. Let's teach them how to dress for the jobs they want, take care of their healthcare needs for a year, educate them in business acumen, elevate their access and the knowledge of tech that can change their lives. Together, we can bend the curve of their future.

A unique function by Curve Benders is their passion for an idea or a personal lens they use to impact others' lives. They create an *Idea Radar* where they send out signals of key topics, people, and focal points of particular interest and value to them. In 2013, Sir Richard Branson created Virgin StartUp, a nonprofit Virgin company for entrepreneurs. They provide government-backed startup loans and one-on-one advice for people looking to launch or grow a business in England or Scotland.[4] Branson recently surprised 800 startup founders at a Digital Meetup. He engaged eternal optimist Simon Sinek on how to start a business and "help us learn how to be human again." But it doesn't just have to be celebrities that create a resounding impact. Adam Braun asked friends and family for donations to build a school in Laos instead of gifts on his 25th birthday. That initial success inspired Braun to start Pencils for Promise, a for-purpose enterprise (a term Braun prefers to not-for-profit), which has since expanded to build more than 400 schools globally.[5]

Curve Benders also have a knack for asking about particularly interesting topics. Then they look for bouncebacks from people who take their information and internalize, synthesize, and apply it. Since they have an insatiable appetite for learning and growing, they want to create an ecosystem where others can dine. Alex Osterwalder, of Strategyzer and *Business Model Generation* fame, did this when he chaired the 11th Global Peter Drucker Forum in 2019 on "The Power of the Ecosystems and Managing in a Networked World." He wanted to know about culture's impact on business model innovation. So, he gathered the most-informed minds in a broad array of ecosystem topics: new means of value creation, rethinking the organization, capitalizing on new technologies, and transforming legacy companies. The brilliant part of this is that Osterwalder is always learning, growing, testing new ideas. He does so by surrounding himself with those who will challenge his assumptions and help him think about the same idea through multiple lenses. He gives to so many and often impacts their lives without either realizing the enormity of his generosity or looking for an accolade.

The key to curve-bending cadence is a diversity of thought. The only way I know how to attain diversity is to collect seeds of ideas, views, and value creation from my peers. I then plant them in others who may be missing out on participating in similar communities. This approach keeps me fresh and demonstrates my potential as a Curve Bender. You also tend to see a lot more refraction points and create curve-bending gravity: the fundamental market pull by others in my relationship ecosystem, who want and need my unique insights, support, or portfolio of relationships to dramatically improve their condition.

SEEKERS AND SOLVERS

Think about eBay, Uber, Airbnb, or Amazon. There's a common thread in their business model and approach to value creation: they bring seekers and solvers together. Seekers have a challenge or an opportunity, which has created a need for which no solution has appeared. Solvers have the direct and relevant knowledge, experience, and wisdom to help address the same challenge or opportunity. Their impediment is that they don't know or have access to one another.

As a Curve Bender, you can do the same with your relationships as a tech marketplace like eBay or Airbnb. The key is not merely to understand what others want (seeking) or may bring to the table (solving), but to uncover their motivations. I've found that otherwise confident executives often overestimate the career risks or potential dilution of their credibility or reputation if they ask for help. They also grossly underestimate the risks of suffering in silence. When you sustain a value-based relationship with others, you can better understand more than what they're trying to do. You can pick apart why, how, what's working, and where they struggle.

You'll experience firsthand how both sides show up in addition to how they position themselves, how succinctly they'll articulate their challenges or opportunities, and how open they are to new ideas. You'll witness how open they are to hearing recommendations to abandon their current idea or path forward. As purveyors of strategic relationships, they become dealers of hope.

Curve Benders are astute observers of the entire picture. Like the Dallas Cowboys' offensive coordinator, they see the entire field. The curve bending opportunity here is to remain calm to observe individual behavior in the face of disappointment, disbelief, or disgust. This response is not necessarily to another individual but the situation. Are they fully in control of their emotions or do their demeanors shift dramatically? You get a succinct validation if their emotions control their thoughts and actions. An interesting quote has been attributed to Warren Buffett: "You will continue to suffer if you have an emotional reaction to everything that is said to you. True power is sitting back and observing things with logic. True power is restraint. If words control you, that means everyone else can control you. Breathe and allow things to pass." Such a stoic response is a superpower, and one that few leaders master. It is also a character trait that independent and wise Curve Benders can observe and point out as a growing edge of someone they genuinely care about. Developing this attribute will make you an exemplary role model in the lives of others.

Lastly, on this topic of seekers and solvers, the idea of proactively gathering fascinating and sharp people together doesn't have to be only in your professional life; it can encompass your entire life. One of my favorite examples is a group of wise, older dads in my community who bring together an informal group of friends each Saturday morning for breakfast. Driven by their faith, they invite less experienced, younger dads to have weekly discussions. Despite their best efforts, most new dads are clueless on fatherhood, so the conversations cover everything from education to dating, college choices, military enlistment, playing for mean coaches, tough conversations on drug and alcohol abuse, and teen suicide. Recently, they've even tackled racial inequality, homelessness, and grace. The "Dads of Wisdom" leader has had a successful professional career, but we all know him as the wise patriarch, a spiritual connector, and a pillar in the character of good men in our community.

COMPOUNDING REFRACTION POINTS

Refraction points in one's growth journey compound over time. With sufficient vibration, timelines on one's growth will ripple outward and upward even if they look flat on a graph (Figure 6.1).

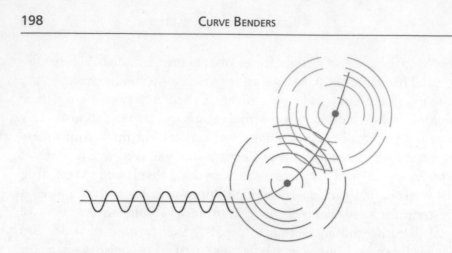

Figure 6.1   The Ripple Effect of Compounding Refraction Points

When you're lucky enough to discover two or more people struggling with a similar or complementary challenge in different contexts, you create exponential value when you compound their refraction points. You become a Curve Bender in both their lives.

One way to think about compounding refraction points is to look more closely at the network effect. NFX, a seed-stage venture firm, created the Network Effects Bible. It tells us that network effects have been responsible for 70% of the technology value created since 1994.[6] NFX identified 14 unique network effects in the past two decades of working with hundreds of companies; their founders are the best form of defensibility, and thus value creation in the digital world. The other three major forms of defensibility are brand, embedding, and scale (Figure 6.2).

If these network effects aren't currently touched, they will soon dramatically impact every industry. These effects are a structure of highly interconnected systems of people or assets that create nodes, links, and network sizes. The breadth and depth of these effects define network density, the directionality of the value creation, the frequency and value of the relationship connections, and critical mass in any network. Network laws and properties define the real value of any participant's network, identity, or anonymity. An organization's network effect is a fascinating study in its impact on market dynamics.

NETWORK EFFECTS MAP

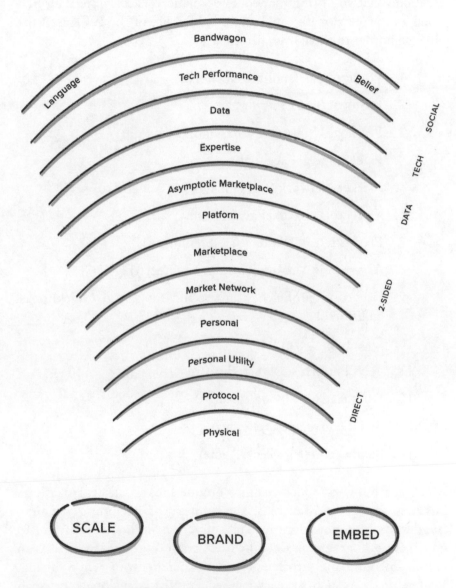

Figure 6.2   The NFX Network Effects

Source: Inspired by James Currier and the NFX Team, "The Network Effect Bible," NFX, https://www.nfx.com/post/network-effects-bible/.

Think about the lives of others that you observe, their challenges, opportunities, and refraction points. Are there specific network effect attributes that you bring that could dramatically accelerate their personal and professional growth? Here is the list of the NFX network effects in order of their strength/impact:

1. Physical (e.g. landline telephones)

2. Protocol (e.g. Ethernet)

3. Personal Utility (e.g. iMessage, WhatsApp)

4. Personal (e.g. Facebook)

5. Market Network (e.g. HoneyBook, AngelList)

6. Marketplace (e.g. eBay, Craigslist)

7. Platform (e.g. Windows, iOS, Android)

8. Asymptotic Marketplace (e.g. Uber, Lyft)

9. Expertise (proficiency in specific tools, e.g. QuickBooks, Salesforce)

10. Data (e.g. Waze, Yelp!)

11. Tech Performance (e.g. Bittorrent, Skype)

12. Language (e.g. Google, Xerox)

13. Belief (currencies, religions)

14. Bandwagon (e.g. Slack, Apple)

Each network effect brings a unique lens to an organization's business model. However, in the context of becoming a Curve Bender and compounding others' refraction points, I want you to consider number 9: *expertise*. The NFX team refers to expertise as an employer requiring proficiency in a specific tool when hiring. Professionals, as such, have a strong incentive to develop expertise in the most widely adopted tools, and they'll list them on their resumes as a strong selling point. Think of a Lean Six Sigma Black Belt, Cisco-certified Network Associate, or a certification from the HubSpot Academy.

For every new person in the labor market who develops expertise in a given product, that product becomes more valuable for all players who have mastered its use. This explains the near-monopoly of tools like Adobe Flash (currently on 95% of all computers on the planet), the preferred multimedia platform of experts in software development, game development, web and mobile applications, and interactive animation.[7] What makes expertise a unique network effect is that it arises from the know-how required of a person to use a particular tool combined with the value transfer mechanism through labor markets.

What if that expertise wasn't from tools? What if it were from a profound relationship with a Curve Bender?

Imagine complementary clusters who dramatically benefit from getting to know, like, trust, learn, and grow from one another. Corporate development and private equity (PE) teams do this all the time: they look for several companies in the same value chain that solve similar yet uniquely different challenges and are, perhaps, serving the same customers. From there, corporate development or PE firms would capitalize on a classic rollup strategy. The same idea applies here. But instead of several companies solving different facets of a problem, you look for an opportunity to help a group of likeminded individuals. These individuals struggle with the same challenge and explore a path that benefits the entire group.

My former Emory Goizueta professor, Jeff Rosenzweig, does this through his ongoing mentor program. He regularly gathers current and past students and introduces these sharp minds to new ideas. He encourages them to discuss the ideas' applications among themselves and determine how they can collaborate to turn great ideas into internship opportunities. They support each other through their respective roles or firms and stay in touch long afterward.

Each of these Curve Benders is compounding refraction points of members of their communities, and their ongoing ripple effects along their own journeys elevates everyone around them.

Curve Benders in Companies

Remember Costco's now-retired Jim Sinegal, who was known for flying around the country, visiting up to 10 stores per day, to learn more about how his business worked? Allegedly, employees greeted him like a celebrity when he arrived at his stores, partly because of his policy of promoting from within, not to mention wages 40% above the industry average. The other part was due to his unpretentiousness. Sinegal famously had the single shortest CEO contract (just one page long) in corporate America and personally handled complaints from customers by telephone. Regardless, Sinegal attributed his and Costco's success to this loyal employee base. "Imagine that you have 120,000 loyal ambassadors out there who are constantly saying good things about Costco," he told ABC News. "It has to be a significant advantage for you."[8]

Curve Benders who lead create meaning for the teams they build and the culture they create. They lead by walking around, shaking individual hands, and taking a personal interest in their employees' lives. These leaders care for their team like family. These intentional and consistent relationship-centric patterns often create learning and growth opportunities on the job, framing not just *how* to achieve but *whom* to become.

They build meaningful and highly collaborative relationship ecosystems in their company's deeply rooted values. They hold a strong belief that connections are "our only sustainable future differentiator." They show up every day with intent and demonstrate a level of engagement endearing to those at the front lines of value creation and value delivery. From the factory floor to market-facing sales reps, the sustained company growth is energized by a commitment to more than paychecks.

Technical startup founders, like Guy Podjarny, often face management challenges. Like most, he began his career in a technical engineering job and became the CEO of Snyk (pronounced "sneak"), an open-source software development approach to security. Sometimes, it makes sense to bring in a seasoned executive to serve as the steward of a hypergrowth startup. Enter board member and investor Peter McKay as Snyk's recent CEO. McKay is a Curve Bender. Since the company's early days, he has been an investor and has known Podjarny in various roles for almost two decades.

McKay brings two decades of executive pedigree, including stints as co-CEO of Veeam and general manager of Americas at VMware, where he led an operation with $4 billion in annual revenues, but he's the quintessential Sherpa of the company's core values. McKay told me, "Having gone through 14 different companies over my career, I've learned a lot. My success as a leader has been supported by my desire to lead, learn, grow, and guide by surrounding myself with the next generation, who may do things very differently than I would." McKay earned his curve bending stripes from his fundamental principles throughout his leadership career: learning from every opportunity and growing his skill set by taking big risks. He credits his achievements to the lessons he has learned from his past experiences. He gets better at what he does by learning more from those he coaches, mentors, and guides.

Pre-pandemic, I enjoyed visiting companies where I could walk around with senior executives and gauge their leadership style. Would a senior executive say hello to frontline employees as we walked the corporate halls like Jim Sinegal? Did they know their names, mention a significant event in their function, or offer to help, coach, or otherwise render assistance? Did they eat in the corporate dining area with the rank and file, or excuse themselves to the executive dining room with the private chef on the 50th floor, not to be bothered? Did they seem approachable, personable, and engaging? Not as a façade, but as an authentic, relationship-centric leader. That's the sign of a Curve Bender.

Curve bending leaders ask frontline employees questions such as, "What frustrated the heck out of you today?" Or, "If you were queen or king for a day, what one thing would you change here?" Organizational hierarchy often creates a candid filter to the top. In the future, that filter will only increase the distance between what's really happening in the organization versus what most leaders will hear, know, or understand. Those employees create the enterprise market value. I coach CEOs to get out of their mahogany row offices and sit next to a call center agent who is taking care of their customers. Go on unannounced sales calls with your young sales reps in the field. Go out to see clients with your field service technicians or delivery drivers. Spend a day on the retail floor, in the distribution center, or on the factory floor. This is how you'll feel how your people, often the organization's only sustainable differentiator, create impact for its key stakeholders.

As Garry Ridge, CEO of WD-40, likes to quote, "Leadership is not about being in charge. It's about taking care of those in your charge." Ask yourself: What percentage of the team members in your charge do you really know? What percentage of your time do you spend investing in your immediate key relationships? Regardless of your company's products or services, fundamentally, we're all in the relationship business. Impact-driven leaders are transformational for people, not the transactions they manage.

One of my favorite questions of senior execs is, "How's your bench, *really*?" In sports, bench strength is a powerful asset, as it implies a depth of available, next-up talent in any role on the team. It conveys flexibility, adaptability, and resilience through foresight planning. Even if one or more of my starting lineups are off, hurt, or face an unforeseen event and can't perform at the necessary level, I'm ready to substitute an equally competent and capable player. This talent depth also implies a competitive environment within the organization where your starting lineup is the best available at that moment in time. Other capable players may not be ready for prime time, or need to work on a key skill, build up their endurance level, recover from a setback, or simply clear their head for consistent competition.

When I engage leaders in their "bench" conversation, I'm exploring their intimate understanding and candid response to the breadth and depth of their next-generation leaders. Their company plus-ones, traditionally referred to in social settings, are the people one level below their direct reports who demonstrate exceptional promise. Most leaders already know their direct reports well. Unfortunately, they're too busy to engage one or two levels below that level and don't have much direct exposure to their high-potentials who are stuck on the corporate bench. That divide shows; in a survey of 1,000 workers at medium- to large-sized companies, fully one-quarter did not know their CEO's name, and one-third said they would not be able to recognize their leader's face in a line-up.[9] Among these employees are some incredible high-potentials.

If you aspire to create a curve bending impact on the people in your organization, you'll need a competent roster of shining stars beyond, below, and around your direct reports. If you get beyond your immediate reporting structure and explore deeper talent in your organization, you'll soon discover that the sharp dashboard your EVP presents in the weekly business plan reviews was developed and updated by a brilliant data architect. You'll discover that the young gun hired from Amazon six months ago has done more to reimagine your outdated processes and how a particular division looks at its market opportunities than the same group had done in the previous two years. You'll see firsthand how young engineers use agile and modular code libraries to create innovative app sprints, and how principles from game design could dramatically elevate your supply chain efficiencies.

Here is an exercise: ask each of your direct reports for a shortlist of their plus-ones. Who is their strong number two? Then grade each individual on their *caliber*, strengths, and growth potential. Is this plus-one truly an A-player with current competencies and a future lens? Carve out the time, resources, and access for the named high-potentials to learn the leadership skills they need to move into more senior roles. I'd encourage spending one day a week with this crop of your athletes to assess their readiness to move from the bench to the starting lineup.

For years, EMC was one of the best-kept secrets in the tech sector. Founded in 1979 in Massachusetts by Dick Egan and Roger Marino, it successfully developed and sold computer memory systems. Later, it developed and sold high-end, disk-based hardware and software. It's best known for its tradition of focused execution and sales excellence. Roger Marino hired motivated recent college grads and developed EMC's assertive sales force. "I hired guys I liked, smart people, athletes, who went out and killed," he told *Boston* magazine.[10] Along the way, EMC acquired VMware and offered 10% of it in an IPO, creating a $19 billion market cap on its first trading day in 2003: RSA Security, Data Domain, Isilon Systems, Pivotal Labs, and all told, around 70 large and small acquisitions. Joe Tucci became CEO of EMC Corporation in 2001 and ultimately sold it to Dell, Inc. in October 2015 for $67 billion.

Here is the fascinating piece of cultural curve bending I discovered. Some 300 or so CEOs or senior executives in the tech infrastructure space began their careers in the mid-1980s to late 1990s at EMC.

"It was an unbelievable culture – hungry, driven, smart, aggressive, focused," said Randy Seidl, now CEO of The Sales Community, Revenue Acceleration, and former SVP and GM of the Americas at Hewlett Packard Enterprise (HPE). Seidl was employee #33 at EMC and added, "We moved fast and got things done. If we didn't know how to do something, we figured it out. Everybody made customer calls. It was a fantastic culture of camaraderie, coaching, mentoring, with incredible peer support."

EMC would ship many of those recent college grads around the world. During Boston College's senior week, Seidl started at EMC as a telemarketer and later ran that inside sales group. Five months after graduating from BC, Seidl was shipped to London to help start EMC's UK operations. Eighteen months later, he went to Sydney to open up the Australia and New Zealand operation. Seidl directly credits Jack Egan for being the unsung hero and the wind beneath the wings of EMC's success. Talk about a curve-bending movement at EMC and their incredible bench strength over the years.

WORKHORSES VERSUS SHOW HORSES

Another incredible opportunity for Curve Benders is your *return on impact* within nonprofit boards. The global pandemic canceled fundraisers and lost donations, which led to scaling back services for the needy. A survey on charities conducted early in the pandemic revealed that 83% were suffering financially, 64% had to cut back on their programming, and 75% had to cancel events.[11] Many charities were left to hope, pray, and wait. Given the disproportionate struggle in the less educated, lower-income sectors, the demand for services, particularly food banks, has been outpacing revenues. Most nonprofits operate on thin margins, and tight restrictions in most government contracts prohibit their ability to get creative in their business model. The IRS publishes clear guidelines for how much "advocacy" a 501(c)(3) nonprofit can do.[12] If they don't keep operating costs down, they're often penalized by the metrics used to evaluate nonprofits. A survey of 3,400 nonprofits revealed that half had 90 days or less of cash on hand, and 19% said they had a month or less.[13]

In the future, I see consolidation of the United States' estimated 1 million philanthropic organizations. Ninety-two percent have annual budgets of less than $1 million.[14] Many nonprofits are governed by weak boards and bureaucrats within an already cash-strapped city and county departments. Most are community-based and focus on a local need.

There are six pressing reasons why nonprofits are ripe for Curve Benders:

1. **Too many overlaps today**, often due to ego, miscommunication, or misperceptions of the organizations' mission, vision, or strategic path forward. I'm empathetic to the unique needs of cancer patients and their loved ones. There is no greater cause than to find a cure. Yet, there has to be a better way to combine the broad resources and efforts of the American Cancer Society, Cancer Survivor's Fund, CancerCare.org, Cancer Research Institute, Children's Cancer Research Fund, Livestrong Foundation, Next Generation Choices Foundation Less Cancer Campaign, Susan G. Komen for the Cure, Breast Cancer Charities of America, Breast Cancer Research Foundation, The National Cancer Institute, CDC's Division of Cancer Prevention and Control, Vineman Cancer Charities Fund, the Department of Defense's Congressionally Directed Medical Research Program, just to name a few of the ones listed on CancerIndex .org, that manage more than $6 billion in cancer research, and support patients and their families.

2. **Outdated Nonprofit Leadership.** Many of the legacy, and often smaller, organizations are led by well-meaning people who are, unfortunately, in the winter of their careers. They aren't tech-, brand-, or business-model-savvy. Worse yet, they're unwilling and unable to attract world-class nonprofit talent and board members. Their missions are incredibly worthy. Yet, their stories are too stale and uninspiring for exceptional talent to want to join. Their boards often lack the innovation mindset to think and lead differently.

3. **Nonprofit Innovation.** There is a reason **charity: water** is a household name. The organization that Scott Harrison, a former New York City club promoter, founded in 2006 has become a fundraising powerhouse in little over a decade. How? They have four enablers. Their brand is clean and simple, with striking aesthetics, often compared to the Nike swoosh and Twitter's iconic bluebird. They use peer-to-peer fundraising, like their birthday campaign, which empowers supporters to own, enjoy, and share their impact at any age! Their business model explicitly links donation sizes to particular resources. Additionally, they use media-like pictures and GPS-specific case studies to tell a story of your investment. When philanthropic fatigue is rampant, and most donors have no idea where their contributions go, charity: water uses graphics like a project map to connect donors with real-world outcomes.

4. **Tech Advancements.** Advancements in technology will address many mundane tasks performed by nonprofits today. While most nonprofits can obtain donated technology, that's not the same as having exceptional talent to use current, much less forthcoming, options.[15]

5. **Mass Capital Infusion.** The Giving Pledge, started by Warren Buffett and Bill and Melinda Gates in 2010, will direct massive resources to solving some of society's most pressing problems. From poverty alleviation, refugee aid, disaster relief, global health, education, women and girls' empowerment, medical research, criminal justice reform, and environmental sustainability to the arts and sciences, there is a great sense of global giving.

6. **Nonprofit M&A.** As the next generation of nonprofit leaders takes over, they'll be more astute in mergers and acquisitions. They will see opportunities to roll up smaller causes in their space.

I believe that one of the most prevailing challenges in nonprofit organizations is their outdated governance model. Years ago, I served on the board of the Centre for Puppetry Arts here in Atlanta. Since 1973, it has introduced millions of visitors to the wonder and art of puppetry, touching the lives of many through enchanting performances, workshops, and the hands-on Worlds of Puppetry Museum. Kermit the Frog and his creator, Jim Henson, cut the ceremonial ribbon in 1978. Since then, it has become the largest organization dedicated to performing arts in puppetry throughout the United States.

A friend/mentor asked me to join the board after he learned of my fond memories of my grandfather putting on puppet shows back in Iran to entertain an army of rambunctious grandchildren. At the time, the center operated a $3 million annual budget and had 75 people on its board! Roughly 10 people did 90% of the work. This dedicated core, the *workhorses*, were there for committee meetings, numerous action items, outreach campaigns, ideation, and brainstorming sessions to fill gaps in resources. Most importantly, we explored net-new growth engines for the nonprofit to create a more sustainable revenue model beyond grants, donations, and ticket sales to shows.

Unfortunately, the leadership's preference was to wrangle in big, local names or recognizable brand organizations. As such, these busy executives may have agreed to lend their name to the board and put on the obligatory fundraising events at their companies or homes from time to time, but they truly did little to move the organization forward. I call this type *show horses*!

As is true with most nonprofit boards, we needed more workhorses and fewer show horses. Curve Benders, by definition, are workhorses. They don't need to join boards (or anything else, for that matter) as badges of honor to make themselves look good. They are builders, creators, and incredible sources of inspiration. Instead of simply lending their name or organization's brand to the nonprofit, they bring their knowledge, experience, and, most importantly, their unparalleled portfolio of relationships to make a fundamental difference for the missions they're passionate about.

I believe nonprofits that compete for our mindshare and wallet share could benefit with fewer show horses. If you are asked to serve, ask specific questions to clarify the board's vision, values, direction, and strategic priorities. If you know who you truly are, what will energize you to make a difference, and what you have no business getting involved with, you can begin to prune the list down to one or two areas where you can create real impact.

As you approach the fall and winter seasons of your career, it'll be important not to lose your psychological edge as a workhorse. A workhorse never fully retires. As for young nonprofit leaders who can benefit from your guidance, you can work together to increase the impact of the cause. Curve Benders who become workhorses in elevating the awareness and impact by a nonprofit don't need the spotlight anymore. They've earned their success, and now, they'd rather be a driving force for other successful missions.

According to an extensive survey of coaches, clients, and HR professionals, 85% of the time, executive coaching is assessed using post-hoc performance reviews, well-being and engagement surveys, measures of learning effectiveness, perceived return on investment, and changes in 360 assessments.[16] Curve Benders often take these measurements and tie them to changes in business outcomes. They wish to ensure that the leaders they choose to work with change their behaviors and that those changed behaviors lead to results. By combining leadership behaviors tailored to specific situations with strategy, resource availability, and economic factors, they help to achieve the organization's goals.

Since Curve Benders have already reached key milestones of their own, their impact on those they choose to work with often turns traditional coaching or mentoring on its head. Instead of focusing only on behavior changes and hoping that they create the desired outcomes, they focus on achieving specific results and explore skills, knowledge, and behavior changes necessary to reach them. Isn't that how we work on the behavior changes and the outcomes we seek for our kids?

For most of your professional life, you've probably advocated for becoming a mentee and learning from others. This book concentrates on finding Curve Benders to help accelerate your journey. I believe you're never too old *or* too young to become a mentor or to find one!

It would behoove you to capture the wisdom from your life at every point in your personal and professional growth journey. When you make time to capture where you've been, what you've done, and how you've failed, you begin to capture real wisdom you could share with the 20-year-old version of yourself. We obviously can't do that, so what if you immersed yourself in opportunities to mentor others?

The lifeblood of most incubators, nonprofit boards, civic communities, and teaching moments isn't content alone. Don't get me wrong; those brilliant HBS case studies provide a worthy analysis of what could have been. My opinion is that the live version is so much richer with its context. Instead of letting others simply read about scenarios in which a leader, a team, or an organization royally screwed up a brilliant opportunity, why not invite them in to an immersive experience?

When we make meaningful contributions, curve bending the lives of others tends to pay dividends in spades. Curve Benders often connect their most valuable relationships with one another, creating additional and highly relevant context in the advice they offer. Curve Benders sponsor or advocate for those they believe in and want to support, regardless of how unpopular their position maybe. Through each of these scenarios, the mentee equally gives back to the Curve Bender in the meaningful connections they make, belonging to a community that cares and drawing inspiration from the relationship that inspires and refills the cup of their Curve Benders.

We could all benefit from more earned wisdom from lived experiences. Curve bending in someone's life isn't an event or a point in time: it's a transition from student to teacher, mentee to mentor. From seeking Curve Benders to becoming a Curve Bender in the lives of others, follow the S-curve of your growth and seek refraction points in the lives of others. Don't wait; be something great in the life of someone else today!

CHAPTER 6 SUMMARY

1. Life isn't just about finding your Curve Bender: it's also about becoming a Curve Bender in the lives of others – that's where you live a life of significance.

2. As a Curve Bender, you can guide others to know themselves, excel at what really matters, and demonstrate character in how they lead.

3. There are three unique relationship development styles: givers, takers, and investors. Givers altruistically give; takers only call when they want something; investors make intentional and prudent investments in others for a long-term value of their relationships.

4. Curve Benders can unite individuals at their refraction points and foster both of their non-linear journeys. A good place to start may be your organization's bench of talent.

5. An incredibly impactful place to make a significant difference is to become a workhorse in supporting nonprofit leaders, willing and able to change, adapt, and evolve through their Curve Benders.

CHAPTER 7

Your Curve Benders Roadmap

> Invest in the future, because that is where you are going to spend the rest of your life.
>
> – Habeeb Akande, *A Taste of Honey and Illuminating the Darkness*

Several of my global clients are proactively planning their strategies for the post-pandemic world. One in the manufacturing sector is surrounded by the uncertainties of IoT, 5G, intelligent automation, availability of raw materials such as crude oil market fluctuations, and autonomous vehicles, to name a few. Another in the cybersecurity space is particularly challenged by the availability of talent, the evolutionary nature of bad actors and cyberthreats, and the expansive never-ending vulnerabilities in the work-from-anywhere world. Interestingly, they all create an arbitrary title for their future paths: Our Company 2030, Strategy 2040, or Vision 2050.

Round numbers (2030, 2040, 2050) are deceiving because they convey a sense of control over the uncertain future in our personal and professional growth journey. They also make good PowerPoint slides for the communication teams – after all, it's easily understood by broad stakeholders, from employees and customers, investors, and the media – about your vision and hopes for the future.

This is the perfect example of linear thinking: trying to control chaos in an uncertain future.

What we need is a non-linear approach, embodied in the **Curve Benders Roadmap**: a framework breaking down the four timelines in your next decade, providing a specific set of repeatable actions to accelerate growth, relationships, relevance, and market value.

Here is the fundamental challenge in creating your Curve Benders Roadmap. All the variables that can act as a headwind, tailwind, or turbulence have different trajectories and unpredictable schedules. Global supply chain dynamics are challenging now, while IoT and intelligent robots are incremental advances, setbacks, and delightful breakthroughs, often spanning a decade or more. Many unknowns will emerge beyond our horizon that cannot possibly be predicted.[1] The challenges you'll face, the obstacles you'll overcome, and the relationships you'll develop and nurture over the next decade can't possibly be assigned to some arbitrary point in time.

Your connections and relationships are contextual – you know many people, but how many are relevant to this particular challenge? Some of the most valuable relationships in your future, you haven't met yet. Others, you're starting to identify as truly transformational and have only begun the journey of nurturing them more consistently. However, others are dormant and carry a unique potential value as your situation or life events alter. The impact of relationships in your future is messier and never preordained. As you read in Chapter 2 on the 15 forces, many are completely out of your control, and the others, for which effort may prove efficacious, will require a team, an organization, or an industry to shape.

Before we get into specifics, here are five core ideas to make your Curve Benders Roadmap significantly more effective:

1. **"Visioning" doesn't replace critical thinking.** A dear friend of mine keeps a poster of the key aspirations in her life in the form of text or pictures she finds endearing. Although I admire her brainstorming and hopes, they're no substitute for strategically discerning where she is today and making the critical investments she needs to make in herself, her business, and her relationships portfolio.

2. **Answers to deep inquiry aren't tied to a fixed date.** One-to-three-year planning is great for operational goals in your life. "I want to go get an MBA" is a brilliant next step in your personal and professional development. Deep uncertainty in your future, such as "How do I become a CEO or a board member

of a publicly traded company?" requires more in-depth inquiry, thinking through multiple possible scenarios, and the answers often aren't tied to a fixed date in your future.

3. **The collision of your inquiry, experimentation, and exploration will shape your future.** Where are you today, and where will you have the most impact tomorrow? How will you shape your future success? How will your role/realm of responsibilities evolve in your organization or industry? What relationships will be most relevant in your evolution – not just at work, but in other facets of your life? These and other questions have unique variables. Only when you make time for deep inquiry, get comfortable experimenting, and develop your exploration skills will you uncover answers that combine to shape your horizon.

4. **Data will be your renewable energy.** The best way to explore your possibilities is through a rigorous analysis of data regarding your present challenges and opportunities. The metrics you create for your growth journey should help you reach critical milestones. The key is to not drain valuable resources in your tactical responses to outside forces in a linear timeline. You can't address long-term uncertainty and risks with rigid, short-term solutions. Disruption in your future will come; the question will always be how prepared and resilient you will be when facing personal or professional disruption.

5. **Keep it simple.** I could've made any reference to long-term planning significantly more complicated. What I've learned over the years is that if you want an idea to be implemented, keep it simple. Get proficient at doing the right things consistently and aim to continue learning more about your journey from now to next.

If you learn how to *manage your present* while you *invent your future*, you'll make the transition to non-linear growth through your strategic relationships, where others can't. The opportunities that non-linear growth can unlock range from accelerating promotions in your current role/realm of responsibilities ahead of others to new opportunities beyond your current organization, more money because of increased perceived value that you bring, a more expansive and quality network, and, most importantly, remaining relevant in the accelerated changes coming for all of us.

To succeed, you'll have to think differently about time, effort, and resources. When considering any future uncertainty – risks, opportunities, or growth – aim to measure certainty and chart your actions versus simply marking the passage of time as milestones.

YOUR FUTURE GROWTH TIMELINE – FOUR PHASES

In this chapter, I outline your Curve Benders Roadmap. There are four timelines, each having a specific set of repeatable actions (Figure 7.1):

1. *Act Now*. **Focus: Next 1 or 2 years.** What should be your short-term focus, based on the available data and evidence you have today? Prioritize these actions, as they'll dramatically enhance your current market value in consistent execution, critical thinking, and discernment of prudent options.

2. *Strategize to Evolve*. **Focus: Next 3 to 5 years.** What strategies will be most useful for you to consider as you evolve in the role, this phase of your life, personally or professionally? Bigger thinking, deeper questions, more strategic analysis of the landscape ahead.

3. *Visualize Non-Linear Growth*. **Focus: Next 6 to 8 years.** This phase is when most fall into the linear growth path; yours will be rare if you integrate strategic relationship questions to think accelerated journeys.

4. *Sequence Your S-Curves*. **Focus: 10+ Years Out.** Given the extreme uncertainties, what will be fundamental enablers of you bridging one of your S-curves to another?

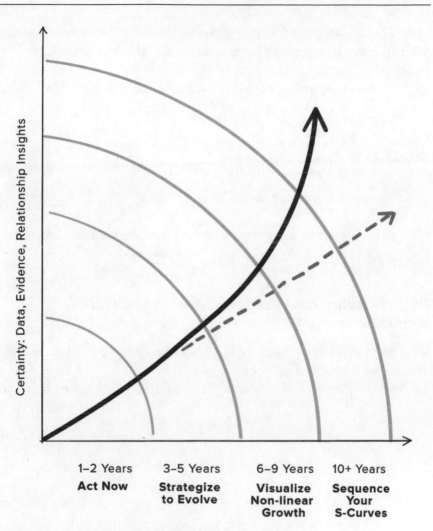

Figure 7.1   Four Timeline Phases in Your Future

YOUR REPEATABLE ACTIONS – FIVE STEPS

Within each of these timeline phases, you'll gather more data, evidence, and relationship insights. The additional certainty, clarity, and line of sight should help you execute five unique specific sets of repeatable steps to accelerate your growth, expand your relationships, reinforce your relevance, and enhance your market value.

This is your "4 × 5 Curve Benders Roadmap," comprised of the following five steps in each of the four phases above (Figure 7.2).

- Step 1: Align Your Personal + Professional Aspirations
- Step 2: Design Effective Inputs
- Step 3: Immersive Inquiry
- Step 4: Invest in Your Relationship Bank
- Step 5: Capitalize Your Curve Benders

Since these five repeatable actions are embedded in each of the four timeline phases, they warrant a brief overview.

Step 1: Align Your Personal and Professional Aspirations

This first step in every phase of your future requires getting your arms around the available data or evidence in the next 12–24 months. What are the key trends and probable events in your company that can

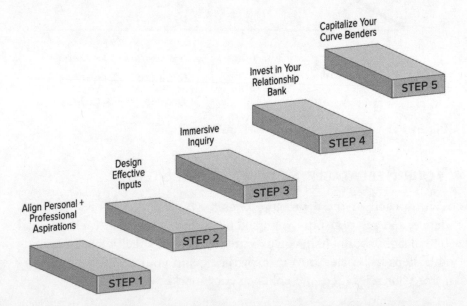

Figure 7.2   **Five Repeatable Actions in Each of the Four Timeline Phases**

directly impact your role/realm of responsibilities? Get tactical and make time to think through questions such as "Where am I now, and where do I want to go, personally and professionally? How can I create the best possible opportunities to get there?" This means having a compelling "Why" in your chosen profession. As we discussed in previous chapters, thinking through how you can be more valuable to others' lives and bend their curve is a worthy consideration here.

Step 2: Design Effective Inputs

Your non-linear growth and success in the Curve Benders Roadmap heavily depend on the breadth, depth, and quality of the strategic relationships you identify, build, nurture, and sustain over time. To find the right strategic relationships at each phase of your growth journey, you need the right inputs.

It's critical in every phase to ask, "What does my lean info diet look like?" I'm a strong advocate of any community that gathers the best actors in that theater. Thinkers 50 has become a reliable resource for identifying, ranking, and sharing our age's management ideas. *Harvard Business Review* and the *MIT Sloan Management Review* have become the definitive sources for intelligent perspectives. The *SSRN*, formerly known as *Social Science Research Network*, is a repository of scholarly research in the social sciences and humanities. Your Curve Benders Roadmap needs intellectual fuel, and although your particular sources for effective input may differ, it's critical to pursue thinking deeper than what an average consumer of this information consumes.

Step 3: Immersive Inquiry

Back in Chapter 3, I made a case for immersive inquiry. It is a fundamental mindset shift. Once you've scanned the market for a cursory view of a topic, it's time to switch from the macro breadth into a deeper dive for depth. Depth is what gets Curve Benders intrigued. They may not agree with your assessment or perspective, but they'll be engaged and curious about how you arrived at your conclusions. Here you'll have the opportunity to enhance or dilute every subsequent interaction. An immersive inquiry is an opportunity to arm yourself with the context necessary to defend your position with facts, data, and insights.

Step 4: Invest in Your Relationship Bank

Think of a relational ecosystem as a solution to a complex problem. It's made up of a dynamic group of independent participants who co-create products or services together. Each participant leverages their unique strengths with a long-term vested interest in the ecosystem's viability and success. So, why would you need one?

As I've outlined throughout this book, I believe the challenges in our future of work, how we live, where and how we disengage to play, and the impact we'll create through giving to others will become increasingly complex. With a great deal of uncertainty, the speed at which we'll need to respond, and the resources required to both address an immediate concern and address longer-term challenges and opportunities, no one leader or company or organization will be able to go at it alone.

Complex challenges and opportunities in our future won't be faced by a single entity. Because of our highly interconnected global economies, multiple participants in very different roles will come together to create unique value propositions, business models, and go-to-market strategies. Thanks to digital transformations, I believe our delineated roles will get increasingly blurred. Producers, suppliers, orchestrators, aggregators, complementors, distributors, manufacturers, wholesalers, retailers, brokers, and agents, as well as those engaged in transportation, logistics, transactions, and perhaps even regulators, will redefine their contributions. In a new way to network, share resources, data, unique insights, and talent, they'll build partnerships to address specific business problems. In short, it all comes back to strategic relationships.

Although the ecosystem concept is not new, a relational ecosystem is a unique approach in each of your Curve Benders Roadmap phases. Specifically, three types of relational ecosystems will serve you well – particularly if you focus on fewer, more strategic relationships now (Figure 7.3):

1. **One-to-One** – A direct connection by a producer and a consumer into a market platform.

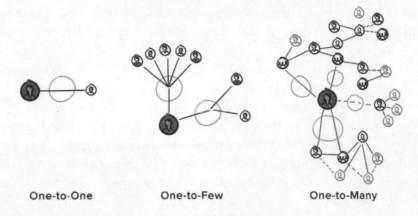

One-to-One   One-to-Few   One-to-Many

Figure 7.3   Three Types of Relational Ecosystems

2. **One-to-Few** – Several suppliers into a core firm, comple-
mented by other participants who contribute their unique
value, to ultimately deliver a value proposition to a target customer.

3. **One-to-Many** – A highly integrated community of likeminded participants, all working to solve different facets of
the same or similar challenges or opportunities. Multiple
variables will force many actors to collaborate, even among
competitors creating coopetition relationships. Consider
the autonomous vehicle sector and the race to create a highly
interoperable environment to manage many different needs.

Step 5: Capitalize Your Curve Benders

Your strategic relationships serve as the common thread between all
four phrases. As you engage them with value-based updates, your progress, and setbacks, celebrate key successful milestones and painful
learning moments (remember, we don't fail; we just keep moving forward), you'll continue to trigger curve-bending moments. As you may
recall from our previous references to Curve Benders, not all relationships will fit that mold, so don't force it. Beyond great bosses, coaches,
and mentors who can help you move the needle on your challenges or
opportunities, Curve Benders are enablers of non-linear growth.

They're often introduced through some of your most strategic and, thus, valuable relationships. You'll want to engage them with your due diligence and give them a glimpse into your critical thinking and relationship-centric approach to complex problem-solving. When, and only when, they observe your passion, tenacity, and commitment to personal and professional growth will they take a more proactive role in your journey. Be cautious not to wear out your welcome, and always keep in mind relationship givers, takers, and investors. Even if you can do nothing now to support their efforts, be sure you're asking consistently. Regardless of how minuscule the request, ensure that you go out of your way to get it done as quickly and well as possible. Just like integrity, they'll check to see if you value their knowledge, wisdom, and relationships.

Before we begin *to crystallize your roadmap, you need to have a clear picture of your top Strategic Relationships to cultivate.* Make a definitive list of strategic relationships you like, trust, and respect in your various ecosystems today (Figure 7.4).

I'd create a simple list outlining your most strategic relationships, their contact info, the context in which they're invaluable to you, and a quick reminder of the last insight you found particularly relevant. These are key members of your relationship bank – in *Relationship*

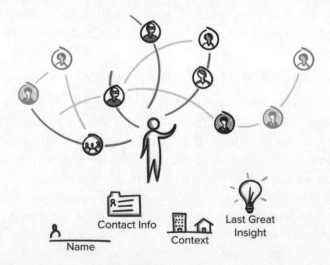

Figure 7.4   Your Relationship Bank

Economics, I refer to them as Your 2AMs, often your most valuable, relevant, and strategic relationships. There's a simple tool you can use to do this on NourGroup.com, but I don't care how you do this, as long as it's regularly updated and easily referenceable and searchable. This is your go-to source for forward-thinking insights. It's critical that you nurture this list with value-add from your side, so you're not perceived to be a relationship taker.

Strategic Relationship	Cell	EM	Context	Last Great Insight
1. John Smith			Technology advancements	10/20 Call on the impact of 5G on IoT
2. Susan Johnson			Diversity, inclusion, equity	6/20 Spoke on the same D&I panel; astute
3. Erica Thompson			Organizational design	8/20 Fabulous conversation on human-centered design and org. structures
4. Pete Gonzales			International expansion	11/20 Virtual presentation on global trade in post-pandemic economies

The above list showing strategic relationships, their context, and ongoing great insights will become abundantly clear if you think of your Curve Benders Roadmap as a radar to scan, internalize, synthesize, respond, gather sufficient data, and course-correct a non-linear path forward.

Military units, often thrust into large-scale crisis and uncertainty, establish granular structures accountable for highly specific tasks, such as operations, communications, and intelligence gathering. They all use *plan-ahead teams* for insights into their decision-making, problem-solving, and communication efforts, particularly when dealing with complex and constantly evolving variables. This strategic approach is so important in planning in uncertain environments that it has been trademarked – the Plan All Hazard Exercise Development and Administration (Plan AHEAD™) is a core tool used in emergency and disaster management across the globe.[2]

Think of the relationships in your Curve Benders Roadmap as a plan-ahead team, charged with collecting forward-looking intelligence, possible scenarios, and options for you to act tactically now while keeping strategic options open in your future. These signal scouts mentioned previously will be best served if you begin with a definitive alignment between your personal and professional aspirations.

PHASE ONE: ACT NOW

Phase One is about taking action now (Figure 7.5).

In the next 12–24 months, what should your short-term focus be, based on the data and evidence you have today? What relational insights can you gather from your most valuable relationships that can pave a path to your continued learning and growth? Get a baseline of your current market value and prioritize short-term investments to enhance and elevate it – specifically, your consistent execution, critical thinking, and discernment of prudent options. This is also the time to clean up your contacts and focus on the top 100–150 most relevant relationships in your work, personal life, play, and giving.

Step 1: Align Your Personal and Professional Aspirations

Make the time to capture where you are today and where you are going, personally and professionally. Make sure you're clear on why your aspirations are important, how you will benefit when you get there, and how you can gauge progress along the journey. Stop worrying about finding the perfect job or even the perfect assignments in any position – I'm not convinced that either exists. The key is always to work in a competitive landscape where you can learn valuable lessons, interact with a broad spectrum of relationship builders and reputation

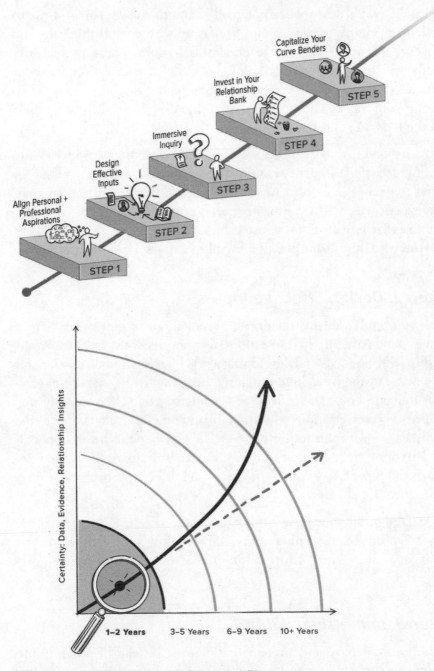

Figure 7.5 Phase One: Act Now, 1–2 Years

breakers (you'll learn what not to do around these people), how to articulate an idea succinctly and back it up with critical thinking, and observe the best and worst leadership behaviors. These prerequisite skills will form and reinforce an unparalleled foundation for your future communication knowledge, empathy, and discipline in collaborating with others, and portfolio of authentic relationships regardless of the logo on your business card.

Beyond just work, make sure you also capture key aspirations in your personal life – be they continued education, a passion to pursue, or ways to disengage. Consider your significant other, make time for quality experiences with family and friends, and choose where to invest. Ensure that your financial house is in order, get help if the topic is not in your wheelhouse, and practice discipline in pursuit of your aspirations.

Step 2: Design Effective Inputs

Ask your most valuable relationships which books they're reading or have found particularly interesting/engaging recently. Immerse yourself in daily podcasts and developing a real interest, if not a passion, for discovery through reading, watching, listening, and generally observing unique perspectives. Seek and immerse yourself in quality and interesting conversations with thought and practice leaders. I've found a discussion with the author of an article or a book to be an opportunity to bring their content to life and make it dramatically more relevant and profitable. You'd be surprised how approachable many (although not all) are.

Designing your lean input sources requires the same diligence now. Cut out the fat, unnecessary, unproductive, or outright toxicity that goes into your information intake because *garbage in, garbage stays*!

Step 3: Immersive Inquiry

Practice immersive and appreciative inquiry. Instead of walking into every meeting with an answer, make the time to capture three to five questions you'd like to ask, three to five questions you're most likely to be asked, and appropriate responses for each. Begin practicing asking questions to understand, clarify, gauge interest, and garner support – if they're not on the same page, learn what it will take to get them there.

Step 4: Invest in Your Relationship Bank

Invest time, effort, and resources in several diverse buckets of strategic relationships. List your most valuable and strategic relationships, and engage them to comprehend where they're going and their plan to get there. If you can understand and contribute to their needs, the relationship's investment becomes one of reciprocal value creation. This will create an opportunity for you to collaborate on a common mission, vision, or potential enemy – like overregulation. A Chinese proverb says, "The best time to plant a tree is 20 years ago. The second-best time is now."

Step 5: Capitalize Your Curve Benders

Focus on elevating the breadth, depth, and quality of your strategic relationships. Think of them as the foundation for you in identifying and accessing Curve Benders. I can't emphasize this point enough: you don't have the bandwidth to invest in every relationship equally. So, it'll be crucial for you to make a list of your most valuable relationships, get your challenge/opportunity on their radar, and keep them abreast of your progress.

It's immensely valuable if I can find a specific opportunity to ask for help and create an environment to contribute – perhaps as an advisor, where and if appropriate, an investor, or a roundtable participant. Invite your strategic relationships to small, highly selective dinners and let them get to know each other. Maybe it's a working meal, and you sketch your challenge/opportunity on an easel and solicit their input. Get very focused on fewer, more value-based strategic relationships.

PHASE TWO: STRATEGIZE TO EVOLVE

Phase two is about creating a vision for your evolution – what will be your best possible choices for the best possible outcomes? (See Figure 7.6.)

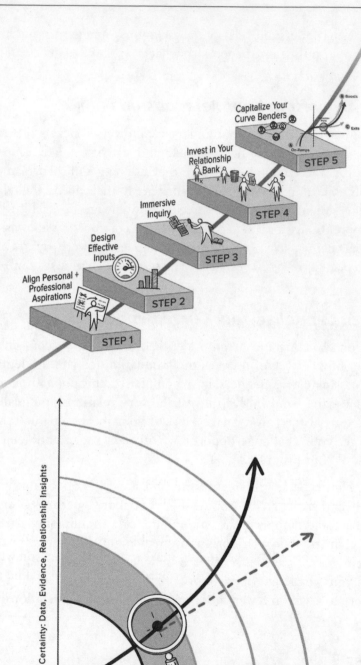

Figure 7.6 Phase Two: Strategize to Evolve, 3–5 Years

In the next three to five years, you'll gather significantly more data, evidence, and relational insights – IF you begin today and build a solid foundation in Phase One: Act Now. Macro thinking here is involved, asking questions like:

- Where are you three to five years from today?
- What are you doing?
- What's getting you up in the morning?
- What keeps you excited about forging ahead?

It's okay not to know – it's not okay to not have a hypothesis here. If you're uncertain, think about all that you enjoy about your life today and would want to extrapolate forward. What type of work, experiences, and relationships bring you real joy? What sludge are you grinding through that just doesn't seem to be worth it, day in and day out? If you don't see a line of sight to any part of your life improving, make plans to begin addressing what you're focused on, are prioritizing, or are sludging through now.

Step 1: Align Your Personal and Professional Aspirations

You'll face less certainty by the 15 forces in how you'll work and live. Your family dynamics will change with life events and priorities. It's important to recalibrate your personal and professional aspirations here. Continue to clarify your vision and the path to reach it. Regularly revisit your prioritized pursuits and make sure you're clear on why you want something and the tradeoffs you're willing to make. The ability to allocate valuable resources down the road heavily depends on your willingness to sacrifice instant gratification now and plan for those investments. Making personal changes now to put you in the best possible position to succeed in that next phase is critical.

Shakespeare wrote, "We must take the current when it serves," which in this context means strategize to evolve your career and life with trends on the rise. Create opportunities to succeed when the tide is unstoppable. I've always preferred to be in and around the tech sector, for its breakneck speed in evolution and the ripple effect it creates in every other facet of our lives. At IBM, I saw the impact of mainframes. In the mid-to-late 1980s, I sold 286 and 486 PCs and Novel networks. We rode the wave of massively parallel processing and high-end graphics at Silicon Graphics to solve complex problems visually. I was president of a startup amid the internet bubble of the 2000s and its recovery. When you align your personal and professional aspirations with trends, your skills will be in greater demand. If you're early in that organization's or industry's S-curve, you'll create expertise in the field, which is often very transferrable to other sectors.

Step 2: Design Effective Inputs

Use process orientation and KPIs to extrapolate future outcomes. Others tend to have more of an outcome-oriented bias. "What do I need to do to reach this milestone in three to five years?" is a common question that comes up in my coaching work. If you elevate the quality of your input, can that help you accelerate your outcomes?

Let's take a sales role as an example. Activities that lead to consistent performance and movement from that front-line selling into sales management and, eventually, sales leadership, are often repeatable, controllable skills that can be consistently improved. Nothing will replace the quality and quantity of sales calls, engaging and influencing the right economic buyers, focusing on solving the right problems, and a strong value proposition for solving it quickly and efficiently. Strategically thinking about your evolution here benefits from KPIs such as sales outcomes, revenue generation, and number of closed deals. What's not a lean source of input are sales anomalies or outliers (such as any deals 3× or greater the size of your average company deal, for example), as they often paint a misleading picture of what the sales rep is doing.

By monitoring and consistently refining your approach to input measures, you gain the following strategic benefits from critical foresight in your evolution:

1. The ability to diagnose challenges before they negatively impact your performance.

2. The opportunity to prioritize specific and targeted develop-
    ment and growth you'll need to reach that next plateau.

3. Robust data that demonstrate results from a set of actions
    now. Learning, adopting, and implementing best practices
    in the sales process example above allows you to teach,
    coach, and mentor others on a similar journey.

4. You focus on the *why* – root causes of events, positive or
    negative – versus just *what* happened.

Step 3: Immersive Inquiry

Commit to become a student of a topic you're passionate about, something that lights you up and fuels your drive forward. Over the past two
decades as a student of business relationships, I've learned that you
begin to develop a brand and gain recognition for your unique expertise. Others begin to read and greatly value your ideas, reference them
in their work with attribution to you, and you develop a reputation as
the go-to person for that unique knowledge, set of skills, or insights.

Management theorist Henry Mintzberg famously defined strategy as 5Ps: plan, ploy, pattern, position, and perspective.[3] In the context of immersive inquiry and your strategy to evolve, I've adapted his
framework to propose a slightly modified version of the 5Ps: *position,
plan, perspective, projects,* and *preparedness:*

1. **What unique *positions* should you take that may be
    counterintuitive, engage, or influence?** The global pan-
    demic challenged the viability of many firms, including
    those in travel, hospitality, and events. It accelerated the
    growth and value propositions by others in home office
    equipment, internet-based communication and collabora-
    tion tools, and home delivery services.

2. **What's your *plan* in thinking beyond the current experi-
    ences and expectations?** All of our experiences and, thus,
    expectations are being raised daily. If I can order a water-
    melon from Whole Foods by 10 a.m. and have it delivered
    for free via my Amazon Prime account in the back of an

Uber car by 2 p.m. the same day, why does it take your company three weeks to deliver an ordered part?

3. **How will your *perspective* evolve as you gather new data and unique insights?** Immersive inquiry can often bring people together and nurture a collective set of insights. It may also push others apart, highlighting a self-centered approach to collaboration with others. Your company's culture, the nature of civic or community organizations you participate in, or philanthropic causes you contribute to may all dramatically change when new data is introduced. How will you recalibrate your lens forward?

4. **What new *projects* should you launch now?** Did you know that the average timeline for a startup to reach a successful exit is estimated to be 9.5 years?[4] If your immersive inquiry leads to specific findings and you're trying to strategize your development in the next three to five years, what projects or critical initiatives should you prioritize, launch, or garner support for now to future-proof your impact?

5. **How *prepared* are you for a very different future?** Most leaders I'm speaking with learned how to live with the global pandemic. Their biggest concern is always the next global disruption. It may not be another global pandemic; it could be a natural disaster or a cyberattack. Their level of preparedness and their own resilience, as well as that of their teams and entire organizations, are highly suspect. How about you in your personal and professional growth journey?

Step 4: Invest in Your Relationship Bank

In this step, you'll begin to realize that beyond the three relational ecosystem types, it's the quality of their participants, fundamental purpose, value creation, and delivery success factors, and the chemistry between the participants that make an enormous difference. You'll begin to gravitate toward highly valuable relational ecosystem orchestrators, coordinators, and complementors. You'll experience a commitment to real innovation (versus innovation theater) and how participants show up and create enormous value by removing bottlenecks, bureaucracies, and redundancies.

Your aim here is to prune potential Fender Benders – energy- and resource-sucking contacts. You'll want to narrow your focus, the value you contribute, and the value that you get from key relationships. I'm a firm believer in staying positive and cordial. Yet, you'll increasingly find demands on your already challenged bandwidth. So, you'll have to narrow the scope of your collaboration and co-creation efforts with fewer, more authentic, and value-based relationships. Even within a one-to-few or one-to-many model, you'll find some individual relationships to be the best fit between your personal and professional growth needs and what the participants bring to the table. Focus on those.

Step 5: Capitalize Your Curve Benders

Focus on a series of touchstone events to attend or immerse yourself among the best thinkers, passionate doers, and those with unique insights for exciting discussions. In the pre-pandemic world, I found great content and connections at South by Southwest (SxSW), TechCrunch Disrupt SF, WSJ.D hosted by *The Wall Street Journal*, the *Fast Company* Innovation Festival, and the Mobile World Congress.

Beyond buying a pass to attend, although a significant first step, aim to create an experience to present your ideas and get other collaborators engaged before, during, and after each event. Could you invite your strategic relationships and ask them to invite someone they believe would greatly benefit from the discussions or contribute to it? Don't make it a production – as a matter of fact, the simpler, the less friction, the more high-value experience, the better. Over the years, I've taken several senior executive teams and their boards to the Consumer Electronics Show (CES) and curated an immersive two-to-three-day experience to witness firsthand how every business (model) currently is or soon will be under attack – often from unknown competitors. This is one example of strategizing to evolve through strategic relationships with prospective Curve Benders.

PHASE THREE: VISUALIZE NON-LINEAR GROWTH

In the next six to nine years, most everyone you know will settle into their stride. They'll get comfortable – and, unfortunately, complacent! That's where you'll have an opportunity to set yourself apart through how you think, plan, prioritize, and execute now. Although not impossible, it'll be more difficult to decide when you get to that future to break away from the pack. Your best bet is to think about those opportunities now. How can you accelerate your growth, dramatically elevate and enhance your portfolio of relationships, become more relevant in response to the critical trends around you, and significantly increase your market value? This is your opportunity to visualize non-linear growth (Figure 7.7).

A single share of Apple, Inc. stock (NASDAQ: AAPL) nine years ago was $22. As of the writing of this book, it's north of $110 per share. That's five times the value. How can you plan a five-time value increase in your knowledge, expertise, breadth, and depth of relationships in the next nine years?

Step 1: Align Your Personal and Professional Aspirations

This step aims to set yourself apart from others you observe to be on a linear path forward. Here you're willing to embrace more uncertainty as you continue to level-set expectations in your personal and professional aspirations. You can't possibly include every detail, or foresee obstacles, or the impact of many of the 15 forces on you that far out. What you *can* do is plan and articulate a clear vision for your journey in the next decade while being open to adapting and iterating your strategy and actions as you get more clarity and make a more significant number of data-driven decisions. This phase involves adopting and adapting to new learnings. This is where you'll also see your most significant aspirational leaps, as new options may become available that were previously unclear or unknown.

According to research, today's college graduates will work for nearly 50 years.[5] Even if you don't have to work for financial reasons, you will want to remain relevant for meaning, purpose, and relationships. This is why non-linear growth is your biggest asset in consistently

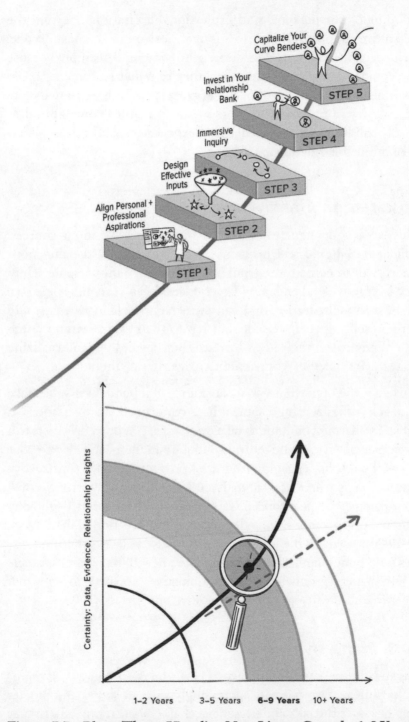

Figure 7.7   Phase Three: Visualize Non-Linear Growth, 6–9 Years

recalibrating your personal and professional aspirations, beyond the three-to-five-month decisions to a longer horizon of the next decade. I often coach managers and leaders not to switch jobs simply because of the compensation structure unless they're under extreme financial stress. The tenure you'll gain in any organization in three to five years or an industry in five to eight years will help mature your skills, dramatically solidify your knowledge and experiences, and create a bedrock of invaluable relationships.

Step 2: Design Effective Inputs

In this step, you begin to filter the highest-quality input sources. Beyond a few digital and print options, I've found visualizing non-linear growth to come more from opportunities to immerse myself in highly interactive and engaging experiences. I can read an article or a book by a thought leader, or I can immerse myself in videos where they're presenting their key ideas, listen to their podcasts, and watch them online project their ideas forward. But beyond just internalizing new ideas, you'll need an opportunity to synthesize them.

Here is the opportunity to make your lean input deliver value: take that input, synthesize it, and apply it in as many quality conversations as possible. By sharing your unique take on an idea, you open up others to a different perspective, create individual inquiry in them, and elevate your brand as thoughtful, engaging, and even provocative (in a constructive manner). This is where you shine. Even if you're entirely wrong, you'll create a dialogue that gets noticed, is appreciated by most forward-thinking leaders and organizations, and often changes the direction of the project, the team, or, perhaps, the organization. Suppose your organization dismisses it, or underappreciates or undervalues new thinking and strategic evolution of ideas, products, projects, or initiatives. You need to know that in order to find/create opportunities to learn and grow.

Step 3: Immersive Inquiry

In this step, immersive inquiry takes a beautiful twist. Here is an example: Non-linear narratives are increasingly used in shows and movies to help discover the past and present of characters (Figure 7.8). Events are portrayed out of chronological order or a logical order presented in the story. The pattern of circumstances needs to jump around and not follow a linear pattern.

When the character development needs more attention, or the story feels stale, screenwriters often shake things up and bounce scenes around. They also include dramatic effects in storytelling, such as stories told in reverse or divergent points of view juxtaposed. This is a more frequent technique for flashbacks, quick cutaway jokes, or bouncing around season to season to reinforce an idea in TV shows. *This Is Us* is one such example. *The Godfather Part II* used this form in jumping between Vito emigrating, Michael's story, and then back to Vito as he grows up and becomes the Godfather.

The screenplay bends time to its advantage, integrates unique aspects of the narrative's characters, and shows us a correlation and causation that we might not pick up on our own. Likewise, we would do well to remember that our growth rarely comes from neat, linear stories. The most significant leaps are often wonderfully non-linear.

What if, instead of merely searching for an answer, in the future of how you worked you were able to bend time and see the results of the questions? Think about it a second – when we ask questions, we're curious about a series of events. What if you could see the answers, and they dramatically accelerated your journey through the inquiry process? That's, in essence, what our S-curves do for us – they accelerate our growth in a dramatically shorter amount of time. In this step and phase, the adaptive and accelerated learning I referenced earlier comes

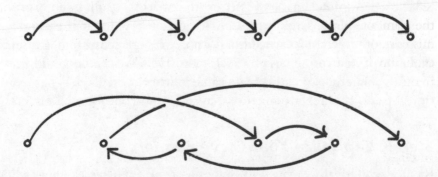

Figure 7.8   Non-Linear Narratives in Shows and Movies

alive. Your inquiry leads to precisely what you need to learn at that moment in time, and you immediately apply it toward the outcomes you're after. *If then* suddenly becomes *if when*.

Step 4: Invest in Your Relationship Bank

In this step, you'll want to link specific relationships in any ecosystem to exponential growth. This approach is consistent with your ongoing pruning efforts. Let's say you began your Act Now phase with 100–150 strategic relationships you believe will be critical to your success. Over the next several phases and years, as you gather more data, evidence, and relationship insights, you'll soon discover that a small subset is consistently proactive. They stay in touch, think of you, and reach out; you've had great success together in the past, and you're clearly on the same personal and professional growth trajectory.

These truly transformative relationships become the opportunity and imperative for your non-linear trajectory. Relational ecosystems comprised of quality participants demonstrate acumen, and soon they become a source of competitive differentiation. These relationships deliver fast and quantifiable results. You find others who are equally passionate about their growth and applying that growth to creativity, scale, and uniquely serving the market, beyond any participant's capabilities.

Research conducted by Deloitte and OpenMatters shows investors placing higher enterprise value on companies deemed network orchestrators than those seen as participants in traditional industries and value chains.[6] Think of mapping your relational ecosystem as the Salesforce AppExchange, touted as the world's leading enterprise cloud marketplace. Salesforce reported that every dollar it earned in 2017 resulted in $3.67 earned by its AppExchange ecosystem, a figure that is expected to increase to $5.18 by 2022.[7] Who else would dramatically benefit, earn, and create value in where you play? What relationships do you need to nurture that surround your Curve Benders?

Step 5: Capitalize Your Curve Benders

By now, you ideally have identified one or more Curve Benders who are passionate about your challenges/opportunities. Your goal here is as diverse a network as possible, as these "weak ties" create entrée to people and perspectives in very different departments, organizations, industries, and even countries.[8] They're incredibly valuable because they often develop relational on-ramps to new information. In contrast, your existing relationships (co-workers, neighbors, partners, vendors, investors, and media contacts) have already provided experiences, insights, and opportunities that are familiar to you.

As you may recall, this is the unique phase where most will continue their linear growth. Your journey will take the desired non-linear path because rather than dismissing the vast network of people you hardly know, you will organize it into a source of ideas, connections, and assistance. In other words, your shallow but wide networks today will become the source for Curve Benders, who can unlock your influence in the next decade.

PHASE FOUR: SEQUENCE YOUR S-CURVES

The next decade is the most exciting, yet uncertain, to me, because I think about where we've been in the past decade. Our lives are almost unrecognizable due to innovations like the Apple iPad, Amazon Alexa, meal kits, wearables, Instagram, consumer drones, Uber, Netflix Originals, Airbnb, 4G, MOOCs, 4K TVs, Nest, DoorDash, Venmo, Slack, Android, LED bulbs, Impossible Burger, Tesla Autopilot, and reusable rockets. How exciting to imagine where we'll be in the next decade! Even more so to get immersed in the next decade of job shifters, industry makers, and life-changing aspirations now. I believe the only way to get there is through non-linear learning and growth, fueled by Curve Benders (Figure 7.9).

Step 1: Align Your Personal and Professional Aspirations

Here, you're adapting to the 15 forces and their impact on your life. In the next decade, we hope you'll have at least one personal S-curve under your belt, and you've experienced firsthand both your willingness and ability to adapt, maneuver, evolve, and learn at an accelerated pace. The key here is to find if you can link one aspiration to the next.

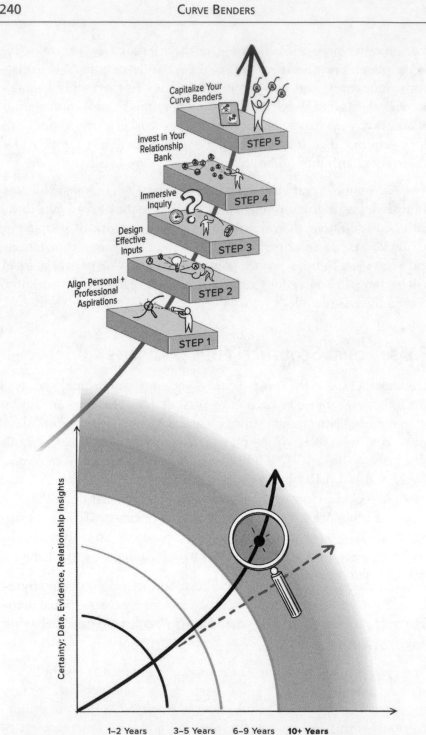

Figure 7.9   Phase Four: Sequence Your S-Curves, 10+ Years

You'll reach that dream job; then what? You'll find a significant other; how will you grow together? Having kids or having kids reach their developmental milestone is often the beginning; what do you aspire to reach, do, or become after that?

As you gain data and evidence, your personal and professional aspirations will evolve. Unlike a traditional goal-setting exercise or rigid questions, like "Where do you want to be in 10 years?," you need to become more methodical in continuous alignment. Think of step one in this phase as your guardrails in the future of how you'll work, live, play, and give. As you make progress on each of these phases, you create a rolling journey of the next phase, assessing key learning and growth experiences along the way. The agility and speed on which you focus your growth trajectory will make a massive difference in the quality of your path forward.

Step 2: Design Effective Inputs

Here, you'll uncover the highly interconnected nature of your lean input sources. You attend one conference and meet a brilliant presenter or someone sitting next to you, who brings up an idea. You internalize it, apply it, benefit from it. You attend the same conference next year and this time present the impact of the concept from the previous year and leave with dozens, if not hundreds, of business cards from others who want to know more, try your idea for themselves, enhance it, elevate it, or build upon it. That conference becomes a vital enabler of your envisioning, linking one personal S-curve to the next. The ideas from that conference become fuel in how you understand, synthesize, and parlay ideas into your personal and professional growth.

As you gain data, evidence, and relationship insights, your strategies will evolve. Instead of purely acting in a highly transactional manner to impact your next 12–24 months, you're thinking and behaving more strategically about the next three to five years. "How will I be more differentiated in the job market than I am today?" is a good question to ask. Ideal is if you tie your evolution to specific consumption goals of input, continuously look to optimize the sources of those inputs, elevate the quality of those inputs, synthesize and socialize them; you'll very quickly discover that, similar to a medical device or a sales process, your design input directly impacts your growth outputs.

Step 3: Immersive Inquiry

I believe we'll ask questions very differently. Immersive inquiry is already dramatically challenged by technologies such as Watson, which can analyze millions of medical records for diagnosis, drug conflicts, and extrapolate possible side effects.[9] So, is it any surprise that your immersive inquiry in the next decade will be fueled by sensors, wearables, and a set of business rules that will predict a logical flow of subsequent questions?

The key will be for you to play chess, thinking several moves ahead in combining what you do know and where you're trying to go in subsequent S-curves sequencing one another, with experiments and explorations of those leaps and bounds. If you didn't use a keyboard today, how could you input data? If the camera on our devices could pick up my hand gestures, could those become the same natural gestures we use to get around our smartphones now? Will we still need and use financial, health, or insurance products and services like we do today?

A strong metric here is to ask, given the *methods* with which you immerse yourself in inquiry, are you able to uncover potential Curve Benders? A reciprocal metric here is how often your immersive inquiry reveals those in need of you to do curve bending for them.

Step 4: Invest in Your Relationship Bank

You're uncertain about the variables that could impact your relational ecosystem. The key is continual creation of relational gravity for you and your ideas. If sequencing one S-curve into another will define the future of how you'll work, then how you extend, expand, and elevate your relationship bank will be its quantifiable set of metrics.

I've found these five questions to be particularly useful now in creating and sustaining relational gravity for the next decade of the work I believe I want to be doing. Start by sharing your insights from your catalyst, immersive inquiry, refraction point, and adaptive learning on your challenge or opportunity, and gauge their immediate reactions. In particular:

1. What questions, which you believe would dramatically elevate my perspective on this topic, am I not asking?

2. Where do you believe this topic (or a particular facet of it) is headed in the next decade? Why or how so, and where did that perspective come from?

3. Have you read anything incredibly insightful on this topic or come across others struggling with similar challenges/opportunities?

4. Do you know of communities of practitioners focused on these challenges/opportunities?

5. You've been kind with your time, insights, and relationship references. How can I be an asset to your efforts?

It's important to focus on a few immersive inquiries about your challenge or opportunity. If you openly share your progress with your most strategic relationships, you'll be surprised how often you tend to stay top of mind with those who can accelerate your progress.

Step 5: Capitalize Your Curve Benders

Look for tools to help you scan the 15 forces and, specifically, the relationship connections between your existing portfolio of relationships and individuals at the epicenter of experiments and exploration of those 15 forces. One fascinating approach here is to explore curve-bending relationships that may be outliers or anomalies. Whether distant from the core of your challenge/opportunity or a relationship from an entirely different perspective, Curve Benders, with a distinctly different point of view, will be invaluable to the expertise of your subject matter.

A regular pattern of reaching out to Curve Benders here will help you identify contrarian networks. Think of them as individuals who want to prove your hypothesis wrong or don't believe that your immersive inquiry has produced meaningful insights. I've found a direct correlation between engaging naysayers and the quality of my ideas. The more your pushback, the more determined I become to solidify my ideas with more rigorous data, empirical evidence, and relationship insights. Remember, this isn't personal – it's the incredibly difficult work necessary to become world-class in your chosen field. Most people don't think and behave in more non-linear curves because they haven't discovered how to sequence one S-curve to the next.

In a decade or more, anomaly detection for Curve Benders specific to your challenge/opportunity will be using methods and algorithms in machine learning that only a few understand today. The key will be your proactive cadence to gauge, update, refresh, apply, and reengage your Curve Benders. They'll be rooting for you.

FINAL STEP: CURVE-BENDING IMPACT

Earlier in this chapter, when I defined your strategic relationships' contextual relevancy as your starting place, I thought it would be appropriate to wrap up this chapter with a revisit to that foundational idea. If you apply rigor and discipline in your execution of a Curve Benders Roadmap, I believe the impact of your portfolio of relationships will emerge (Figure 7.10).

Keep this information updated as a living, breathing list of your most valuable and strategic relationships. You could certainly add a

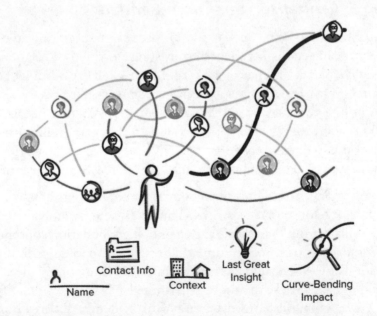

Figure 7.10   Your Relationship Bank and Its Curve-Bending Impact

column to the right of each contact, titled "Curve-Bending Impact." You can download a template of this chart at nourgroup.com:

Strategic Relationship	Cell	EM	Context	Last Great Insight	Curve-Bending Impact
1. John Smith			Technology advancements	10/20 Call on the impact of 5G on IoT	1/21 Instrumental in elevating my personal tech stack
2. Susan Johnson			Diversity, inclusion, equity	6/20 Spoke on the same D&I panel around BLM; astute	2/21 Introduced me to head of D&I and XYZ company over dinner
3. Erica Thompson			Organizational design	8/20 Fabulous conversation on human-centered design and org. structures	3/21 Brilliant joint article in the *WSJ* on chief entrepreneur
4. Pete Gonzales			International expansion	11/20 Virtual presentation on global trade in post-pandemic economies	4/21 Jointly delivered a series of virtual interactive roundtables on getting demand back

You'll want to measure investments in the relationship by both sides. I like quality joint projects and net-new opportunities to create awareness for our respective areas of expertise. Appreciate and plan to reciprocate with passion whenever friends and colleagues think of you for opportunities to co-create value for a targeted executive community.

As I advocated in *Relationship Economics*, opportunities to enhance your relationships' quality, breadth, and depth are a valiant pursuit. Here are several evergreen questions when it comes to your Relationship Bank:

- Did my relationship with these individuals materially improve my condition?

- Did I contribute to their personal and professional growth, such that they've become advocates of our relationship?

- Am I more expert in subject-matter (depth) or am I more proficient in the field's tangential areas (breadth) because of this relationship?

- Did this person elevate my behavior in my growth areas?

CHAPTER 7 SUMMARY

1. The Curve Benders Roadmap has four distinct timeline phases: Act Now, Strategize to Evolve, Visualize Non-Linear Growth, and Sequence Your S-Curves. Each phase brings more data, evidence, and insights.

2. Within each phase, your Curve Benders Roadmap has five repeatable actions: Align Your Personal and Professional Aspirations, Design Effective Inputs, Immersive Inquiry, Invest in Your Relationship Bank, and Capitalize Your Curve Benders.

3. When you consistently align personal and professional aspirations, you create a plan-ahead team. They collect forward-looking intelligence for you and brainstorm possible scenarios for tactical actions now while keeping strategic options for your future.

4. When you design effective inputs, you ensure your information diet is lean, enriching, and strengthening. You are eliminating toxic and unnecessary information.

5. Immersive inquiry is a fine method to arm yourself to defend your position with facts, data, and insights.

6. Investing in your relationship bank to your network helps you weather any storm the 15 forces may bring.

7. As you demonstrate passion and prudence to your Curve Benders, they will plan for your non-linear growth. Aim to capitalize them in the process continually.

Final Thoughts

Ihope you found the ideas here relevant and took away insights, quotes, and actionable advice.

I'm grateful for unique bosses, colleagues, and partners throughout my life. More recently, coaches, mentors, and admirable clients have made my life choices – whether advising leaders and their boards, speaking to global audiences, educating leaders, or coaching executives – an absolute joy.

I've learned much from rather unlikely sources: my children, neighbors, and past grad professors reconnected after 20 years. As I think about my Curve Benders, here are 10 final thoughts.

1. **If you want anything in life, you have to go after it.** I came to this country with $100, a suitcase, limited English, and few family ties. I feel blessed every day to live the American Dream. We all fail; we are victims of wrongdoing or suffer the consequences of others' actions or failures to act. The key is to leave these states ASAP. You can spend much time, effort, and energy being upset about a job layoff or you can spend them on finding your next job. I've discovered that hustle and tenacity are incredible pathfinders to luck!

2. **Curve Benders seldom stroll into your life; you must seek them out.** Nothing will replace your due diligence, deep inquiry, being your best every day, and time with people you don't have to impress.

3. **A solid foundation at home will give you the necessary confidence to explore your future.** Wendy and I will celebrate our 25-year anniversary in 2021. She has been our family's solid foundation and enabled all the risks I've taken

to try new ideas, expand, fail, learn, and grow. Find your Rock of Gibraltar and source of your faith, support, and guidance. Then figure out the rest together.

4. **Become an expert first, then an advisor, speaker, author, coach, or mentor a distant second.** My business doesn't depend on an industry associations' alphabet soup of credentials after my name. I've gained business because I've become a student of business relationships and their applications in driving growth, promoting innovation, and visual storytelling.

5. **Uncertainty doesn't have to equal chaos.** While no one can see the future, the difference between thriving and struggling to survive is planning ability and to plan and develop resilience.

6. **Only you can define your market value.** Care less about what other people think, say, or do. Small minds will always squash big ideas. Invest in you – education is something that no one can ever take away from you and is the best enabler of your non-linear growth, and thus future success.

7. **It's tough to bend curves with people you don't know.** The premise of this book reinforces two previous books in the series, *Relationship Economics* and *Co-Create*. In the previous books, I've written about how to turn some of your everyday contacts into more strategic relationships. Some of those relationships will help you co-create new possibilities. Curve Benders will shape your future success and significance. You must deliberately choose the relationships in which you invest to be able to innovate with them. Serial iteration and innovation with them over a lifetime let them become your Curve Benders and let you do the same for others.

8. **Kindness and grace go a long way in becoming a Curve Bender in others' lives.** Our society says that money and status prove success. Change that view by showing that grace and kindness are just as important. I believe it; you should, too.

9. **If you're the smartest person in the room, you are in the wrong room.** Never lose your humility to learn, grow, fail, learn, try again, fail again, only to surprise yourself with just how far you've come.

10. **You can watch disruption happen, chose to be a part of the wave, or find opportunities to lead it.** Wouldn't you rather be racing a motorcycle than watching a race? If I'm ever in the lead, that's just icing on the cake.

Here is to your Curve Bending Movement.

– Nour

NOTES

INTRODUCTION: DON'T DOUBT WAZE!

1. CNBC International TV, "Punctuated Equilibrium and Investing in Moments of Change | CNBC Conversation," YouTube Video, 2:01, October 5, 2019, https://www.youtube.com/watch?v=?ce4IW-5Ruc.
2. "Punctuated Equilibrium," Wikipedia, https://en.wikipedia.org/wiki/Punctuated_equilibrium.
3. National Education Association of the United States Committee of Ten on Secondary School Studies, "Report of the Committee of Ten on Secondary School Studies: With the Reports of the Conferences Arranged by the Committee," published for the National Education Association by the American Book Co., p. 17, https://archive.org/details/reportcommittee00studgoog/page/n43/mode/2up.
4. Tasha Eurich, "What Self-Awareness Really Is (and How to Cultivate It)," *Harvard Business Review*, January 4, 2018, https://hbr.org/2018/01/what-self-awareness-really-is-and-how-to-cultivate-it.

CHAPTER 1: WORK–LIFE BLENDING

1. Penelope Christensen, "Understanding Names in Genealogy," June 2012 course. The National Institute for Genealogical Studies.
2. "What Does Your Last Name Say About You?," Ancestry, July 1, 2014,https://blogs.ancestry.com/cm/there-are-7-types-of-english-surnames-which-one-is-yours/.
3. "Be Rich: Our Annual Generosity Campaign," Buckhead Church, https://buckheadchurch.org/be-rich.
4. Danielle Muoio, "Amtrak Will Start Using High-Speed Trains in 2021 – But Your Trip Will Still Take Just as Long," *Business Insider*, December 7, 2016, https://www.businessinsider.com/why-amtrak-acela-high-speed-trains-not-faster-2016-12.
5. Christopher Quinn, "Leadership Atlanta Names Class of 2021," *Atlanta-Journal-Constitution*, June 2, 2020, https://www.ajc.com/news/local/leadership-atlanta-names-class-2021.

6. "Understanding the Value Agenda," CEO.Works blog, September 19, 2018.

7. Personal interview with Sandy Ogg of CEO.Works, January 2019.

8. Annette LaPrade, Janet Mertens, Tanya Moore, and Amy Wright, "The Enterprise Guide to Closing the Skills Gap: Strategies for Building and Maintaining a Skilled Workforce," IBM Institute for Business Value, September 2019, https://www.ibm.com/thought-leadership/institute-business-value/report/closing-skills-gap#.

9. "More Than a Third of Babies Born in 2012 Will Live to 100, Report Predicts," *The Guardian*, March 26, 2012, https://www.theguardian.com/society/2012/mar/26/third-babies-2012-live-100.

CHAPTER 2: 15 FORCES IMPACTING YOUR FUTURE

1. A.L. Duckworth, C. Peterson, M.D. Matthews, and D.R. Kelly, "Grit: Perseverance and Passion for Long-Term Goals," *Journal of Personality and Social Psychology* 92, no. 6 (2007): 1087.

2. M. Credé, M.C. Tynan, and P.D. Harms, "Much Ado about Grit: A Meta-Analytic Synthesis of the Grit Literature," *Journal of Personality and Social Psychology* 113, no. 3 (2017): 492–511.

3. "Eric R. Kandel – Facts," NobelPrize.org, July 6, 2020.

4. Samantha Jordan, Gerald Ferris, Wayne Hochwarter, and Thomas Wright, "Toward a Work Motivation Conceptualization of Grit in Organizations," *Group & Organization Management* 44, no. 2 (2019): 320–360.

5. "Driving Impact at Scale from Automation and AI," McKinsey Digital, February 2019, https://www.mckinsey.com/~/media/McKinsey/Business Functions/McKinsey Digital/Our Insights/Driving impact at scale from automation and AI/Driving-impact-at-scale-from-automation-and-AI.ashx.

6. Mary Baker, "9 Future of Work Trends Post-COVID-19," Gartner, June 8, 2020, https://www.gartner.com/smarterwithgartner/9-future-of-work-trends-post-covid-19/.

7. "Olympics 2012: Michael Phelps Has Mastered the Psychology of Speed," *Washington Post*, YouTube, June 15, 2012, https://www.youtube.com/watch?v=Htw780vHH0o&feature=youtu.be.

8. FINA, "Coaching the Best Swimmer of All Time: Michael Phelps – Session 1, FINA Golden Coaches Clinic, 2016," YouTube, February 13, 2017, https://www.youtube.com/watch?v=N0Kma3WLbTQ.

9. Kathleen Stansberry, Janna Anderson, and Lee Rainie, "Experts Optimistic About the Next 50 Years of Digital Life," Pew Research Center, October 28, 2019, https://www.pewresearch.org/internet/2019/10/28/experts-optimistic-about-the-next-50-years-of-digital-life/.

10. Richard Watson, "Timeline of Emerging Science & Technology (2014 to 2030+)," What's Next: Top Trends, June 27, 2014, https://toptrends.nowandnext.com/2014/06/27/timeline-of-emerging-science-technology-2014-2050/.

11. iShares by BlackRock, "Own the Future of Innovation," May 2020, https://www.ishares.com/us/literature/brochure/megatrends-101-future-of-innovation.pdf.

12. Christopher Groskopf, "Projected Median Age of the US Population, through 2060," https://theatlas.com/charts/rkeE6oqa

13. Wolfgang Lutz, Anne Goujon, Samir KC, Marcin Stonawski, and Nikolaos Stillianikis (Eds.), "Demographics and Human Capital Scenarios for the 21st Century," European Commission, https://ec.europa.eu/jrc/sites/jrcsh/files/lutz_et_al_2018_demographic_and_human_capital.pdf.

14. United Nations, "World Population Ageing, 2019," https://www.un.org/en/development/desa/population/publications/pdf/ageing/WorldPopulationAgeing2019-Highlights.pdf.

15. United Nations, "World Migration Report," June 2020, https://www.un.org/sites/un2.un.org/files/wmr_2020.pdf.

16. BlackRock, "Megatrends: Demographics and Social Change," July 2020, https://www.blackrock.com/uk/intermediaries/themes/thematic-investing/megatrends-explained/demographics-social-change.

17. D.R. Vogel, G.W. Dickson, and J.A. Lehman, "Persuasion and the Role of Visual Presentation Support: The UM/EM Study," MIS Research Center, School of Management, University of Minnesota, June 1986, http://thinktwicelegal.com/olio/articles/persuasion_article.pdf.

18. Angela Ahrendts, "Burberry's CEO on Turning an Aging British Icon into a Global Luxury Brand," *Harvard Business Review*, January–February 2013, https://hbr.org/2013/01/burberrys-ceo-on-turning-an-aging-british-icon-into-a-global-luxury-brand.

19. Benjamin Obeng, "Why This Billion Dollar Beauty Brand Could Do with Angela Ahrendts' Saving Touch," *Medium*, August 26, 2019, https://medium.com/@benjosh243/why-this-billion-dollar-

beauty-brand-could-do-with-angela-ahrendts-saving-touch-968b98413394.

20. Lucinda Shen, "The 20 Biggest Companies That Have Filed for Bankruptcy Because of the Coronavirus Pandemic," *Fortune*, June 29,2020,https://fortune.com/2020/06/29/companies-filing-bankruptcy-2020-during-coronavirus-pandemic-covid-19-economy-industries/.

21. Klaus Schwab and Saadia Zahidi, "5 Trends in the Global Economy – and Their Implications for Economic Policymaking," World Economic Forum, October 9, 2019, https://www.weforum.org/agenda/2019/10/global-competitiveness-report-2019-economic-trends-for-policymakers/.

22. Global Future Council on Cities and Urbanization, "Data Driven Cities: 20 Stories of Innovation," World Economic Forum, October 2017, http://www3.weforum.org/docs/Top20_Global_Data_Stories_report_2017.pdf.

23. Andrew S. Winston, "The World in 2030: Nine Megatrends to Watch," *MIT Sloan Management Review*, May 7, 2019.

24. Joe Rennison, Eric Platt, and Dave Lee, "Amazon Secures Record Low Borrowing Costs," *Financial Times*, June 1, 2020, https://www.ft.com/content/a5b6138b-df18-497f-bed1-57a0f75bfc1f.

25. "Workers Who Could Work from Home, Did Work at Home, and Were Paid for Work at Home, by Selected Characteristics, Averages for the Period of 2017–2018," U.S. Bureau of Labor Statistics Economic News Release, last modified September 24, 2019, https://www.bls.gov/news.release/flex2.t01.htm.

26. Janna Anderson and Lee Raini, "Concerns about Democracy in the Digital Age," Pew Research Center, Internet and Technology, February 21, 2020, https://www.pewresearch.org/internet/2020/02/21/concerns-about-democracy-in-the-digital-age/.

27. Michael Sheetz, "Watch Out, UPS. Morgan Stanley Estimates Amazon Is Already Delivering Half of Its Packages," CNBC, December 12, 2019, https://www.cnbc.com/2019/12/12/analyst-amazon-delivering-nearly-half-its-packages-instead-of-ups-fedex.html.

28. Brooklin from OrderMetrics, "The Amazon Seller Metrics That Matter Most," *Repricer Express*, May 20, 2020, https://www.repricerexpress.com/amazon-seller-metrics/.

29. "Global Warming Could Render the Assets of Many Financial Companies Worthless, Mark Carney Warns," *Financial Post*, December 30, 2019, https://financialpost.com/news/fp-street/boes-carney-says-finance-must-act-faster-on-climate-change.

30. Parag Khanna, "All Roads Need Not Lead to China," *Noema*, July 13, 2020, https://www.noemamag.com/all-roads-need-not-lead-to-china/.

31. Kieron O'Hara and Wendy Hall, "Four Internets: The Geopolitics of Digital Governance," Centre for International Governance Innovation, December 7, 2018, https://www.cigionline.org/publications/four-internets-geopolitics-digital-governance.

32. Mariana Mazzucato, "Mission-Oriented Innovation Policy," https://marianamazzucato.com/research/mission-oriented-innovation-policy/.

33. Sean Fleming, "World Order Is Going to Be Rocked by AI – This Is How," World Economic Forum, February 13, 2020, https://www.weforum.org/agenda/2020/02/ai-looks-set-to-disrupt-the-established-world-order-here-s-how.

34. Todd Harrison, Kaitlyn Johnson, Thomas G. Roberts, Tyler Way, and Makena Young, "Space Threat Assessment 2020," Center for Strategic and International Studies, March 2020, https://aerospace.csis.org/wp-content/uploads/2020/03/Harrison_SpaceThreat Assessment20_WEB_FINAL-min.pdf.

35. "Global Counterspace Capabilities," Secure World Foundation, July 2, 2020, https://swfound.org/counterspace/.

36. Samuel Brannen, Kathleen H. Hicks, Seth G. Jones, Rebecca Hersman, and Todd Harrison, "World Order After Covid-19," Center for Strategic and International Studies, May 28, 2020, https://www.csis.org/analysis/world-order-after-covid-19.

37. "Global Trends 2030: Alternative Worlds," National Intelligence Council, December 2012, https://www.dni.gov/files/documents/GlobalTrends_2030.pdf.

38. UN Intergovernmental Panel on Climate Change (IPCC) 2019 report, https://www.ipcc.ch/.

39. Jérémie Mouginot et al., "Forty-Six Years of Greenland Ice Sheet Mass Balance from 1972 to 2018," *Proceedings of the National Academy of Sciences of the United States of America*, May 7, 2019, https://www.pnas.org/content/116/19/9239.

40. "China – Gross Domestic Product per Capita Based on Purchasing Parity in Current Prices," World Data Atlas, https://knoema.com/atlas/China/GDP-per-capita-based-on-PPP.

41. "The World in 2050," PWC Global, February 2017, https://www.pwc.com/gx/en/issues/economy/the-world-in-2050.html.

42. Saeid Golkar, "There Is No Hope for Political Reform Led by Iranian Moderates," *Aljazeera*, September 5, 2019, https://www.aljazeera.com/indepth/opinion/hope-political-reform-led-ira-nian-moderates-190828141846978.html.

43. "Commodification of Cyber Capabilities: A Grand Cyber Arms Bazaar," 2019 Public-Private Analytic Exchange Program, U.S. Department of Homeland Security, https://www.dhs.gov/sites/default/files/publications/ia/ia_geopolitical-impact-cyber-threats-nation-state-actors.pdf.

44. "An Update to the Economic Outlook: 2020 to 2030," Congressional Budget Office, July 2, 2020, https://www.cbo.gov/publication/56442.

CHAPTER 3: ACCELERATED RELEVANCY

1. "Growing a Resilient Business Outside of Silicon Valley," IDEO U Creative Confidence Podcast, May 8, 2020, https://www.ideou.com/blogs/inspiration/growing-a-resilient-business-outside-of-silicon-valley.

2. "What Is a Unicorn Startup?" CBInsights, September 2020, https://www.cbinsights.com/research-unicorn-companies.

3. Michael Canic, "To Make Real Change Happen, Embrace the Joy of Pain," *Chief Executive*, September 1, 2020, https://chiefexecutive.net/to-make-real-change-happen-embrace-the-joy-of-pain/.

4. Patricia Cobe, "Restaurants Blow Up Their Business Model to Survive Post-Covid," Restaurant Business Online, June 4, 2020, https://www.restaurantbusinessonline.com/operations/restaurants-blow-their-business-models-thrive-post-covid.

5. Marcel Schwantes, "This Famous Albert Einstein Quote Nails It: The Smartest People Today Display This 1 Trait," *Inc.*, February 15, 2018, https://www.inc.com/marcel-schwantes/this-1-simple-way-of-thinking-separates-smartest-people-from-everyone-else.html.

6. H. Beyer and K. Holtzblatt, *Contextual Design: Defining Customer-Centered Systems* (San Francisco, CA: Morgan Kaufmann Publishers, 1998).

7. Drucker Institute, Drucker Archives, https://www.drucker.institute/about/drucker-archives/.

8. Prasad Balkundi and Martin Kilduff, "The Ties That Lead: A Social Network Approach to Leadership," *The Leadership Quarterly* 17, no. 4 (2006): 419–439.

9. Smitri Bhagat, Moira Burke, Carlos Diuk, Ismail Onur Filiz, and Sergey Edunov, "Three and a Half Degrees of Separation," Facebook Research, February 4, 2016, https://research.fb.com/blog/2016/02/three-and-a-half-degrees-of-separation/.

10. Phil Rosenzweig, *The Halo Effect: . . . And the Eight Other Business Delusions That Deceive Managers* (Simon & Schuster, 2014).

11. "What the Baader-Meinhof Phenomenon Is and Why You May See It Again . . . and Again," *Healthline*, December 17, 2019, https://www.healthline.com/health/baader-meinhof-phenomenon.

12. Sunnie Giles, "How to Fail Faster – And Why You Should," *Forbes*, April 30, 2018, https://www.forbes.com/sites/sunniegiles/2018/04/30/how-to-fail-faster-and-why-you-should/#44dba31fc177.

13. Stacy Liberatore, "Average Person Has Over 6,000 Thoughts per Day, According to Study That Isolated a 'Thought Worm' in the Human Brain Showing When an Idea Begins and Ends," *Daily Mail*, July 16, 2020, https://www.dailymail.co.uk/sciencetech/article-8531913/Average-person-6-000-thoughts-day-according-study-isolated-thought-worm.html.

14. Friedrich Nietzsche, *Thus Spoke Zarathustra: A Book for Everyone and Nobody* (Oxford University Press, 2008).

15. For a solid introduction to Chaos Theory as applies to the psychological mind, see Robin Robertson and Allan Combs, eds., *Chaos Theory in Psychology and the Life Sciences* (Psychology Press, 2014).

16. Laura Nash and Howard Stevenson, "Success That Lasts," *Harvard Business Review* 82, no. 2 (2004): 102–109.

17. "'You've Got to Find What You Love,' Jobs Says," *Stanford News*, July 14, 2005, https://news.stanford.edu/2005/06/14/jobs-061505/.

18. Steve Glaveski, "Where Companies Go Wrong with Learning and Development," *Harvard Business Review*, October 2, 2019, https://hbr.org/2019/10/where-companies-go-wrong-with-learning-and-development.

19. Charles Conn and Robert McLean, "Six Problem-Solving Mindsets for Very Uncertain Times," *McKinsey Quarterly*, September 15, 2020, https://www.mckinsey.com/business-functions/strategy-and-corporate-finance/our-insights/six-problem-solving-mindsets-for-very-uncertain-times.

CHAPTER 4: CURVE BENDERS AS RISK MITIGATORS IN YOUR PERSONAL S-CURVE

1. Matthew Rabin and Max Bazerman, "Fretting about Modest Risks Is a Mistake," *California Management Review* 61, no. 3 (2019): 34–48.
2. Rob Wile, "A Venture Capital Firm Just Named an Algorithm to Its Board of Directors – Here's What It Actually Does," *Business Insider*, May 13, 2014, https://www.businessinsider.com/vital-named-to-board-2014-5.
3. N. Sarwat and M. Abbas, "Individual Knowledge Creation Ability: Dispositional Antecedents and Relationship to Innovative Performance," *European Journal of Innovation Management*, September 28, 2020, https://www.emerald.com/insight/content/doi/10.1108/EJIM-05-2020-0198/full/html.
4. Inspired by "Early Warning Systems for Pandemics: Lessons Learned from Natural Hazards," US National Library of Medicine, National Institute for Health, Elsevier Public Health Emergency Collection, May 16, 2020, https://www.ncbi.nlm.nih.gov/pmc/articles/PMC7228879/.
5. Based on Kim Scott's book *Radical Candor: How to Get What You Want by Saying What You Mean* (Pan McMillan UK, 2018).
6. George Loewenstein, "The Psychology of Curiosity: A Review and Reinterpretation," *Psychological Bulletin* 116, no. 1 (1994): 75–90.
7. Jim Harter, "Employee Engagement on the Rise in the U.S.," Gallup, August 26, 2018, https://news.gallup.com/poll/241649/employee-engagement-rise.aspx.
8. "Creating a Learning Culture," WD-40 company website, https://wd40careers.org/our-tribe.
9. Abraham Carmeli and Zachary Sheaffer, "How Learning Leadership and Organizational Learning from Failures Enhance Perceived Organizational Capacity to Adapt to the Task Environment," *The Journal of Applied Behavioural Science* 44, no. 4 (2008): 468–489.

10. Stephanie Yan, "5 Years Ago, Bernie Madoff Was Sentenced to 150 Years in Prison – Here's How His Scheme Worked," *Business Insider*, July 1, 2014, https://www.businessinsider.com/how-bernie-madoffs-ponzi-scheme-worked-2014-7.

11. Douglas Heaven, "Elizabeth Holmes: The Hypnotic Tale of the Rise and Fall of Theranos," *NewScientist*, March 21, 2019, https://www.newscientist.com/article/2197299-elizabeth-holmes-the-hypnotic-tale-of-the-rise-and-fall-of-theranos/.

12. "Bridges," Explain That Stuff!, June 23, 2019, https://www.explainthatstuff.com/bridges.html.

13. Nevitt Sanford, *Where Colleges Fail: A Study of the Student as a Person* (Jossey-Bass, 1967), p. 98.

14. Charles B. Handy, *The Empty Raincoat: Making Sense of the Future* (New York: Random House, 1995).

15. Everett Rogers, *Diffusion of Innovations*, 5th ed. (Free Press, 2003).

16. Mario Coccia and Joshua Watts, "A Theory of the Evolution of Technology: Technological Parasitism and the Implications for Innovation Management," *Journal of Engineering and Technology Management* 55 (2020): 101552, https://doi.org/10.1016/j.jengtecman.2019.11.003.

17. Roberto Mangabeira Unger, *The Knowledge Economy* (Verso Books, 2019).

CHAPTER 5: ORGANIZATION OF THE FUTURE

1. Anna Thorsen, "Why Millennials Are Choosing Startups over Corporations," Valuer, January 15, 2019, https://www.valuer.ai/blog/why-millennials-are-choosing-startups-over-corporations.

2. "CEO's Curbed Confidence Spells Caution," 22nd Annual Global CEO Survey, PWC, 2019, https://www.pwc.com/mu/pwc-22nd-annual-global-ceo-survey-mu.pdf.

3. Rachel Feintzeig, "Recession Rises on List of CEO Fears in 2020," *Wall Street Journal*, January 2, 2020, https://www.wsj.com/articles/recession-rises-on-list-of-ceo-fears-for-2020-11577962921.

4. Brad Smart, "How to Avoid the 3 Biggest Problems in Your Hiring Process and Save Millions," Growth Institute, 2019, https://blog.growthinstitute.com/topgrading/3-problems-hiring-process.

5. "A Culture of Innovation: Similarities in Canadian and American Corporate Innovation Cultures," An Impact Brief, University of

Toronto Impact Centre, May 2016, https://narwhalproject.org/wp-content/uploads/2017/10/A-Culture-of-Innovation.pdf.

6. George R. Crowley and Russell S. Sobel, "Adam Smith: Managerial Insights from the Father of Economics," *Journal of Management History*, September 2010.

7. Jim Connell, Gary C. Edgar, Bill Olex, Robin Scholl, Todd Shulman, and Russ Tietjen, "Troubling Successes and Good Failures: Successful New Product Development Requires Five Critical Factors," *Engineering Management Journal* 13, no. 4 (2001): 35–39.

8. Steve Blank, "Why Companies Do 'Innovation Theater' Instead of Actual Innovation," *Harvard Business Review*, October 7, 2019, https://hbr.org/2019/10/why-companies-do-innovation-theater-instead-of-actual-innovation.

9. Michael Ringel, Ramón Baeza, Raholl Panandiker, and Johann D. Harnoss, "Successful Innovators Walk the Talk," BCG, June 22, 2020, https://www.bcg.com/publications/2020/most-innovative-companies/successful-innovation.

10. Michael Ringel, Ramón Baeza, Raholl Panandiker, and Johann D. Harnoss, "Tomorrow's Innovation Leaders Are Made Today," Boston Consulting Group, April 13, 2020, https://www.bcg.com/publications/2020/six-moves-for-innovation-during-recovery.

11. Ringel, Baeza, Panandiker, and Harnoss, "Successful Innovators Walk the Talk."

12. Douglas R. Vogel, Gary W. Dickson, John A. Lehman, "Persuasion and the Role of Visual Presentation Support: The UM/3M Study," MIS Research Center, School of Management, University of Minnesota, June 1986, http://misrc.umn.edu/workingpapers/full-papers/1986/8611.pdf.

13. Amy Huber, *Telling the Design Story: Effective and Engaging Communication* (Taylor & Francis, 2017).

14. "Creating Resilient Leadership Develop Program to Navigate Change," Herrmann International Blog, https://blog.thinkherrmann.com/.

15. Ford Motor Company, Corporate Governance and Policies, Sustainability and Innovation Committee Charter, https://corporate.ford.com/content/dam/corporate/us/en-us/documents/governance-and-policies/company-governance-sustainability-and-innovation-committee-charter.pdf.

16. "Where Have All the Long-Tenured CEOs Gone?" Korn Ferry Institute, https://www.kornferry.com/insights/articles/where-have-all-the-long-tenured-ceos-gone.

17. "The CEO 100, 2019 Edition," *Harvard Business Review*, November–December 2019, https://hbr.org/2019/11/the-ceo-100-2019-edition#the-ceo-life-cycle.

18. Minna Saunila, "Innovation Capability in Achieving Higher Performance: Perspectives of Management and Employees," *Technology Analysis & Strategic Management* 29, no. 8 (2017): 903–916.

19. Beverley Head, "How Do We Lift Our Innovation Game?" *Company Director* 35, no. 10 (2019): 22.

20. Kosmas Papadopoulos, "Board Refreshment: Finding the Right Balance," Harvard Law School Forum on Corporate Governance, September 1, 2018, https://corpgov.law.harvard.edu/2018/09/01/board-refreshment-finding-the-right-balance/.

21. Peter Weill, Thomas Apel, Stephanie L. Woerner, and Jennifer S. Baner, "It Pays to Have a Digitally Savvy Board," *MIT Sloan Management Review*, March 12, 2019, https://sloanreview.mit.edu/article/it-pays-to-have-a-digitally-savvy-board/.

22. Tobias Kollmann, Andreas Kuckertz, and Christoph Stöckmann, "Continuous Innovation in Entrepreneurial Growth Companies: Exploring the Ambidextrous Strategy," *Journal of Enterprising Culture* 17, no. 03 (2009): 297–322.

23. D. Daniel Keum, "Innovation, Short-Termism, and the Cost of Strong Corporate Governance," *Strategic Management Journal*, June 28, 2020, https://doi.org/10.1002/smj.3216.

CHAPTER 6: CURVE BENDING IN THE LIVES OF OTHERS

1. John Maxwell, "Moving from Survival Mode to Significance," John C. Maxwell (blog), November 3, 2015, https://www.johnmaxwell.com/blog/moving-from-survival-mode-to-significance/.

2. Alan J. Gow, Alison Pattie, Martha C. Whiteman, Lawrence J. Whalley, and Ian J. Deary, "Social Support and Successful Aging: Investigating the Relationships Between Lifetime Cognitive Change and Life Satisfaction," *Journal of Individual Differences* 28, no. 3 (2007): 103–115.

3. Jenny Santi, "The Secret to Happiness Is Helping Others," *Time*, August 4, 2017, https://time.com/collection-post/4070299/secret-to-happiness/.

4. Virgin StartUp website: https://www.virginstartup.org/.
5. Adam Braun, "How One Small Pencil Built Hundreds of Schools, Fathom, https://fathomaway.com/interview-pencils-of-promise-ceo-adam-braun/.
6. James Currier and the NFX Team, "The Network Effect Bible," NFX, https://www.nfx.com/post/network-effects-bible/.
7. Zach Whittaker, "Mapping the World's Most Popular Software in Users," *ZDNet*, August 29, 2010, https://www.zdnet.com/article/mapping-the-worlds-most-popular-software-in-users/.
8. Alan B. Goldberg and Bill Ritter, "Costco CEO Finds Pro-Worker Means Profitability," ABC News, August 10, 2006, https://abc-news.go.com/2020/Business/story?id=1362779.
9. Rose Leadem, "A Quarter of Employees Say They Don't Know Their CEO's Name," *Entrepreneur*, May 4, 2017, https://www.entrepreneur.com/article/293827.
10. Andrew Rimas, "Act Two – Roger Marino," *Boston Magazine*, May 15, 2006, https://www.bostonmagazine.com/2006/05/15/act-two-roger-marino-part-one/.
11. "Impact of the Pandemic & Economic Shutdown on the Nonprofit Sector," *Charity Navigator*, April 17, 2020, https://www.charitynavigator.org/index.cfm?bay=content.view&cpid=7900.
12. "The Future of Nonprofits: An Interview with Tom Harvey," University of Notre Dame, October 13, 2020, https://www.notredameonline.com/resources/nonprofit-leadership/the-future-of-nonprofits-an-interview-with-tom-harvey-part-ii/.
13. "2018 State of the Nonprofit Sector Survey," Nonprofit Finance Fund (2018 survey of 3,400 nonprofit leaders across all 50 states), https://nff.org/learn/survey.
14. "Nonprofit Impact Matters: How America's Charitable Nonprofits Strengthen Communities and Improve Lives," 2019 Annual Report, National Council of Nonprofits, https://www.nonprofit-impactmatters.org/site/assets/files/1/nonprofit-impact-matters-sept-2019-1.pdf.
15. Suzanne Laporte, Douglas Kelly, and Tosin Agbabiaka, "Can Technology Transform the Nonprofit Sector?" *Yale Insights*, May 29, 2018, https://insights.som.yale.edu/insights/can-technology-transform-the-nonprofit-sector.
16. "Info 2020 – 15th Annual Industry Review from Sherpa Coaching, Executive Coaching Survey," Sherpa Coaching, https://www.sherpacoaching.com/annual-executive-coaching-survey/.

CHAPTER 7: YOUR CURVE BENDERS ROADMAP

1. Sang M. Lee and Silvana Trimi, "Innovation for Creating a Smart Future," *Journal of Innovation & Knowledge* 3, no. 1 (2018): 1–8.
2. Leo Frishberg, "Looking Back at Plan AHEAD™: Exercising User-Centered Design in Emergency Management," *CHI'05 Extended Abstracts on Human Factors in Computing Systems*, 2005, pp. 988–1003.
3. Henry Mintzberg, "The Strategy Concept 1: Five Ps for Strategy," *California Management Review* 30, no. 1 (Fall 1987): 11–24.
4. Keith C. Brown and Kenneth W. Wiles, "The Growing Blessing or Unicorns: The Changing Nature of the Market for Privately Funded Companies," *Journal of Applied Corporate Finance*, August 20, 2020, https://onlinelibrary.wiley.com/doi/abs/10.1111/jacf.12418.
5. D. Lain, M. van der Horst, and S. Vickerstaff, "Extending Working Lives: Feasible and Desirable for All?," in *Current and Emerging Trends in Aging and Work*, edited by Sara J. Czaja, Joseph Sharit, and Jacquelyn B. James (London: Springer, 2019), 101–119.
6. Barry Libert, Bill Ribaudo, and Megan Beck Fenley, "Adopting Digital Age Business Models to Improve Shareholder Value," *Deloitte, CFO Journal*, on *Wall Street Journal*, August 11, 2014, https://deloitte.wsj.com/cfo/2014/08/11/adopting-digital-age-business-models-to-improve-shareholder-value/.
7. Molly Hoffmeister, "A Look at Partnering in the $859B Salesforce Ecosystem," *Medium*, November 7, 2017, https://medium.com/inside-the-salesforce-ecosystem/a-look-at-partnering-in-the-859b-salesforce-ecosystem-f1e8dc13627d.
8. Mark S. Granovetter, "The Strength of Weak Ties," *American Journal of Sociology* 78, no. 6 (May 1973): 1360–1380, https://sociology.stanford.edu/sites/g/files/sbiybj9501/f/publications/the_strength_of_weak_ties_and_exch_w-gans.pdf.
9. Mohamed Nooman Ahmed, Andeep S. Toor, Kelsey O'Neil, and Dawson Friedland, "Cognitive Computing and the Future of Health Care: The Cognitive Power of IBM Watson Has the Potential to Transform Global Personalized Medicine," *IEEE Pulse* 8, no. 3 (2017): 4–9.

ACKNOWLEDGMENTS

Almost two decades ago, I embarked on a journey to advise, educate, and coach leaders to think differently about the value of their business relationships. I wanted to help them get beyond the perception of transactional contacts and networking as a "soft skill." Those who invested the time, effort, and resources saw firsthand that business relationships could be quantifiable, should be intentional, and must become more strategic in their lives.

Those who have gone beyond the intellectual understanding of my ideas in the *Relationship Economics* book, to internalize and apply them, have been able to translate concepts like Relationship Currency®, Reputation Capital®, and Professional Net Worth® into new roles, promotions, a new level of team dynamics, and organizational transformation success. An estimated 10,000+ individuals have taken the Relationship Economics Quiz on NourGroup.com, and we have a treasure trove of insights to publish in the third edition of the book in 2021.

More recently, *Co-Create* book ideas have helped global enterprises create net-new profitable growth engines, deepen existing customer and partner relationships to new levels, and co-create strategic opportunities in global sales, customer experience, and real innovative products and services. To date, we've trained almost 35,000 frontline contributors, managers, and executives in the Co-Create workshops. In preparation for the paperback second edition, we're creating a robust assessment to gauge your creativity, collaboration, and propensity to embrace change – critical attributes in successful co-creation, also available on NourGroup.com.

With *Curve Benders*, I aim to create a movement in the future of how we'll work, live, play, and give. As discussed in this book, I believe potent forces will create headwind, tailwind, and turbulence in our future. To remain relevant, we're all going to have to learn and grow at an accelerated pace. Certain relationships in our lives will transform linear learning for many into a non-linear path for a few. I call them Curve Benders, and beyond searching for one, I believe that every one of us has an incredible opportunity and an awesome responsibility to become a Curve Bender in the lives of others. I hope you'll join us.

This chapter of my professional life wouldn't be possible without an incredible group of global clients, to whom I'm indebted for their trust, vote of confidence in our work together, and friendship. I admire how they steer complex organizations in challenging circumstances and uncertain times with their steadfast leadership. Although we may not always agree, I'm grateful for their willingness to listen, internalize my ideas, and find opportunities to implement some of them to create enterprise value in their respective organizations. You fuel my learning, resolve, and aspirations. Thank you.

I've long believed that we're all products of the advice we take. I would be remiss not to mention past mentors such as Bruce Kasanoff, Alan Weiss, PhD, and Marshall Goldsmith – three definitive Curve Benders in my life. Many thanks to friends and colleagues in the MG100 community for their love and support, Thinkers 50 for their gatherings of the best of the global management thinkers, and brilliant institutions such as the Global Drucker Forum for fresh-perspective management. Thought leaders contributing to and recognized by these communities inspire me to think beyond the impact of business relationships on our present and imagine value creation possibilities through our strategic relationships in the future.

This book would not have been possible without Ben Bradbury's content architecture guidance or Lin Wilson's masterful illustrations both on the cover and throughout the chapters. I'm grateful for your commitment to our work together. Adrien and Natalie – thank you for your research and editing support.

I'm delighted to publish *Curve Benders* with longtime friend Shannon Vargo at John Wiley & Sons. Huge thanks to Shannon for investing in me and this idea, and Sally Baker for marshaling this work through the publishing process.

Lastly, I'm grateful to Mom and Dad back in Iran. Although the global pandemic has made it more difficult for us to see each other, you're in my thoughts and prayers daily.

I wrap up this acknowledgment the same way I begin every chapter – with an inspiring quote:

Change can be frightening, and the temptation is often to resist it. But change almost always provides opportunities – to learn new things, to rethink tried processes, and to improve the way we work.

> – *Klaus Schwab, founder and executive chairman,*
> *World Economic Forum*

With my best,
Nour

About the Author

A senior leadership/board advisor, educator, executive coach, and bestselling author, David Nour is internationally recognized as the leading expert on the applications of strategic relationships in profitable growth, sustained innovation, and lasting change. Nour is the author of 11 books translated into eight languages thus far, including bestsellers *Relationship Economics*® (Wiley) and *Co-Create* (St. Martin's Press).

Nour serves as a trusted advisor to global CEOs and coaches leadership teams and rising entrepreneurs. He is CEO of The Nour Group, Inc., an innovation advisory firm focused on fueling net-new enterprise growth. Recent client engagements span leading global companies, including Adtran, Cipla, Cox, Delta Air Lines, Dovel Technologies, Dell EMC, Disney, Humana, Oceaneering, Samsung Electronics, and The Wine Group.

In addition to advisory and executive coaching, Nour delivers an estimated 50 customized keynotes annually for global brands, association conferences, and academic forums on strategic business relationships' economic value. Tailoring content for audiences from boardrooms to ballrooms, delivered in person or high resolution virtually, he shares unique insights and an independent perspective, peppered with interactive moments and real-world takeaways, to inspire people to think and behave differently in the face of continued global disruptions.

Nour has served as an adjunct professor at the Goizueta Business School at Emory University, was named to the Thinkers50 Radar Class of 2021, and Global Gurus Top 30 Leadership Professionals lists. He is a member of the FBI Citizens Academy, the Association for Corporate

Growth, and the National Association of Corporate Directors (NACD), where he has earned the Governance Fellow accreditation.

A *Forbes* leadership contributor on the future of work, and an *Inc.* contributor on relationship economics, Nour's unique insights have been featured in a variety of prominent publications, including *The Wall Street Journal*, *The New York Times*, *Fast Company*, *Huffington Post Business*, *Entrepreneur*, and *Knowledge@Wharton*. He's also the host of the popular Curve Benders podcast.

Born to middle-class educators in Iran, Nour arrived in the United States in 1981 with a suitcase, $100, and no English fluency. He lived with an aunt and uncle in the Atlanta suburbs, where he finished high school and became an Eagle Scout. He graduated from Georgia State University with a bachelor's degree in business management and went on to earn an Executive MBA from the Goizueta Business School at Emory University.

He resides in Atlanta, Georgia, with his family. Learn more at www.NourGroup.com.

OTHER BOOKS BY THE AUTHOR

Curve Benders is David Nour's 11th book since 2008. A prolific writer, Nour has spent the past two decades researching, advising, and coaching leaders – in essence, becoming a student of business relationships – how individuals, teams, and organizations deliver unprecedented growth through a unique return on their strategic relationships. Think of his books *Relationship Economics*, *Co-Create*, and *Curve Benders* as his "Star Wars trilogy":

- In *Relationship Economics*, Nour introduced the idea of intentional, strategic, and quantifiable business relationships accelerating business outcomes.

- In *Co-Create*, he provided a canvas for the application of strategic business relationships in iteration, innovation, and disruption opportunities.

- In *Curve Benders*, he focuses on a roadmap of how strategic relationships can dramatically alter our non-linear growth trajectory against the forces that will shape the future of how we'll work, live, play, and serve others.

Following are just some of his other books available from NourGroup.com.

RELATIONSHIP ECONOMICS – FORTHCOMING THIRD EDITION (WILEY, 2021)

In our current turbulent global economy, multicultural management teams must execute seamlessly in an environment of increasingly more sophisticated and demanding relationship ecosystems. This book, forthcoming in its third edition in 2021, is the how-to guide. Its applications are beyond just getting and giving business cards or connecting with others on LinkedIn, or how to get the most out of a conference. It's a fundamental shift in one's mindset, skillset, and roadmap on the strategic, intentional, and quantifiable business relationships' value to deliver extraordinary results.

CO-CREATE (ST. MARTIN'S PRESS, 2017)

In our dynamic world, no one has all the answers. What if two or more of your most valuable and strategic relationships came together to create something far beyond what anyone thought imaginable? With a long-term vested interest in its success, could this initiative, campaign, product, service, or unique outcome deliver profitable, net-new growth opportunities? More importantly, could it transform the relationship to something more profound, more meaningful, and dramatically more impactful, often impenetrable by competitors? In *Co-Create*, Nour makes more than a compelling case to innovate through your strategic relationships; he provides a proven roadmap to do so.

RETURN ON IMPACT (JOSSEY-BASS, 2013)

Access to information is instantaneous. Social tools put professional networks within arm's reach. What leadership strategies will allow your organization to create and support differentiating value and nurture ongoing relationships with your members? In *Return on Impact: Leadership Strategies for the Age of Connected Relationships*, Nour charts the implications of a socially enabled world and the reinvention – in structure and governance, talent acquisition, listening practices, and business and revenue models – that leaders of organizations must undertake to fuel growth in the next decade.

CONNECTABILITY (MCGRAW-HILL, 2010)

Drawing from the powerful lessons of emotional awareness and relationship dynamics, this book promotes a sophisticated yet simple method for developing superior partnerships, guaranteed to consistently create quality results. Even the best-intentioned team players too often focus more on communicating their ideas than hearing and understanding what others have to say. *ConnectAbility* changes all this, using eight steps to foster optimum communications.

THE ENTREPRENEUR'S GUIDE TO RAISING CAPITAL (PRAEGER, 2009)

Written to help entrepreneurs navigate the capital-raising maze, this book shows how to attract financing to fund the startup and growth phases any business moves through. Nour provides real-life, pragmatic advice from entrepreneurs who have successfully raised capital from friends, family, angel investors, banks, and institutional investors such as venture capital and private equity firms.

INDEX

5Ps. *See* Plan, Ploy, Pattern, Position, and Perspective